d Sons & Co.

Lower Deck

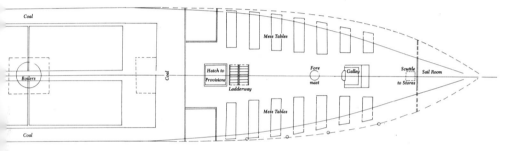

Inboard Works

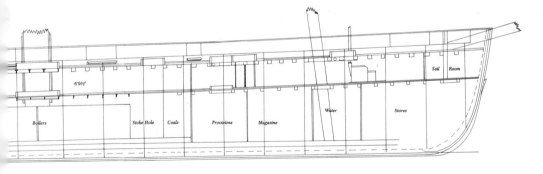

SOUTHERN

THUNDER

EXPLOITS OF THE CONFEDERATE STATES NAVY

BY

R. Thomas Campbell

 Burd Street Press

This Burd Street Press book
was printed by
Beidel Printing House, Inc.
63 West Burd Street
Shippensburg, PA 17257 USA

In respect for the scholarship contained herein, the acid-free paper used in this book meets the guidelines for permanence and durability of the Committee on Production Guidelines for Book Longevity of the Council on Library Resources.

For a complete list of available publications
please write
Burd Street Press
Division of White Mane Publishing Company, Inc.
P. O. Box 152
Shippensburg, PA 17257 USA

Library of Congress Cataloging-in-Publication Data

Campbell, R. Thomas, 1937–
     Southern thunder : exploits of the Confederate Navy / by RThomas
Campbell.
          p.   cm.
     Includes bibliographical references and index.
     ISBN 1-57249-029-2 (alk. paper)
     1. Confederate States of America. Navy--History. 2. United
States--History--Civil War, 1861-1865--Naval operations,
Confederate.   I. Title.
E596.C365   1997   96-37062
973.7'57--dc21   CIP

Dedication

To Those Who Wore The Navy Gray,
And The Loved Ones They Left Behind.

Table of Contents

Illustrations

*P*reface

Thousands of volumes have been written concerning the great land campaigns and the respective commanders who led their troops to victory or defeat during the War Between the States. Comparatively little has been published, however, concerning the navy's role in that terrible conflict. This is especially true in respect to the Confederate States Navy. The many and diverse operations engaged in by the Confederate navy are unfamiliar to most casual students of the war. Other than the mislabeled battle between the "*Monitor* and the *Merrimac*," most profess little knowledge of any other operations involving the naval arm of the Confederacy. Only one work attempts to tell the entire story of the Southern navy, and that is J. Thomas Scharf's *History of the Confederate States Navy*, published in 1887. Written prior to the compilation of the *Official Records*, and while a commendable work, it suffers from lack of detail in areas of naval operations in which Scharf was not actively involved. Unfortunately, only a handful of Confederate naval leaders wrote their memoirs after the cessation of hostilities, and because of this, the researcher is left many times with only fragments, and the mostly Federal reports in the *Official Records*.

There is enough evidence, however, to piece together a truly amazing account of the Confederate navy's accomplishments. Against unbelievable odds, the Confederate navy fought valiantly to the bitter end with innovation, resourcefulness, and remarkable courage. By so doing, it contributed greatly to the South's defense at the time of her greatest peril. As was noted in my first work entitled, *Gray Thunder*, the story of the Confederate navy is not just the story of cruisers, ironclads, and gunboats; it is a very real human drama of dedicated and devoted officers and men, fighting desperately for a cause in which they earnestly believed. The Constitutional principles of states' rights and the guarantee that the people had the authority to choose their own government were the ideals over which they fought. Names such as Semmes, Kell, Brown, Gift, Read, Maury, Buchanan, and others to whom the reader will be introduced in these pages, echo down through the ages as naval commanders, fully equal in brilliance of leadership and devotion to duty as Robert E. Lee or "Stonewall" Jackson.

By selecting particular exploits, this work is intended to give the reader a glimpse of the challenges confronting the Confederate navy in its numerous accomplishments, as well as its many defeats. The navy of the Confederate States was officially established by an act of the Confederate Congress on February 21, 1861. It existed for almost four years and nine months until, finally, its last flag was lowered by the CSS *Shenandoah* at Liverpool, England, on November 6, 1865. During this period the Confederate government proceeded to build a courageous and innovative naval force. The fact that they achieved all that they did, in spite of the South's limited resources, is what makes the study of the Confederate navy so intriguing. For all those who wore the navy gray, this is their story.

Acknowledgments

I wish to acknowledge the help and assistance of my wife, Carole. Without her encouragement, her patience, and especially her editing expertise, this book would not have been possible.

All photos, unless otherwise noted, are courtesy of the Naval Historical Foundation, Washington, D.C.

Chapter One

"Give Me That Ship, ..."

The flickering light of the headlamp struggled to pierce the darkness as the regular passenger train from West Point to Montgomery rumbled through the night. Sitting by a window, gazing into the Alabama blackness, was a neatly dressed man in civilian attire who only days before had resigned his commission as a naval officer in the service of the United States.

The air had become soft and balmy, though I had left a region of frosts and snow only two days before, wrote Raphael Semmes. *The pine woods were on fire as we passed through them, the flames now and then running up a lightwood tree, and throwing a weird and fitful glare upon the passing train. The scene was peculiarly Southern, and reminded me that I was drawing near my home and my people, and I mechanically repeated to myself the words of the poet:*

> *"Breathless there a man with soul so dead,*
> *Who never to himself hath said,*
> *This is my own, my native land!"*

And my heart, which up to that moment had felt as though a heavy weight were pressing upon it, began to give more vigorous beats, and send a more inspiring current through my veins. Under this happy influence I sank, as the night advanced and the train thundered on, into the first sound sleep which had visited my weary eyelids since I resigned my commission, and read at the

1

foot of the letter accepting my resignation, my name inscribed as plain "Esq."
This night-ride through the burning pine woods of Alabama, afterward stood
as a great gulf in my memory, forming an impassable barrier, as it were, be-
tween my past and my future life. It had cost me pain to cross the gulf, but
once crossed, I never turned to look back.[1]

***

Situated high on the bluffs, overlooking a bend in the Alabama River, the Confederate capitol at Montgomery, Alabama was overflowing with excitement in the spring of 1861. Everywhere, crowds of men and women could be seen gathered on street corners and the sprawling lawns of the exquisite mansions, all anxiously discussing the latest news. The city's three hotels, the Exchange, Montgomery Hall, and the Madison, were thronged with guests, and no additional rooms were available. It was April, and word had only recently been received that Fort Sumter in Charleston harbor, South Carolina had fallen to the forces of General Beauregard. The Northern government, under Abraham Lincoln, had issued a call for 75,000 volunteers to "suppress the rebellion," and ominous war clouds of a Northern invasion hung heavily over the city and the new nation. Day and night, the dusty streets were filled with the sights and sounds of marching men, most without weapons, trooping out to makeshift camps of instruction in the countryside. Others, meanwhile, were marching with spirited steps toward the railroad station for the long ride to Virginia.

In the improvised office of Stephen R. Mallory, the recently appointed Secretary of the Confederate Navy, an important meeting was in session. Commander Raphael Semmes was intently studying a list of ships, handed to him by the Secretary, which had been surveyed at New Orleans by Commodore Rousseau and his board of officers. Semmes, who was originally from Maryland, but had resigned from the "old service" when his resident state of Alabama seceded, had only recently returned from a fruitless trip to the Northern states, where he had searched various ports looking for vessels that could be purchased and converted into commerce-raiding warships. As he scanned the report, one of the vessels on the paper caught his eye. Semmes explained:

A board of naval officers was already in session at New Orleans, charged with
the duty of procuring as speedily as possible, some light and fast steamers to be let
loose against the enemy's commercial marine, but their reports up to this time,
had been but little satisfactory. They had examined a number of vessels, and found
some defects in all of them. The Secretary, speaking of the discouragement pre-
sented by these reports, handed me one of them, which he had received that morn-
ing from the board. I read it and found that it described a small propeller steamer
of five hundred tons burden, sea-going, with a low-pressure engine, sound, and

capable of being so strengthened as to be enabled to carry an ordinary battery of four, or five guns. Her speed was reported to be between nine and ten knots, but unfortunately, said the Board, she carries but five days' fuel, and has no accommodations for the crew of a ship of war. She was accordingly condemned. When I finished reading the report, I turned to the Secretary and said, "Give me that ship; I think I can make her answer the purpose."[2]

The vessel to which Semmes referred was the screw steamer *Havana*, which had become stranded at New Orleans when Federal blockaders appeared off the mouth of the river. Against the advice of the naval board, Secretary Mallory purchased the packet ship, which had recently been engaged in regular runs between New Orleans and Havana, and ordered Semmes to take command of her as the CSS *Sumter*. Eager to begin the conversion of the *Havana*, Semmes left Montgomery the following day on board the splendid double-decked steamboat, *Southern Republic*, which was bound for Mobile. Arriving in New Orleans on April 22, Semmes reported to district commander Captain Lawrence Rousseau, and immediately took possession of the *Sumter*.

I found her only a dismantled packet-ship, Semmes wrote, *full of upper cabins and other top hamper, furniture, and crockery, but as unlike a ship of war as possible. Still, I was pleased with her general appearance. Her lines were easy and graceful, and she had a sort of saucy air about her which seemed to say, that she was not averse to the service on which she was about to be employed.*[3]

No warship had ever been fitted out at New Orleans, and finding a suitable shipyard and skilled workers to accomplish the conversion proved troublesome. James Martin, owner of the Atlantic Dry Dock Company across the river at Algiers, agreed to try, and was awarded the contract by the Navy Department. Semmes soon became embroiled in all the myriad details that an experienced facility would easily have handled as routine.

I now took my ship actively in hand, Semmes recorded, *and set gangs of mechanics at work to remove her upper cabins, and other top hamper, preparatory to making the necessary alterations. These latter were considerable, and I soon found that I had a tedious job on my hands. It was no longer the case, as it had been in former years, when I had occasion to fit out a ship, that I could go into a navy-yard with well provided workshops and skilled workmen ready with all the requisite materials at hand to execute my orders. Everything had to be improvised, from the manufacture of a water tank, to the "kids and cans" of the berth deck messes, and from a gun carriage to a friction primer. I had not only to devise all the alterations but to make plans and drawings of them, before they could be comprehended.*[4]

Weighing 437 tons and measuring 184 feet in length and 30 feet in beam, the *Sumter* had all her upper works dismantled and removed down to the main deck. Hammocks, bedding, guns, gun carriages, and ammunition were ordered, and the main deck was strengthened to support the six ton weight of a five gun battery. These guns consisted of four 32-pounders in broadside and one 8-inch pivot-mounted shell-gun amidship. A berth deck for the accommodation of the crew was built, and officers' quarters were constructed, including a cabin for Semmes. Her rig was altered to a barkentine (three masts instead of two) which would improve her efficiency under canvas. A new set of sails was ordered, and her smokestack was hinged to allow lowering while under sail, which would alter her silhouette. Top speed under steam and canvas combined would be a disappointing nine-to-ten knots, and without a lifting device for her propeller, she was at a distinct disadvantage under sail alone. The engine, which was a low pressure direct-acting type, was partially above the waterline and thus exposed to enemy fire. Workmen constructed a massive bulkhead consisting of large wooden beams held together by heavy iron bars which would help protect the engine and other machinery. Even with expanded coal bunkers holding 114

Semmes and his officers pose for the photographer on the deck of the *Sumter*, just prior to sailing from New Orleans. Note the blue Confederate uniforms, the reluctant switch to gray having not yet taken place. *Seated left to right*: Lieutenant William E. Evans, Commander Raphael Semmes, First Assistant Engineer Miles J. Freeman. *Standing left to right*: Surgeon Francis L. Galt, Lieutenant John M. Stribling, Lieutenant John M. Kell, Lieutenant Robert T. Chapman, and Marine First Lieutenant Becket K. Howell.

tons, only eight days' supply of fuel could be carried, and this would prove to be a severe limitation.

It took two months of tedious work to make the alterations, and an impatient Semmes was plagued by constant delays and shortages. The battery of five guns, originally ordered from the Confederate naval yards at Pensacola and Charleston, failed to materialize. They were finally reordered from the Gosport Navy Yard at Norfolk, but weeks passed with still no word of their arrival in New Orleans. In exasperation, Semmes finally dispatched Lieutenant Robert T. Chapman in search of them. Chapman located the cannon lying in a ditch along the rail line, where they had been thrown to make room for army freight.[5]

Meanwhile, the Navy Department had assigned the *Sumter's* officers, and First Lieutenant John McIntosh Kell was ordered to report as executive officer. Semmes had known the brawny Georgian in the "old service," where he had once defended him in a court-martial. A man of great courage and completely devoted to the Southern cause, Kell had resigned his commission within an hour after his state seceded. The *Sumter's* commander, who preferred to remain aloof from his officers and men and run his ship through his first lieutenant, would find Kell an ideal executive officer. The two would team together again later in the war as commander and executive officer on the deadly *Alabama*. Additional lieutenants assigned were Robert T. Chapman from Alabama, John M. Stribling from South Carolina, and William E. Evans, who was also from South Carolina. (A complete roster of *Sumter's* officers can be found in Appendix A.)[6]

While the elaborate conversion was in process, sailors began arriving to enlist in the 92 man crew. With many seafaring men trapped in New Orleans by the suddenness of the war and the blockade, there was no shortage of candidates. As Semmes and Kell interviewed prospective crew members, those who were accepted were housed on board the receiving ship CSRS *St. Philip* which was berthed nearby. The *St. Philip* had previously been the *Star of the West* when she attempted to run reinforcements into Fort Sumter in Charleston harbor and was fired upon by Southern gunners on January 9, 1861. Captured along the Gulf coast in April by Texas forces, she was transferred to Confederate service and renamed *St. Philip* in honor of the fort guarding the Mississippi below New Orleans.[7]

Included among the men who chafed at the inactivity and swatted mosquitoes each day on the *St. Philip*, were three sergeants and seventeen privates of the Confederate States Marine Corps under the command of Lieutenant Becket K. Howell. A brother-in-law to President Davis, Howell served as marine commandant not only on the *Sumter*, but would later serve as the only representative of the marines on the

CSS *Alabama*. Semmes would have reason to lament that his marines on the *Sumter*, being mostly foreign born, were the *most indifferent set of men I have in the ship. It is very difficult to "lick them into shape."*[8]

At last, with the carriage for the 8-inch pivot gun finished, the water tanks installed, ammunition and small arms stowed away, coal in the bunkers, and the crew taken on board, Semmes was prepared to put the *Sumter* into commission. On June 3, 1861, President Davis' fifty-third birthday, a moving ceremony was enacted on the deck of the first Confederate cruiser. A bright new Stars and Bars, presented by the ladies of New Orleans, was raised to the peak, and while guns roared and bands played, the jaunty little *Sumter's* lines were cast off, and she steamed up the river in grand style on a trial run. It would take two additional weeks before Semmes felt that all was ready. Time was critical, however, as the Federal blockade was drawing its noose more tightly around the Crescent City.[9]

On the 18th of June, after all the vexatious delays, . . . Semmes wrote, *I got up anchor and dropped down to the Barracks below the city a short distance, to receive my powder on board, which for safety, had been placed in the State Magazine. At 10:30pm of the same day, we got up steam, and by the soft and brilliant light of a moon near her full, threw ourselves into the broad and swift current of the Father of Waters, and ran rapidly down to the anchorage between Fort Jackson and Fort St. Philip, where we came to at 4:00am.*[10]

Semmes' purpose in anchoring at the forts was to await a favorable opportunity to run past the Federal blockading ships which were guarding the passes leading to the Gulf. Three channels lead from the Head of the Passes to the open sea: Pass a L'Outre, South Pass, and Southwest Pass. By the time the *Sumter* rode at anchor between Forts Jackson and St. Philip, the passes were guarded by the 21-gun *Brooklyn*, the 16-gun *Powhatan*, the 32-gun *Niagara*, and the 52-gun *Minnesota*, all of which were steam and sail powered. All of these warships were faster than the little *Sumter* and capable of smashing her to pieces with one single broadside.[11]

As the soft veil of night fell over the river on the evening of June 21, Semmes received a dispatch from the privateer *Ivy*, that the *Powhatan*, which had been blockading the Southwest pass, had left her station in chase of a sail. *I immediately ordered steam to be raised, and getting up my anchor, steamed down to the Head of the Passes*, Semmes recounted, *where the river branches into its three principal outlets. Arriving here at half past ten P. M. I dispatched a boat to the light house for a pilot; but the keeper 'knew nothing' of the pilots, and was unwilling to come on board himself, though requested. The night wore away and nothing could be done.* Daylight revealed that the *Powhatan* had returned to her station.

Later the same day, Semmes dispatched another request for a pilot, however, the master of the pilot's association sent word that none were available. Most of the pilots were of Northern birth, and they were not eager to help a Confederate cruiser get to sea. About this time a telegram was received from the commander of the forts stating that the captain of the pilots' association reported that "no pilots were on duty." Semmes was incensed! Summoning Lieutenant Stribling, Semmes ordered him to proceed to the pilot station in the *Ivy*, and bring the pilot master on board the *Sumter*. If the pilot master refused, Stribling was to place the master under arrest, along with all the pilots, and forcibly bring them on board.

Soon the pilot master and several unenthusiastic pilots were standing on the deck of the *Sumter*. Semmes lectured the group on their responsibilities to the Confederate government, and directed that they choose from among themselves, one who would remain on board for one week's service. With the choice made and the rest of the pilots dismissed, Semmes and the men and officers of the *Sumter* settled into a monotonous routine of fighting boredom and mosquitoes, while watching for an opportunity to dash by the blockaders.[12]

After several false starts, caused by one or more of the blockaders being erroneously reported missing, Semmes received definite word on June 30, that the *Brooklyn* had left her station off Pass a L'Outre and was nowhere in sight. *The crew, who had been "cleaning themselves" for Sunday muster, at once stowed away their bags*, Semmes wrote; *the swinging-booms were gotten along side, the boats run up, and in ten minutes, the steam was again hissing as if impatient of control. The men ran round the capstan in "double quick," in their eagerness to get up the anchor, and in a few minutes more, the ship's head swung off gracefully with the current, and, the propeller being started, she bounded off like a thing of life on this new race which was to decide whether we should continue to stagnate in the midsummer in the marshes of the Mississippi, or reach those "glad waters of the dark blue sea."*[13]

As the anchor was being raised, Semmes noticed that the pilot, who was standing nearby, appeared ashen and pale. Upon inquiry, he nervously declared that he was unfamiliar with the Pass a L'Outre, for he was a "Southwest Pass pilot." Again Semmes' anger boiled over, and turning to Kell, he ordered the jack raised as a signal for a new pilot. Kell remembered that Semmes demanded that the pilot "take us out and if he ran us ashore or put us in the hands of the enemy he would swing him to the yardarm as a traitor."[14] Based on previous experience, Semmes expected no response from the pilot station. He was determined to attempt the passage over the bar himself, however, with or without a pilot.

When the officers of the *Brooklyn* spotted the ominous black smoke pouring from the *Sumter's* funnel, they gave up their chase of the distant sail and commenced to retrace their course to the mouth of Pass a

L'Outre. *We had nearly equal distances to run to the bar,* Semmes noted, *but I had the advantage of a four knot current. Several of my officers now collected around me, and were discussing the chances of escape.. "What think you of our prospects," said I, turning to one of my lieutenants, who had served a short time before on board the Brooklyn, and knew well her qualities. "Prospect, sir! not the least in the world — there is no possible chance of escaping that ship. Even if we get over the bar ahead of her, she must overhaul us in a very short time. The Brooklyn is good for fourteen knots an hour, sir." "That was the report," said I, "on her trial trip, but you know how all such reports are exaggerated; ten to one, she has no better speed, if so good, as the Sumter." "You will see, sir," replied my lieutenant; "we made a passage in her, only four months ago from Tampico to Pensacola, and averaged about thirteen knots the whole distance."*[15]

Semmes resolved to outrace the *Brooklyn* to the bar. Without an experienced pilot, he was taking a dangerous chance of running the *Sumter* aground. Suddenly, one of his officers called his attention to a boat that was rapidly approaching. *Casting my eyes in the given direction, I saw a whale-boat approaching us pulled by four stout blacks, who were bending like good fellows to their long ashen oars, and in the stern sheets was seated, sure enough, the welcome pilot, swaying his body to and fro as his boat leaped under the oft-repeated strokes of the oars, as though he would hasten her already great speed. But more beautiful still was another object which presented itself. In the balcony of the pilot's house, which had been built in the very marsh, on the margin of the river, there stood a beautiful women, the pilot's young wife, waving him on to his duty with her handkerchief. We could have tossed a biscuit from the Sumter to the shore, and I uncovered my head gallantly to my fair countrywomen. A few minutes more, and a tow-line had been thrown to the boat, and the gallant young fellow stood on the horseblock beside me.*[16]

The rakish little *Sumter*, with her freshly-painted black hull, was now in a race for her life. Semmes would have to reach and cross the bar at the mouth of the Pass a L'Outre before the *Brooklyn* arrived, if he wanted any chance of outrunning her once in the Gulf. Approximately seven or eight miles out in the Gulf, Semmes could see his enemy. Black smoke poured from her funnel, and all her sails were thrown to the wind as she bounded over the ocean swells heading straight for the bar. Officers on her quarterdeck, including her commander Captain Charles H. Poor, peered anxiously through telescopes at the "Rebel pirate" making a dash for freedom. The *Brooklyn's* guns had a maximum range of four miles, and Captain Poor knew that if he could draw two or three miles closer, they could open fire.

Running with the four-knot current of the river, Semmes was determined to win the race. Down below, sweating Engineer Miles J. Freeman exerted every effort to obtain one more pound of steam and one more revolution per minute out of the propeller. With volumes of smoke and hissing steam, the *Sumter* pounded on, her slender bow parting the muddy Mississippi and sending plumes of spray flying to either side. The end of the river and the bar were rapidly approaching. Sweeping by the lighthouse wharf, brightly colored handkerchiefs fluttered from the hands of Southern ladies as they cheered the men of the new Confederate cruiser.

Half a mile or so from the light-house, Semmes wrote, *and the bar is reached. There was a Bremen ship lying aground on the bar, and there was just room, and no more, for us to pass her. She had run out a kedge, and had a warp attached to it* (an anchor attached to a line) *that was lying across the passage-way. The crew considerately slackened the line as we approached, and in another bound the Sumter was outside the bar, and the Confederate flag was upon the high seas! We now slackened our speed for an instant, ...to haul the pilot's boat alongside, that he might return to the shore. As the gallant young fellow grasped my hand, and shook it warmly, as he descended from the horseblock, he said, "Now, Captain, you are all clear; give her h-ll, and let her go!"*[17]

Semmes had won the race, yet the *Brooklyn* was now dangerously close. Kell estimated her at three-and-one-half to four miles, and she was coming on with a vengeance. Semmes ordered a lieutenant to cast a lead to check the *Sumter*'s speed. "Nine and a half knots, Sir!" came the cry. Engineer Freeman was summoned, and upon inquiry, informed Semmes that the engine was doing its very best . . . *"though,"*

The *Sumter* running out of New Orleans past the USS *Brooklyn* on June 30, 1861. Actually, the two vessels were much farther apart than depicted in this wartime lithograph.

said he, "there is a little drawback just now, in the 'foaming' of our boilers, arising from the suddenness with which we got up steam; when this subsides, we may be able to add half a knot more."

Both ships now loosed and set all available sails. Smoke continued to pour from the funnels of both vessels as the engineers and firemen strove for one additional turn per minute of their propellers. Semmes had a slight sailing advantage over the *Brooklyn* as the *Sumter's* rig, with large fore and aft sails, allowed her to sail more closely into the wind. *I resolved at once to hold my wind so closely,* Semmes explained, *as to compel her to furl her sails, though this would carry me a little athwart her bows, and bring me perhaps a little nearer to her, for the next half hour or so. A rain squall now came up, and enveloped the two ships, hiding each from the other. As the rain blew off to leeward, and the Brooklyn reappeared, she seemed fearfully near us, and I had begun to fear I should realize the foreboding of my lieutenant.*

Although Semmes had resolved to "never look back," the memories of his recent service in the navy that was now pursuing him, caused him to delight in the sight of the splendid *Brooklyn*: *I could not but admire the majesty of her appearance, with her broad flaring bows, and clean and beautiful run, and her masts and yards, as taut and square as those of an old time sailing frigate. The stars and stripes of a large ensign flew out from time to time, from under the lee of her spanker, and we could see an apparently anxious crowd of officers on her quarter deck, many of them with telescopes directed toward us. She had evidently, I thought, gained upon us, and I expected every moment to hear the whiz of a shot; but still she did not fire.*

Semmes was now beginning to have grave concerns that they might not be able to outrace the onrushing *Brooklyn*. He called for Paymaster Henry Myers to bring the ship's papers on deck and be ready to toss them overboard at a moment's notice. As fortune would have it, some good news now reached the quarterdeck: *At this crises,* Semmes explained, *the engineer came up from below, bringing the welcome intelligence that the "foaming" of his boilers had ceased, and that his engine was "working beautifully," giving the propeller several additional turns per minute. The breeze, too, favored me, for it had freshened considerably; and what was still more to the purpose, I began to perceive that I was "eating" the Brooklyn "out of the wind;" in other words, that she was falling more and more to leeward. I knew, of course, that as soon as she fell into my wake, she would be compelled to furl her sails. This she did in half an hour or so afterward, and I at once began to breathe more freely, for I could still hold onto my own canvas. ... We now began to gain quite perceptibly on our pursuer, and at half-past three, the chase was abandoned, the baffled Brooklyn retracing her steps to Pass a L'Outre, and the Sumter bounding away on her course seaward.*[18]

Semmes declined to fire a gun in triumph, for his powder was much too precious for that. He did, however, send his crew into the rigging where three thunderous cheers for the Confederate flag echoed over the pristine blue waters of the Gulf.

While the *Brooklyn* had given up the chase, the *Sumter* was not out of danger. Numerous Union warships were off the coast of the Confederate States, and it was imperative to avoid any sighting. Semmes set a course for the south coast of Cuba, and though two other vessels were spotted at long range, they did not discover the Confederate cruiser, and sundown found the *Sumter* alone in the Gulf and speeding southeast. As darkness spread its welcome mantle over the ocean, the men of the *Sumter* were awed by the appearance of the Great Comet of 1861 which left a fiery trail across the sky. The crew, still excited over the fortuitous escape from the *Brooklyn*, considered the comet a good omen. With this confirmation of continued good luck, a round of grog was served as the Confederate warship, with all her lights extinguished, sped onward through the night.

There was time now for reflective thought, and Semmes was filled with emotion this night: *As I leaned on the carriage of a howitzer on the poop of my ship, and cast a glance toward the quarter of the horizon whence the land had disappeared, memory was busy with the events of the last few months. How hurried and confused they had been! It seemed as though I had dreamed a dream, and found it difficult, upon waking, to unite the discordant parts. A great government had been broken up, family ties had been severed, and war — grim, ghastly war — was arraying a household against itself. A little while back, I had served under the very flag which I had that day defied. Strange revolution of feeling, how I now hated that flag! It had been to me as a mistress to a lover; I had looked upon it with admiring eyes, had dallied with it in hours of ease, and had recourse to it in hours of trouble, and now I found it false! What wonder that I felt a lover's resentment?*[19]

A cloudless daybreak revealed the *Sumter* on course, under sail and steam, and headed for the western tip of Cuba. Semmes' plan was to round Cape Antonio at the western end of the island, enter a Cuban port for coal, and continue on to Barbados for an additional supply. From there he would head for Cabo de Sao Roque off the coast of Brazil, where, because of the currents and winds, most of the world's north-south commerce passes. Semmes described this area as "the turning point of the commerce of the world."

With the lookouts reporting no sightings from the mastheads, and the *Sumter* sailing through a calm sea, Semmes graphically described the scene on the cruiser's deck the first day: *The awnings were soon spread, and the usual routine of a man-of-war at sea commenced. The crew was mustered in clean apparel at quarters at nine o'clock, and a division of guns was exercised, the rest of the crew being dispersed in idle groups about the deck;*

Commander Raphael Semmes, captain of the CSS *Sumter*. Semmes posed for the photograph in New Orleans shortly before the *Sumter* sailed in June of 1861.

the old salts overhauling their bags, and seeing that their tobacco and soap, and needle and thread were all right for the cruise, and the youngsters discussing their recent escape. . . . We held our course during the rest of this day. . . . An occasional swash of the sea against the ship's side, the monotonous beating of time by her propeller, an occasional order from the officer of the deck, and the routine "calls" of the boatswain's whistle as dinner or grog was piped, were the only audible sounds, beyond the usual hum of conversation among the crew.[21]

The morning of July 3 found the cruiser off Cape Corrientes and running between the Isle of Pines and the Cuban coast. No sails had been sighted until mid-afternoon when the cry, "Sail Ho!" came from the masthead. Upon questioning, the lookout reported two sails straight ahead off the bow. Raising the British ensign to the peak, Semmes signaled the first vessel to heave to, but after sending a boarding party to examine her papers, she proved to be a Spanish brig. The *Sumter's* captain offered his apology, and she was allowed to continue. Replacing the English colors with the Confederate ensign, Semmes fired a round across the second vessel's bow, and she hove to as her United States' colors unfolded to the breeze.

She was the *Sumter's* first prize, and inspection established her as the *Golden Rocket*, a three-masted square-rigger of 607 tons out of Bangor, Maine, bound in ballast for Cienfuegos, Cuba, for a load of sugar. The boarding party returned with the ship's captain, William Bailey, who carried with him the *Golden Rocket's* papers. Bailey was escorted to Semmes' cabin, and the Confederate commander began a process that would be repeated many times in the next three years. After being examined closely, the documents clearly evidenced that the *Golden Rocket* was American, and with no cargo to consider, Semmes quickly decided her fate. It was not easy, however, for him to consign her to the flames. It would take a while to harden the Confederate commander's heart against an enemy who was even now invading and plundering his homeland. *"My duty is a painful one, to destroy so noble a ship as yours,"* Semmes announced to Captain Bailey, *"but I must discharge it without vain regrets; and as for yourself, you will only have to do, as so many thousands have done before you, submit to the fortunes of war — yourself and your crew will be well treated on board my ship."*[22]

It was dark by the time the boarding party had removed the *Golden Rocket's* crew and such supplies as they needed, including the vessel's chronometer. Semmes sent a boat into the darkness to set the *Golden Rocket* ablaze, and he eloquently described this burning of his first prize of war:

The wind by this time had become very light, and the night was pitch-dark — the darkness being of the kind graphically described by old sailors, when they say, you may cut it with a knife. ... The boat which had been sent on this errand of destruction, had pulled out of sight, and her oars ceasing to resound, we knew that she had reached the doomed ship, but so impenetrable was the darkness that no trace of the boat or ship could be seen, although the Sumter was only distant a few hundred yards. Not a sound could be heard on board the Sumter, although her deck was crowded with men. Every one seemed busy with his own thoughts, and gazing eagerly in the direction of the doomed ship, endeavoring in vain to penetrate the thick darkness. Suddenly, one of the crew exclaimed, "There is the flame! She is on fire!" The decks of the Maine-built ship were of pine, caulked with old-fashioned oakum, and paid with pitch; the wood-work of the cabin was like so much tinder, having been seasoned by many voyages in the tropics, and the forecastle was stowed with paints and oils. The consequence was that the flame was not long in kindling, but leaped, full grown, into the air, in a very few minutes after its first faint glimmer had been seen.

The boarding officer, to do his work more effectually, had applied the torch simultaneously in three places, the cabin, the mainhold, and the forecastle; and now the devouring flames rushed up these three apertures with a fury which nothing could resist. The burning ship, with the Sumter's boat in the act of shoving off from her side; the Sumter herself, with her grim, black sides, lying in repose like some great sea-monster, gloating upon the spectacle, and the sleeping sea, for there was scarce a ripple upon the water, were all brilliantly lighted. The indraught into the burning ship's holds and cabins added every moment new fury to the flames, and now they could be heard roaring like the fires of a hundred furnaces in full blast.

The crew of the *Golden Rocket*, along with the men of the *Sumter*, lined the rail and stared in awestruck silence as the flames built into a raging crackling inferno. *The prize ship had been laid to, with her main-topsail to the mast, and all her light sails, though clewed up, were lying loose about the yards,* Semmes continued. *The forked tongues of the devouring element, leaping into the rigging, newly tarred, ran rapidly up the shrouds, first into the tops, then to the topmast-heads, thence to the top-gallant, and royal mast-heads, and in a moment more to the trucks; whilst this rapid ascent of the main current of fire was going on, other currents had run out upon the yards, and ignited all the sails. A top-gallant sail, all on fire, would now fly off from the yard, and sailing leisurely in the direction of the light breeze that was fanning, rather than blowing, break into bright and sparkling patches of flame, and settle, or rather silt into the sea. The yard would then follow, and not being wholly submerged by its descent into the sea, would retain a portion of its flame, and continue to burn as a floating brand for some minutes. At one time the intricate network of the cordage of the burning ship was traced, as with a pencil, upon the black sky beyond, the many threads of flame twisting and writhing like so many serpents that had received their death wounds. The mizzen-mast now went by the board, then the fore-mast, and in a few minutes afterward, the great main-mast tottered, reeled, and fell over the ship's side into the sea, making a noise like that of the sturdy oak of the forests when it falls by the stroke of the axeman.*[23]

The destruction of the *Golden Rocket* was an emotional trial for both Semmes and Kell. They had spent nearly their entire adult lives protecting the flag that they had just destroyed. For a sailor, it was also especially difficult to witness the destruction of a fine ship. Years later the pain was still evident as Kell wrote: *It was a sad sight to a sailor's eyes, the burning of a fine ship. We had not then grown accustomed to the sight with hardened hearts.*[24]

The next day July 4, 1861, was cloudy with passing rain squalls off the Isle of Pines, but the *Sumter* stopped and boarded two more vessels. They were the 200-ton brig *Cuba* and the 245-ton brig *Machias*. Both had just departed Trinidad-de-Cuba with a load of sugar and molasses and were destined for English ports. The ships were obviously American, but their manifests confirmed that their cargoes belonged to neutrals, which meant Semmes could not burn them without violating Spanish neutrality. After transferring needed supplies to the *Sumter*, Semmes put a prize crew of four men on both vessels and took them in tow. His intent was to take them into the port of Cienfuegos, Cuba, and to request that Spanish authorities hold them until they could be adjudicated by a Confederate court. Britain and France had issued proclamations prohibiting both belligerents from bringing prizes into their ports, but it was Semmes' hope that Spain had not, as yet, followed their example. Under international law the cargo was private property belonging to neutrals; however, the ships were legal prizes for the captors. With Southern ports blockaded, Semmes' only choice was adjudication in a neutral port, if allowed, or bonding of the vessels and their cargoes. (A bond was a monetary amount set on the value of the prize, to be paid to the Confederate States at the end of the war.)

As the *Sumter* steamed for Cienfuegos, Semmes found the cruiser's speed so diminished by the weight of the towed vessels, that he cast off the tow line to the *Cuba* and instructed the prize crew to proceed on their own to the Cuban port. The following morning, the *Cuba* was nowhere in sight. It was months later when Semmes learned that during the night the *Cuba's* crew overpowered the prize crew of four men, and putting them in irons, set sail for New York.[25]

Toward evening on July 5, as the *Sumter* was approaching the Cienfuegos lighthouse with the *Machias* still in tow, two more American vessels were spotted. Semmes described their capture: *As we approached the lights, we descried two more sails in the southeast, making an offing with all diligence, to which we immediately gave chase. They were eight or ten miles distant from the land, and to facilitate our pursuit, we cast off our remaining tow, directing the prize-master to heave to off the lighthouse and await our return. We had captured three prizes in twenty-four hours, and as here were probably two more, I could perceive that my crew was becoming enamored of their business, pretty much as the veteran fox-hunter does in view of the chase. They moved about with great alacrity in obedience to orders; the seamen springing aloft to furl the sails like so many squirrels, and the fireman below sending up thick volumes of black smoke from the furnaces. The Sumter, feeling the renewed impulse of her engines, sprang forward in pursuit of the doomed craft ahead as if she too knew what was going on.* They proved to be the 284-ton *Ben Dunning* of Maine, and the 192-ton *Albert Adams,* of Massachusetts, both laden with Spanish-owned sugar, bound for European markets.[26]

Hastily throwing a small prize crew on both brigs, Semmes ordered them to "hold on" to the light of the lighthouse until morning when he intended to take them into port. The master of one of the captured vessels, who had his wife on board, informed Semmes that she and a lady companion were seriously ill with yellow fever. Semmes assured the captain that they would be well treated, and even offered to send the *Sumter's* surgeon on board the brig to attend to the ladies.

The next morning dawned bright and clear, and as the *Sumter* was about to lead her three prizes up the small river to Cienfuegos, the officer of the deck spotted a plume of smoke coming down the river from the city. Climbing into the rigging for a better view, he announced that a small steam tug was towing two barks and a brig down stream, and that all three vessels were flying United States' colors. Not wanting to violate Spanish territorial waters, which extended three miles from land, Semmes kept the *Sumter* motionless and watched as the little tug cast off her tow lines and bid her charges farewell. Meanwhile, so as not to cause suspicion, the Spanish jack was hoisted at the fore as a signal for a pilot. To further the illusion of a simple merchant steamer, Semmes ordered the yards disarranged, and sent most of the crew below. With the three heavily laden ships continuing toward the open sea, the steam tug pulled alongside the *Sumter*, and a Spanish pilot jumped on board, inquiring if Semmes wished him to take the ship up the river to Cienfuegos.

I replied in the affirmative, Semmes wrote, and said to him pleasantly, "but I am waiting a little to take back those ships you have just towed down." "Diablo!" said he, "how can that be; they are Americano del Norte, bound to Boston and la Nueva York!" "That is just what I want," said I. "We are Confederados, and we have laguerra with the Americanos del Norte!" "Caramba!" said he. "That is good; give her the steam quick, Captain!" "No, no," replied I, "wait awhile. I must pay due respect to your Queen, and the Captain-General; they command in these waters, within the league, and I must wait until the ships have passed beyond that."[27]

When the three ships were approximately five miles from land, as estimated by both Semmes and the Spanish pilot, orders were shouted and the *Sumter* bounded after them. The Spanish colors were quickly hauled down, and the Confederate ensign was rushed up the halyards, while a blank cartridge fired from the pivot gun brought all three into the wind. They were the 429-ton bark *West Wind* of Westerly, Rhode Island, the 463-ton bark *Louisa Kilham* of Boston, and the 300-ton brigantine *Naiad* of New York. All were loaded to capacity with Spanish-owned sugar. Prize crews were sent aboard, and Semmes now prepared to take his six captives into the Cuban port.

As the *Sumter* steamed cautiously up the narrow river leading toward Cienfuegos, musket fire suddenly flashed across her bow. The shots were fired by Cuban sentries stationed at a small white fort that was guarding the entrance to the harbor. Because all the captive vessels were still flying United States' colors, which were easily recognized by the Cuban sentries, Semmes signaled the prize crews to continue and ordered the *Sumter* stopped. Sending Lieutenant Evans to the fort, the *Sumter's* captain politely asked the commandant the reason for the musket fire. A Spanish officer, who met Evans at the boat ramp, explained that neither he nor his men had ever seen a Confederate flag, and he was concerned that the mysterious cruiser might be a pirate coming to sack the town. Later that afternoon the fort's commandant paid Semmes a visit, and over a glass of wine in Semmes' cabin, offered his apology and granted permission for the *Sumter* to proceed.[28]

It had been only one week since the *Sumter* had outrun the *Brooklyn* and escaped from New Orleans. While seven Northern merchant vessels had been captured, with one being destroyed, the *Sumter* was already down to only one day's supply of coal in her bunkers. Semmes sent Lieutenant Chapman ashore in search of the precious commodity and pondered the dangerous consequences of leaving a trail of frequent coaling stops for the Union navy to follow.

Chapman carried with him a letter from Semmes to Don Jose de la Pozuela, governor of Cienfuegos, which outlined the Confederate commander's views concerning the disposition of his prizes and the diplomatic position that he hoped Spain would adopt. Using his extensive knowledge of international law, Semmes argued that the Confederacy was a *de facto* government and was entitled to belligerent rights. A rule excluding Confederate prizes from Spanish ports, even if applied to both belligerents, would be, he contended, an injustice to the Confederate States. With Southern ports blockaded, and neutral ports denied, Confederate cruisers would be prevented from bringing their prizes into a port for adjudication, and they would have no choice but to destroy them on the high seas. Federal warships, on the other hand, could always sail their prizes to a Northern port. Semmes asserted that the only means of proving Spanish ownership of the vessels' cargoes was for a Confederate States prize court to examine the evidence. How could they do this if the prizes could not be taken into a Confederate or neutral port? Semmes pointed out to the governor, that while the cargoes were neutral, the ships themselves were fair prizes rightfully belonging to the Confederate States. Semmes closed by requesting that an independent agent be appointed to retain the prizes while Spanish authorities considered his arguments.

While the *Sumter* was loading coal, a dispatch arrived from Governor Pozuela, stating the Spanish government's position in regards to the prizes. Neither side, it stated, would be permitted to bring prizes into Spanish ports, and Semmes' prizes would be retained until the home government in Madrid decided what to do with them. Unknown to Semmes, was that Queen Isabella on June 17, had issued a proclamation based on the same neutrality policies as Britain and France. Appointing a Spanish agent to administer the prize affair in the name of the Confederate States, Semmes hurried the *Sumter*'s preparations for sea. Aware that there was a telegraph line between Cienfuegos and Havana, he knew it would not take Federal warships long to learn of his presence. At 11:00 p.m. on the night of July 7, 1861, the *Sumter* steamed back out to sea and shaped a course toward the Island of Barbados. Months later, Semmes learned that the Spanish government, not wanting to incur the wrath of the United States, handed the prizes back to their original owners, claiming that they were taken illegally within Spanish waters.[29]

Soon after departing Cienfuegos, the weather worsened, and for six days the frail *Sumter* battled gale-force winds and heavy seas. So little progress was made, that Semmes had to change his plans for stopping at Barbados for coal. With only two days' supply of the precious fuel remaining, the fire in the furnace was banked, and the propeller was ordered uncoupled. Sailors scurried aloft to loose the topsails, and a course was set under sail for the island of Curacao, Netherlands Antilles. On the storm-tossed night of July 13, Semmes recorded in his journal: *Heavy sea all night, and ship rolling and tumbling about, though doing pretty well. The propeller revolves freely, and we are making about five knots.* At daylight a sail was reported, but the sea was too rough to give chase.[30]

A surprising fact concerning Raphael Semmes, was that despite years of service on the oceans of the world, he suffered from acute seasickness. On the night of July 10, as the *Sumter* plowed through heavy seas, Semmes struggled out of his hammock and began to climb the ladder to the main deck. His journal entry recorded the next few moments: *At 1:30 this morning I went upon the companion ladder to give some directions to the officer of the deck ... and while so doing I felt a sudden sickness of the stomach and reeling of the brain. I laid my head on my arm, thinking the sensation would pass off, but in a moment more I lost consciousness and tumbled from the top to the bottom of the ladder upon the cabin floor.... Confined to my hammock during the day.*[31]

The weather moderated as the *Sumter* approached the Spanish Main, but adverse currents forced the use of steam again. On July 16, the *Sumter* rounded the northwest corner of the island of Curacao, which lay only a short distance off the Venezuelan coast. Later in the day, she arrived off the picturesque village of Santa Ana, and hoisting a jack and firing a gun, signaled for a pilot. Although a Dutch pilot came on board, he stated that it was now too dark, and the *Sumter* would have to wait until morning.

When the United States consul learned that a "Rebel pirate" was lying off shore and preparing to enter the harbor, he hurried to the governor to present his protests. Convinced by the consul that the *Sumter* was a privateer, the governor sent word in the morning that unless the cruiser was in distress, it could not enter the harbor. Again, Semmes sat down in his cabin and wrote a lengthy letter explaining the existence of the Confederate States and his ship's qualifications as a warship of that nation. Handing Lieutenant Chapman the finished letter, he instructed his officer to present the Confederate commander's compliments to the governor, give him the letter, and await a response.

After the lapse of an hour or two and becoming impatient, Semmes recorded, *I told my first lieutenant that as our men had not been practiced at the guns for some time, I thought it would be as well to let them burst a few of our eight-inch shells at a target. Accordingly the drum beat to quarters, a great stir was made about the deck, as the guns were cast loose, and pretty soon, whiz! went a shell across the windows of the council-chamber which overlooked the sea; the shell bursting like a clap of rather sharp, ragged thunder a little beyond, in close proximity to the target. Sundry heads were seen immediately to pop out of the windows of the chamber, and then to be withdrawn very suddenly, as though the owners of them feared that another shell was coming, and that my gunners might make a mistake in their aim. By the time we had fired three or four shells, all of which burst with beautiful precision, Chapman's boat was seen returning, and thinking that our men had had exercise enough, we ran out and secured the guns.*

My lieutenant came on board smiling, and looking pleasantly as men will do when they are bearers of good news, and said that the governor had given permission to enter. We were lying close in with the entrance, and in a few minutes more, the Sumter was gliding gracefully past the houses on either side, as she ran up the little canal, or river, that split the town in two. The quays were crowded with a motley gathering of townspeople, men, women, and children, to see us pass, and sailors waved their hats to us from the shipping in the port. Running through the town into a land-locked basin in its rear, the Sumter let go her anchor, hoisted out our boats, and spread her awnings,—and we were once more in port.[32]

The *Sumter* spent a week at Curacao, and while Kell kept part of the crew busy painting and caulking, those not on duty were given shore liberty. In addition, the first lieutenant also contracted with a local shipyard to replace the fore-topmast which had been damaged in the rough weather of recent days. The *Sumter* had been at sea less than a month, but already her engine and boilers were in need of repairs. Consequently, the engineers spent hours scraping and cleaning the boilers, fire boxes, and flues. With her bunkers filled with 115 tons of English coal, and with monkeys, which had been brought on board by the adventuresome crew, swinging from the rigging, the *Sumter* sailed out to sea on July 24. Semmes described their departure: *Accordingly, at twelve o'clock precisely, on the day last above mentioned ... the Sumter, bidding farewell to her new made friends, moved gracefully out of the harbor—this time amid the waving of handkerchiefs in female hands, as well as of hats in the hands of the males; the quay, being lined as before, to see us depart. The photographer took a last shot of the ship as she glided past his sanctum, and we looked with some little interest to the future numbers of that "Journal of Civilization," vulgarly yclept "Harpers Weekly," for the interesting portrait.* A few months later, Semmes did see the photo in *Harpers Weekly*, which obediently listed it as a picture of the "Rebel pirate."[33]

As the *Sumter* sailed out into the blue waters of the Caribbean, the Federal consul at Santa Ana was rushing an urgent dispatch to his superiors in Washington. The consul confidently reported that the "Rebel Pirate" was headed for the commercial crossroads of Canal de la Mona between Santo Domingo and Puerto Rico. Semmes, who kept his own consul and rarely confided his intentions to anyone except his first lieutenant, had purposely spread the word among some of the crew that they were headed toward this area of the Caribbean. It had not taken long for the Federal representative at Curacao to overhear this bit of "intelligence" from the *Sumter's* boisterous sailors making their rounds of drinking establishments on the island. This simple spreading of false information would become the trademark of Raphael Semmes, not only with the cruise of the *Sumter*, but later with the *Alabama* as well. While Union Secretary of the Navy, Gideon Welles, was rushing warships to the coast of Puerto Rico, the *Sumter* was capturing enemy merchant vessels along the coast of Venezuela.[34]

Chapter Two

Farewell at Gibraltar

The fiery disk of the morning sun rose quickly over the clear waters of the Caribbean on July 24, 1861. It was the day after the *Sumter's* departure from Curacao, and through the bluish morning haze, the sunlight revealed the mystic and majestic mountains of Laguayra, rising thirty miles to the west along the Venezuelan coast. With the advent of daylight and limitless visibility, the *Sumter's* lookout was not long in crying "Sail ho!" from the masthead. The vessel sighted was off the port bow and after a short chase, the schooner *Abby Bradford* from New York bound for Puerto Cabello, Venezuela, was brought into the wind. *We knew our prize to be American long before she showed us her colors,* Semmes explained. *She was a "down-east" fore and aft schooner, and there are no other such vessels in the world. They are as thoroughly marked as the Puritans who build them, and there is no more mistaking the "cut of their jib."*

No attempt had been made to cover her cargo of flour and provisions, which Kell estimated at $25,000, with neutral certificates, but Semmes suspected that it was owned by a Venezuelan merchant. Determined to try his hand at convincing Venezuelan authorities to allow him to bring his prizes into their ports, Semmes sailed for Puerto Cabello, entering the sleepy harbor with the *Abby Bradford* in tow on July 26. Dispatching a letter to the local governor, the Confederate commander requested permission to place the *Abby Bradford* in the custody of the Venezuelan government, until she could be adjudicated by a Confederate court.[1]

First Lieutenant John McIntosh Kell, executive officer of the *Sumter*. This superb photgraph of Kell, resplendent in his new blue Confederate uniform, was taken in New Orleans the day before the *Sumter* sailed.

The small seaports along the Venezuelan coast were heavily dependent upon American ships for carrying their products to world markets, and the ever present United States consul had little trouble in convincing the governor that it would not be in his best interest to deal with the "Rebel pirate." Within a few hours, Semmes received an official letter ordering him to depart within twenty-four hours. Placing a prize crew on board the *Abby Bradford*, with the *Sumter's* quartermaster, Eugene Ruhl in charge, Semmes ordered him to sail the schooner to New Orleans. The Confederate commander was also very careful to instruct Ruhl to make landfall west of the city in one of the many secluded coves along the Louisiana coast. The following morning the *Sumter* steamed out of Puerto Cabello, followed by the *Abby Bradford*, and Ruhl set sail for the Confederacy. Unfortunately, Ruhl failed to follow Semmes' instructions. Instead of entering one of the desolate coves along the coast, he attempted to enter New Orleans itself and was captured by a Federal blockader.[2]

Soon after seeing the *Abby Bradford* off, another sail was discovered making its way along the Venezuelan coast. With light winds and a calm sea, the 295-ton bark *Joseph Maxwell* of Philadelphia, became an easy capture and the *Sumter's* tenth prize. The *Joseph Maxwell* had just departed Laguayra, where she had unloaded a portion of her cargo and was proceeding to Puerto Cabello to off-load the remainder. After an examination of her papers, Semmes determined that a portion of the remaining cargo belonged to a Venezuelan merchant in Puerto Cabbello.

Heaving the bark to in charge of a prize crew, Semmes recorded, *I took her master on board the Sumter, and steaming back into the harbor, sent Paymaster Myers on shore with him to see if some arrangement could not be made, by which the interests of the neutral half-owner of the cargo could be protected; to see, in other words, whether this prize, in which a Venezuelan citizen was interested, would not be permitted to enter and remain until she could be adjudicated. Much to my surprise, upon the return of my boat, the paymaster handed me a written 'command' from the governor to bring the Maxwell in and deliver her to him until the 'Venezuelan courts' could determine whether she had been captured within the marine league or not! This insolence was refreshing. I scarcely knew whether to laugh or be angry at it.*

Noting that Venezuelan soldiers were manning the rusting guns of an old stone fort nearby, an angry Semmes ordered Kell to beat to quarters. With the *Sumter's* crew standing by their loaded guns, the Confederate cruiser turned and steamed defiantly back out to sea. The *Joseph Maxwell's* draft of thirteen feet precluded taking the prize into a small isolated Confederate port, and no sailing vessel would stand a chance of successfully running the blockade into one of the principal harbors. Not willing to burn the prize because of her neutral cargo, Semmes placed Midshipman William A. Hicks in command and ordered him to take the bark to Cienfuegos. There, Hicks was to leave the ship in charge of an agent until a Confederate court could settle the ownership of her cargo. Semmes was obviously still unaware of Spain's neutrality proclamation. Hicks sailed the bark to Cienfuegos, but was ordered to leave. A short distance outside of the harbor, he mistook a Spanish vessel for a Federal warship, and in his eagerness to escape, ran the *Joseph Maxwell* aground. Abandoning the prize, Hicks and his crew returned to Cienfuegos in one of the bark's open boats, where some time later he made his way back to the Confederacy.[3]

For the next several days, the *Sumter* steamed eastward along the Venezuelan coast with little traffic being encountered. It was the rainy season in this part of the world, and visibility was down to less than a mile. *On board ship,* Semmes wrote, *we looked like so many half-drowned rats. The officer of the deck, trumpet in hand, was ensconced to his ears in his India-rubber pea jacket, his long beard looking like a wet mop, and little rills of rain trickling down his neck and shoulders from his slouched "Sou'wester." The midshipman of the watch had taken off his shoes, and rolled up his trousers, and was paddling about in the pools on deck as well pleased as a young duck. And as for the old salt, he was in his element. There was plenty of fresh water to wash his clothes in, and accordingly the decks were filled with industrious washers, or rather scrubbers, each with his scrubbing-brush and a bit of soap, and a little pile of soiled duck frocks and trousers by his side.*[4]

On July 30, with her coal bunkers almost empty, the *Sumter* ran through the Bocas del Drago, or Dragon's Mouth, into the Gulf of Paria, and entered the harbor of Port of Spain in the island of Trinidad. This was the first English port visited by the *Sumter,* and soon her decks were crowded with well-wishers and curiosity seekers. One of these was the master of a Baltimore brig that was preparing to depart Port of Spain, who asked Semmes if he intended on capturing his vessel. Semmes assured him that even though Maryland had been prevented from leaving the Union, the Confederacy considered her a friend, and he would have nothing to fear from the *Sumter*. The master was elated, and returning to his ship, sailed the next day.

While the *Sumter* was being loaded with coal, a British 12-gun steam frigate arrived in port. Semmes was impressed by the courtesies that the officers of this warship, the *H.M.S. Cadmus*, extended to him and his officers, but was amused by one of the English officer's visit to the *Sumter*. A young lieutenant who came on board was invited by Semmes into the Confederate commander's cabin where, after the usual pleasantries, the lieutenant informed Semmes that he had been instructed by his captain to ask to see Semmes' commission. With tongue-in-cheek, Semmes replied that he would be only too happy to present his commission,—provided that the English officer displayed his first. The lieutenant had come prepared.... "*Here is her majesty's commission,*" Semmes wrote later, *unrolling at the same time a large square parchment, beautifully engraved with nautical devices, and with sundry seals pendent therefrom. In return I handed him a small piece of coarse and rather dingy paper, at the bottom of which was inscribed the name of Jefferson Davis. He read the commission carefully, and when he had done, remarked, as he handed it back to me, "Mr. Davis has a smooth, bold signature."*[5]

It took four days to load what turned out to be inferior coal, and six more days were lost while excessive corrosion was cleaned from the boilers. Finally, on August 5, the *Sumter* steamed out of Port of Spain and turned her head eastward along the coast of Trinidad.

The next day the cruiser entered the Atlantic Ocean and set a course that would take her along the northern coast of Brazil. Initially, the weather was good with calm seas, and the *Sumter* made steady progress steaming along at eight knots. Semmes was disappointed, however, that a vessel required a thirteen mile chase before a blank cartridge from the rifled pivot brought her to. She proved to be a Dutch brig. Another sail was spotted at approximately twelve miles, but Semmes felt the chase was not worth the consumption of coal it would require to overhaul her. The weather began to deteriorate, and soon the *Sumter* was rolling and pitching in an angry sea. The wind came whistling through her rigging directly off the bow, and together with the strong ocean currents, impeded her progress considerably. Adding to the woes, Engineer Freeman now reported that evidently they had been cheated by the coal merchant in Port of Spain, and the *Sumter's* bunkers contained considerably less fuel than they had estimated.

Things were beginning now to look decidedly serious, Semmes recorded. *I had but three days of fuel on board, and upon consulting my chart, I found that I was still 550 miles from my port, current taken into account. It was not possible for the dull little Sumter to make this distance in the given time if the wind and current should continue of the same strength. I resolved to try her, how-ever, another night, hoping that some change for the better might take place.*

Semmes' journal entry for August 11, records the conditions en-countered at daybreak the following day: "*The morning has dawned with a fresh breeze, and a rough sea into which we have been plunging all night, making but little headway. The genius of the east wind refuses to permit even steam to invade his domain, and drives us back with disdain. His ally, the current, has retarded us sixty miles in the last twenty-four hours! I now no longer hesitated, but directing the engineer to let his fires go down, turned my ship's head to the westward, and made sail; it being my intention to run down the coast to Cayenne in French Guiana, with the hope of obtaining a fresh supply of fuel at that place.*[6]

On August 15, as the guns from the surrounding forts roared in celebration of Louis Napoleon's birthday, the *Sumter* sailed into the harbor of the French penal colony at Cayenne. Semmes sent Lieuten-ant Evans and Paymaster Myers to call upon the governor to request permission to coal, but they were the recipients of a most unfriendly reception. The governor insisted that the *Sumter* would have to be quar-antined for five days, and that there was absolutely no coal to be had at any price. Once again, Semmes had run afoul of a United States consul who wielded much influence over a foreign colony. Within an hour after the return of Evans and Myers, the *Sumter* was steaming down the coast in the direction of Netherlands, Guiana. Semmes hoped that the industrious Dutch would prove more receptive.[7]

On the evening of August 18, the *Sumter* dropped anchor at the shal-low mouth of the Surinam River which leads to the town of Paramaribo. *Soon after we came to anchor,* Semmes related, *we descried a steamer in the west, steering for the mouth of the river. Nothing was more likely than that, by this time, the enemy should have sent some of his fast gun-boats in pursuit of us, and the smoke of a steamer on the horizon, therefore, caused me some uneasi-ness.... The steamer now approaching, having been descried at a great distance by the curling of her black smoke high into the still air, night set in before she was near enough to be made out. We could see her form indistinctly, in the darkness, but no certain conclusions could be arrived at as to her size or nation-ality. I at once caused my fires to be lighted, and beating to quarters, prepared my ship for action. We stood at our guns for some time, but seeing, about ten P. M., that the strange steamer (had) come to anchor some three or four miles outside of us, I permitted the men to leave their quarters, cautioning the officer of the watch, however, to keep a bright lookout during the night for the ap-proach of boats, and to call me if there should be any cause for alarm.*

Semmes was troubled as he turned in. He suspected that the stranger was a warship, but whose warship, he did not know. As he tossed and turned in his bunk, he weighed the facts in his mind. The steamer had anchored with no lights showing and seemed to be paying no attention to the *Sumter*. She could not be a mail packet, he reasoned, for they always ran well-lighted. In addition, a mail packet's commander would have had knowledge of the entrance to the river and would not have stopped to wait for daylight. Perhaps this was a trick being practiced by a clever Federal captain who was trying to put his ship as close as possible to the *Sumter* with the intent of attacking her at first light. The more Semmes pondered, the more he was convinced that she was a warship of some kind. *...It was of no use to speculate upon the chances of her being an enemy,* he concluded; *daylight only could reveal that. In the meantime, the best thing we could do would be to get a good night's rest, so as to rise refreshed for the morning's work, if work there should be.*[8]

As daylight began to edge its way over the eastern horizon, the long roll of the drum broke the silence on the *Sumter*. Men tumbled out of their hammocks and fumbled in the darkness getting dressed. Hastening through dimly lit passageways, they clambered up the ladders to the main deck, and rushing to their division, hurriedly cast loose the guns and made them ready to fire. Other crew members were busy raising the anchor, while down below, steam began hissing through the valves in the engine room. From the horse block, Semmes, with his marine glass to his eyes, could see that the mysterious steamer was also getting under way, and that she was turning directly toward the *Sumter*. Orders were passed to the engine room, and Engineer Freeman threw the levers and opened the valves to start the engine. As the cruiser began to move, the helmsman spun the wheel, bringing the *Sumter* around to meet the oncoming stranger head on.

As the two vessels drew closer, Semmes could see that the mysterious steamer was a side-wheeler and about the same size as the *Sumter*. They appeared to be evenly matched. Neither vessel as yet, had shown her colors, and Semmes ordered the French ensign hoisted to force the approaching ship to reveal her nationality. To the astonishment of everyone on the *Sumter*, the tricolor was hoisted to the mizzenmast of the approaching steamer. Here was an embarrassment! A Confederate cruiser, impersonating a French warship, was coming face to face with a real French warship! Quickly the French flag was hauled down, and the Confederate colors thrown to the breeze.[9]

The stranger was the French warship *Vulture*, which had run short of fuel while conveying convicts to the penal colony at Cayenne, and she, too, was headed up the Surinam River to Paramaribo. After exchanging pleasantries, the French side-wheeler took on a pilot, and with the *Sumter* following in her wake, both vessels steamed up the river. The *Sumter's* anchor had barely splashed into the pristine waters of Paramaribo harbor, when the American consul, Henry Sawyer, conveyed his protests to the governor. His arguments that the Confederate cruiser was a privateer and a "pirate" were ignored, and the *Sumter's* officers and men received a warm reception in this Dutch possession.

Although it had been less than three weeks since her overhaul in Trinidad, the *Sumter* was now in need of more repairs, and of course, her coal supply was nearly depleted. In spite of the offer of the American consul to purchase all the coal in Paramaribo, which would keep it from the "pirate," the *Sumter's* bunkers were soon overflowing with the "black gold." At Kell's suggestion, two water tanks were dismantled and the area was used for the stowage of additional coal, thereby extending the ship's steaming capacity from eight days to twelve.

While this work was being accomplished, Semmes took the rare opportunity to go ashore and attend Catholic mass. *The church was a neat, well arranged wooden building, of large dimensions,* he wrote, *and filled to overflowing with devout worshippers. All the shades of color, from "snowy white to sooty" were there, and there did not seem to be any order in the seating of the congregation, the shades being promiscuously mixed. The preacher was fluent and earnest in action, but his sermon, which seemed to impress the congregation, being in that beautiful and harmonious language which we call "low Dutch," was entirely unintelligible to me. The Latin mass and ceremonies—which are the same all over the world—were, of course, quite familiar, and awoke many tender reminiscences.*[10]

Newspapers from the island of Barbados, brought on board by visiting French and Dutch officers, revealed to Semmes that the Federal warship *Keystone State* had stopped there on July 21, while searching for the *Sumter*, and another article reported the dispatching of the heavy steamers *Niagara* and *Crusader* to Cienfuegos, Cuba. The false information planted by Semmes had worked, and so far, the Union warships were following a cold trail. On August 30, after leaving word that he was sailing for Barbados to look for the *Keystone State*, the *Sumter* dropped down river to the bar and was anchored for the night while last minute tasks were taken care of. The next morning, amid gently rolling swells and a fresh wind from the northeast, she stood out to sea and headed north. Once out of sight of land, however, Semmes ordered Kell to change course to the southeast, and the Confederate cruiser headed for the shipping lanes off the coast of Brazil.[11]

Cruising south, the *Sumter* crossed the mouth of the great Amazon River, and pushed on toward the Brazilian port of São Luis. As usual, coal was soon in short supply, and a sail that was sighted in the distance on September 4 was not chased in order to conserve the precious fuel. No other ship was spotted, and Semmes began to suspect, correctly as it turned out, that commerce was being diverted from the shipping lanes as the word spread concerning the presence of the

Sumter. Soon after he crossed the equator, Semmes ordered the Stars and Bars hoisted, even though there were no other beings to witness the ceremony. This was the first instance of the Confederate flag being carried to the Southern Hemisphere. Cruising through the shallow waters off the coast of Brazil, Semmes reached the passage to São Luis harbor too late in the evening to hazard an entrance. In the morning, with no pilot boat in sight, Semmes determined to steam through the shallow water on his own.

We rounded safely the shoals of Mount Itacolomi, and passed the middle ground of the Meio, Semmes recorded later, *and I was already congratulating myself that the danger was past, when the ship ran plump upon a sandbank and stopped! She went on at full speed, and the shock to those standing on deck was almost sufficient to throw them off their feet. We had a skillful leadsman in the chains, and at his last cast, he had found no bottom with eight fathoms of line, all that the speed of the ship would allow him to sink. Here was a catastrophe! Were the bones of the Sumter to be laid to rest on the coast of Brazil, and her commander and crew to return to the Confederate States and report to the government that they had lost its only ship of war! This idea flashed through my mind for an instant, but only for an instant, for the work of the moment pressed. The engineer on duty had stopped his engine without waiting for orders as soon as he felt the ship strike, and I now ordered it reversed. In a moment more the screw was revolving in the opposite direction, and the strong tide which was running out, catching the ship on the port bow at the same time, she swung round to starboard, and slid off the almost perpendicular edge of the bank into deep water, pretty much as a turtle will drop off a log. The first thing I did was to draw a deep breath, and the second was to put on an air of indifference, as if nothing had happened, and tell the officer of the deck, in the coolest manner possible, to "let her go ahead."* A nearby fisherman, seeing the *Sumter's* difficulty, came on board and offered to safely guide the Confederate cruiser. With his help, the *Sumter* was soon at anchor in the harbor of São Luis, and as Semmes recorded: *The Confederate States flag waved in the Empire of Brazil.*[12]

While the *Sumter* was being coaled and provisioned, Semmes went ashore on September 8, and registered at the Hotel de Porto to rest and recover from his constant bouts with seasickness. The owner of the hotel, Señor Porto, who had once followed the sea, was now a man with considerable influence in government affairs. He and Semmes soon became friends, and with Porto's assistance, the *Sumter's* commander was able to procure everything that he needed for his ship. By September 15, she had been painted, coaled, repaired, and provisioned. And Semmes was out of cash. Borrowing $2,000 from J. Wetson, a prosperous Texan now living in São Luis, Semmes sailed in mid-afternoon, and soon the little *Sumter* was plowing her way through the gentle swells of the Atlantic Ocean. Four days after the departure of the Confederate cruiser, the powerful USS *Powhatan*, commanded by David Dixon Porter, steamed into the harbor of São Luis.[13]

Semmes ordered the *Sumter's* course set for the equatorial calm belt which begins at about five degrees north latitude. Here, where there would be calm seas, variable winds, and numerous rain showers, the *Sumter* could lie in wait under easy sail, and observe all the homeward-bound traffic that historically traverses this area. If an American vessel was spotted, Semmes could quickly order steam raised and accomplish the capture without the expenditure of excessive fuel. The *Sumter* reached the calm belt on September 24, and on the next day, the welcome cry of "Sail ho!" resounded from the masthead.

It had been almost two months since the Confederate cruiser had captured an enemy merchant ship, and with the cry from aloft, the excited crew raced to their stations. Within thirty minutes, the sails were snugly furled, steam was hissing in the engine room, and the *Sumter* was charging across the smooth sea in hot pursuit. With little wind to fill the stranger's sails, the *Sumter* approached rapidly, and when near enough for a hail, ordered the merchant vessel to heave to. At the same time, the Confederate colors were being rushed up the halyards. With no opportunity for escape, the captured vessel quickly obeyed. She was the *Joseph Park*, a 244-ton brigantine from Boston, six days out of Pernambuco, and was in ballast, because she could not obtain a cargo from merchants who had heard that the *Sumter* was at São Luis. Semmes was amused by an entry in the *Joseph Park's* log, written by her captain at the start of her voyage, stating that, "We have a tight, fast vessel, and so we don't care for Jeff. Davis."

After removing such articles as provisions, sails, and cordage from the prize, Semmes transferred the *Joseph Park's* crew of seven to the *Sumter* and sent a prize crew on board the captured vessel. Placing Lieutenant Evans in command, he instructed Evans to remain within seven or eight miles of the *Sumter* during the daylight hours, closing in to three or four miles at night, and to act as a scout for the cruiser. In this way, the "eyes" of the *Sumter* would cover a greater area of the vast sea around them.[14]

The two ships cruised slowly together for several days, but not a single sail was sighted. Finally, on September 29, a disappointed Semmes signaled the *Joseph Park* to draw in close, and removing the prize crew, he instructed Lieutenant Kell to give the men a little gunnery practice. A layer of darkness had spread over the placid ocean by the time the firing ceased, and the guns were secured. As the crew watched, a boat pulled away from the side of the *Sumter*, and immediately, the *Joseph Park* burst into flames. The fire spread quickly and

The *Sumter* firing on the brigantine *Joseph Parks*, September 25, 1861. Semmes had used the *Joseph Parks* as a scout for several days; however, no sails were sighted. Finally, with the prize crew removed, Kell exercised the cruiser's guns on the doomed brig.

within a few minutes, she was a raging inferno. As the boat hurried to return, the lurid light from the crackling flames reflected off the still waters of the ocean and danced against the black hull of the *Sumter* as she stood off several hundred yards. The fire, racing up the rigging and outlining the merchant vessel against the nighttime sky, marked a dramatic change in the Confederacy's war at sea. No longer was there any hope of taking a prize into a neutral port for adjudication. From now on, Semmes and other Confederate commanders would have no choice but to apply the torch.

Semmes spent the next ten days cruising slowly within the calm belt, but only neutral sails were sighted. Meanwhile, Porter with the *Powhatan*, had left São Luis and was still doggedly searching for the *Sumter*. On the dark night of October 5, 1861, lookouts on the *Powhatan* spotted a flickering light on the distant horizon, and the Federal cruiser sped toward the glow. Suddenly, the light disappeared. Later, after reading the account of the *Sumter's* positions during her cruise and comparing it to that of the *Powhatan*, Porter concluded that it was indeed the *Sumter* he had sighted across the wide expanse of darkened ocean. Semmes agreed, after comparing the two reports, that the light came from the *Sumter*, but while Porter estimated the distance as 75 miles, Semmes placed the two ships at only 40 miles apart. Close enough, Semmes concluded, that on a clear day they could have seen each other's smoke.[15]

More than a month had passed without the *Sumter's* crew capturing a prize. Semmes was convinced the word had spread concerning the Confederate cruiser, and Northern captains were steering clear of the normal shipping lanes. It was now approaching the end of October, and the crew was preparing for the usual Sunday muster when the cry "Sail ho!" echoed from the masthead. Muster preparations were quickly forgotten, as sailors scurried about the deck and into the rigging to unfurl the sails. Firemen and engineers hurried down the ladders to the engine room, and soon black smoke was pouring from the *Sumter's* stack as she bounded over the calm sea in hurried pursuit. The distant vessel was a fast one, and it took the better part of the day to draw within firing range. Finally, at approximately 3:00 p.m., the pivot gun crew fired a single blank cartridge, and the merchant ship quickly rounded into the wind. She was the *Daniel Trowbridge* of New Haven, a 200-ton schooner out of New York and bound for Demerara in British Guiana. Her hold was crammed with provisions and delicacies of great variety, and it took the *Sumter's* crew two days to transfer all the food stuffs to the cruiser's lockers. Once all the beef, pork, canvassed hams, ship-bread, fancy crackers, cheese, and flour was on board the *Sumter*, the *Daniel Trowbridge* was set ablaze.[16]

After the sailing from São Luis, Semmes had overhauled and stopped fifteen neutrals and captured only two Northern merchantmen. He did not consider his cruise a failure, however, because newspapers acquired from many of the neutral ships were replete with articles describing the demoralization within the Northern merchant marine service. Scores of American ships were laid up in various ports, because they could not secure cargoes, and insurance rates for shippers transporting in American bottoms were increasing to prohibitive levels. Semmes was also aware that at least four or five Federal warships were searching for him, which meant that there were fewer Union ships in the blockading fleets surrounding the Confederate coast. With coal again running short from the constant chasing of neutral sails, the *Sumter* entered the harbor of Fort de France on the island of Martinique, on November 9, and dropped anchor.

Semmes paid a personal call on Maussion de Cande, governor of the island, who was also a rear admiral in the French navy, and requested permission to purchase coal from the government stocks. Cande greeted Semmes cordially, and stated that he could purchase all the supplies that Semmes needed, but he would have to do so from the commercial facilities across the bay at St. Pierre. While Semmes dispatched Lieutenant Chapman and Paymaster Myers across the bay in search of coal and warm pea jackets for the crew, Kell granted shore liberty to the men who were not on duty. Soon the town was alive with drunken revelers, as the Confederate sailors made their rounds of the grog shops. Semmes reported that his men "behaved tolerably well," but narrated an amusing story:

Poor Jack! How strong upon him is the thirst for drink! ... It was about nine p.m., and I was below in my cabin, making preparations to retire. Presently I heard a plunge into the water, a hail, and almost simultaneously, a shot fired from one of the (Marine) sentinel's rifles. The boatswain's-mate's whistle now sounded, as a boat "was called away," and rapid shuffling of feet was heard overhead, as the boat was being lowered. Upon reaching the deck, I found that one of the fireman, who had come off from "liberty" a little tight, had jumped overboard, and in defiance of the hail, and shot of the sentinel, struck out lustily for the shore. The moon was shinning brightly, and an amusing scene now occurred. The boat was in hot pursuit, and soon came upon the swimmer; but the latter, who dived like a duck, had no notion of being taken. As the boat would come up with him, and "back all," for the purpose of picking him up, he would dive under her bottom, and presently would be seen either abeam or astern, "striking out," like a good fellow again. By the time the boat could turn and get headway once more, the swimmer would have some yards the start of her, and when she again came up with him, the same tactics would follow. The crew, hearing what was going on, had all turned out of their hammocks, and come on deck to witness the fun; and fun it really was for some minutes, as the doubling, and diving, and twisting, and turning went on—the boat now being sure she had him, and now sure she hadn't. The fellow finally escaped and probably a more chop-fallen boat's crew never returned alongside of a ship, than was the Sumter's that night. An officer was now sent on shore in pursuit of the fugitive. He had no difficulty in finding him. In half an hour after the performance of his clever feat, the fireman was lying—dead drunk—in one of the 'cabarets,' in the sailor quarter of the town. He had no intention of deserting, but had braved the sentinel's bullet, the shark—which abounds in these waters—and discipline— all for the sake of a glass of grog.[17]

On November 13, the *Sumter* raised her anchor and steamed across the bay to St. Pierre to begin loading the coal for which Chapman and Myers had contracted. While there, Kell took advantage of the excellent dockyard facilities to replace the foreyard and to scrape and repair the boilers. On the next day, at 2:30 in the afternoon, as the coaling continued and mechanics were busy working on the boilers, the 8-gun steam sloop USS *Iroquois*, captained by Commander James S. Palmer, rounded the north end of the island. Palmer attempted to disguise his ship by flying the Danish colors and keeping all his gun ports closed, but Semmes, noting the crisp lines of a warship, was not fooled.

We caught sight of the enemy first, Semmes related. *He was crawling slowly from behind the land which had hidden him from view, and we could see a number of curious human forms above the rail bending eagerly in our direction. The quarterdeck in particular was filled with officers, and we were near enough to see that some of these had telescopes in their hands, with which they were scanning the shipping in the harbor. We had a small Confederate States flag flying, and it was amusing to witness the movements on board the Iroquois, the moment this was discovered. A rapid passing to and fro of officers was observable, as if orders were being carried in a great hurry, and the steamer, which had been hitherto cautiously creeping along, ... sprang forward under a full head of steam. At the same moment, down came the Danish and up went the United States flag. "There she comes with a bone in her mouth!" said the old quartermaster on the look-out; and no doubt Captain Palmer thought to see every moment, the little Sumter flying from her anchors.*[18]

Semmes' lack of concern was based on the fact that the *Sumter* was anchored in a French port under the protection of the French flag. He knew he could not outrun nor outfight the *Iroquois*, but trusted to the adherence by the Federal captain, to the rules of international law. Any hostile action toward the *Sumter* in a French port would constitute an act of war against France itself. In addition, international law required a belligerent vessel to remain in port for twenty-four hours after the departure of an enemy. With this in mind, Semmes resigned himself to a waiting game with the Federal warship, and the coaling and re-pairs continued, much to the annoyance of the commander of the *Iroquois*. Palmer steamed into the harbor and lowered a boat which communicated with the American consul. He did not anchor, how-ever, and thus he did not fall under the twenty-four hour rule. Soon the *Iroquois* could be seen outside of the bay, steaming slowly back and forth beyond the three mile limit.

Later that evening, Semmes had turned in at his usual hour, but was hurriedly awakened a few minutes after midnight. *At half-past one o'clock, the officer of the deck came down in great haste to say that the Iroquois had again entered the harbor, and was steaming directly for us. I ordered him to get the men immediately to their quarters, and followed him on deck as soon as I could throw on a necessary garment or two. In a very few minutes, the battery had been cast loose, the decks lighted, and the other preparations usual for battle made. It was moonlight, and the movements of the enemy could be distinctly seen. He came along, under low steam, but so steadily, and aiming so directly for us, that I could not doubt it was his intention to board us. The men were called to "repel boarders," and for a moment or two, a pin might have been heard to drop on the Sumter's deck, so silent was the harbor, and so still was the scene on board both ships. Presently, however, a couple of strokes on the enemy's steam gong were heard, and in a moment more, he sheered a little, and lay off our quarter motionless. It was as though a great sea-monster had crawled in under cover of the night, and was eyeing its prey, and licking its chops in anticipation of a delicious repast. After a few minutes of apparent hesitation and doubt, the steam gong was again struck, and the leviathan—for such the Iroquois appeared alongside the little Sumter—moving in a slow and graceful curve, turned and went back whence it came. This operation, much to my astonishment, was repeated several times during the night. Captain Palmer was evidently in great tribulation.*[19]

The next morning, the governor, upon hearing of the illegal and threatening actions of the Federal warship, dispatched the French war steamer *Acheron* to St. Pierre, with orders to enforce French neutrality. Commander Palmer was told that he would have to either anchor in the harbor or remain outside the marine league. Palmer choose to attempt to blockade the *Sumter* from outside the large crescent-shaped bay, and took a position where he could move either north or south, depending upon the direction that the *Sumter* might attempt to escape. Knowing that Semmes' only chance for slipping by him would be on a dark night, Palmer secretly arranged to have signal lights hoisted to the masthead of the Northern schooner *Windward*. The number of lights displayed would indicate the direction that the "Rebel pirate" was taking.

Semmes learned of this arrangement and protested vigorously to French authorities. Palmer, knowing the criticism he would receive back home if he let the *Sumter* slip by him, was desperate to prevent her escape, and therefore ignored the French orders to remove the warning lights. The citizens of Martinique anticipated a confrontation at any time, and the surrounding vantage points were crowded every day with curious spectators. Semmes, in his usual off-handed manner, encouraged these rumors which kept the lone Federal cruiser on constant alert. But Semmes had no intention of challenging the heavily armed Union warship. His mind was on running, not fighting. Messengers had brought warnings that other Federal cruisers were on their way, and if they joined the *Iroquois* outside of the harbor, his chances for escape would be slim. He had to act and act quickly. What the *Sumter* needed most was a moonless night. Pulling the almanac off his cabin shelf, Semmes found that on November 23, the moon would not rise until shortly after 11:00 p.m. The Confederate commander felt that "this would be ample time in which to escape or be captured."

I gave orders to the first lieutenant, to see that every person belonging to the ship was on board at sundown, Semmes wrote, and directed him to make all the necessary preparations for getting (up) *his anchor, and putting the ship under steam, at eight P. M.—the hour of gunfire; the gun at the garrison to be the signal for moving.* Shortly before the sounding of the eight o'clock gun, all was ready on board. Unneeded spars had been lowered to the deck, and every available sail had been set. The *Sumter's* crew was standing silently by their loaded guns, each man, no doubt, deep in his own thoughts. Below, firemen continued to swing shovels of precious coal into the roaring furnace, while steam hissed through the pipes and valves. Engineers, oil cans in hand, hurried about lubricating and checking the machinery one more time. All was dark and quiet on the main deck, and the hum of humanity coming from the marketplace on shore was easily audible. Semmes anxiously paced the horse block. The *Sumter* was ready.

The muffled windless on board the Sumter was quietly heaving up the anchor, Semmes wrote. *It is already up, and the "cat hooked," and the men "walking away with the cat." The engineer is standing, lever in hand, ready to start the engine, and a seaman, with an uplifted ax, is standing near the taffarel to cut the sternfast. One minute more and the gun will fire! Everyone is listening eagerly for the sound. The Iroquois is quite visible through our glasses, watching for the Sumter like the spider for the fly. A flash! and an almost simultaneous boom of the eight o'clock gun, and without one word being uttered on board the Sumter, the ax descends upon the fast, the engineer's lever is turned, and the ship bounds forward under a full head of steam.*

The *Iroquois*, at 1,016 tons, was much heavier than the *Sumter*, and she was at least two to three knots faster. Her armament included a rifled 50-pounder, two 11-inch smoothbores, and four 32-pounders. A confrontation with these heavy guns would be fatal for the frail Confederate cruiser. Semmes continued his description of this night: *A prolonged and deafening cheer at once arose from the assembled multitude in the market place. Skillful and trusty helmsmen, under the direction of the "master," bring the Sumter's head around to the south, where they hold it so steady that she does not swerve a hair's breadth. There is not a light visible on board. The lantern in the captain's cabin has a jacket on it, and even the binnacle is screened so that no one but the old quartermaster at the "con" can see the light or the compass. The French steamer-of-war Acheron lay almost directly in our course, and as we bounded past her, nearly grazing her guns, officers and men rushed to the side and in momentary forgetfulness of their neutrality, waved hats and hands at us.*

Semmes had stationed one of his lieutenants where he could observe the schooner *Windward*, and within a few minutes, the officer came running aft shouting, "*I see them, sir! I see them!—look sir, there are two red lights, one above the other at the Yankee schooner's masthead.*" *Sure enough,* Semmes continued, *there were the lights; and I knew as well as the exhibitor of them, what they meant to say to the Iroquois, viz.: "Look out for the Sumter, she is standing south!"*

The *Sumter* continued on her southerly course, her billowing black smoke disappearing into the dark night. Only the steady thump of the engine and the gentle swishing of the water being parted by her graceful bow broke the deadly silence. Her crew stood motionless by their guns, straining to see into the darkness, and realizing that at any moment, an 11-inch shell might come crashing into their sides.

I ran a few hundred yards farther on my present course and then stopped, Semmes explained. *The island of Martinique is mountainous, and near the south end of the town, where I now was, the mountains run abruptly into the sea, and cast quite a shadow upon the waters for some distance out. I had the advantage of operating within this shadow. I now directed my glass toward the Iroquois. I have said that Captain Palmer was anxious to catch me, and judging by the speed which the Iroquois was now making toward the south in obedience to her signals, his anxiety had not been at all abated by his patient watching of nine days. I now did what poor Reynard sometimes does when he is hard pressed by the hounds—I doubled. Whilst the Iroquois was driving like mad under all steam for the south, wondering, no doubt at every step, what the d——l had become of the Sumter, this little craft was doing her level best for the north end of the island.*

Shortly after the *Sumter* had reversed her course and headed north, an engineer rushed up on deck from below to find Semmes. The bearings holding the propeller shaft were overheating, he reported, and it was absolutely necessary that they stop to allow them to cool. For twenty long minutes, the *Sumter* lay motionless opposite Martinique while engineers poured water on the overheated bearings. Fortunately, because of the mountainous backdrop, she was still invisible to the *Iroquois*. Finally, with her bearings cooled, the *Sumter* raced on toward the open sea. Soon a welcome rain squall overtook the speeding Confederate warship and enveloped her in its protective folds. By the time the moon broke over the eastern horizon, the little *Sumter* was steaming by the island of Dominica with no pursuer in sight, and Semmes wrote ... *it is safe to say, that the next morning, the two vessels were one hundred and fifty miles apart!*[20]

The following day, the powerful USS *Dacotah* arrived off Martinique to join the *Iroquois*, but the *Sumter* was gone.

Semmes now ordered the cruiser's course set eastward with the intent of crossing the Atlantic to seek better hunting grounds on the far side of the ocean. He was also concerned about the condition of his vessel, and hoped that in a European port, he might have the *Sumter* repaired, or if that was not feasible, obtain a more seaworthy craft. On November 25, 1861, two days after her night escape from the *Iroquois*, a large three-masted square-rigger approached the *Sumter* from head on. When she was sufficiently near, Kell had the United States' colors run up and a blank cartridge fired. The 1,083-ton *Montmorenci*, of Bath, Maine, also hoisted American colors, and obediently rounded into the stiff wind. Her large cargo of coal was headed for St. Thomas and was protected by authentic British certificates of ownership. Kell valued the cargo at $20,000, and because the vessel could not be burned without violating British neutrality, she was released on a ransom bond.[21]

While running through heavy seas the next day, the lookout again cried, "Sail ho!" It took a few hours of hard steaming to catch the small 121-ton schooner, but soon the customary boom of the pivot rifle brought her to a stop. She proved to be the *Arcade* from Portland, Maine, and was loaded with American-owned barrel staves bound for Guadeloupe. After removing the small crew, she was quickly set ablaze, the seasoned staves adding fuel to the brilliant flames, which lighted the ocean for many hours after darkness had settled. When told that an exquisite telescope taken from the *Arcade* had been awarded to her master for bravely saving lives in a ship disaster, Semmes had the fine spyglass returned.[22]

On December 3, the *Sumter* was approximately 400 miles southeast of Bermuda when the lookout spotted a vessel approaching from dead ahead. With the Confederate cruiser already under sail, her fires banked, and her smokestack lowered, she looked the part of an innocent merchant ship plodding her way eastward. Flying the French flag, the *Sumter* waited for the approaching vessel to draw near, and as she came abeam, the Confederate ensign replaced the one from France and a gun was fired. The 1,100-ton *Vigilant*, from Bath, Maine, completely taken in by the disguise, quickly hauled up, backed her main topsail, and waited for the boarding party. Semmes removed a 9-pounder gun, ammunition, and some small arms before setting her ablaze.

The weather now began to worsen and soon the *Sumter* was plowing through turbulent seas. For days, the pounding on the fragile hull continued, and the thermometer began to fall as they sailed farther into the Northern Hemisphere. Semmes' journal reflected the strain on him while crossing the Atlantic during this stormy December: *We carried very short sail, and most of the time we were shut down below,—that is, such of the crew as were not on watch,—with tarpaulin-covered hatches, and a cold, driving rain falling almost incessantly. What with the howling of the gale as it tears through the rigging, the rolling and pitching of the ship in the confused and irregular sea, and the jog, jog, jog of the pumps through half the night, I have had but little rest.* The pumps had to be manned constantly as the steady pounding had started a serious leak around the *Sumter's* propeller shaft, and this could not be repaired without entering a dry dock.[24]

On December 8, in spite of the howling winds and raging sea, the whaling bark *Eben Dodge* was captured. She was headed for the Pacific whaling grounds, but had sprung some of her spars and was leaking badly from the battering of the storms. The *Sumter's* boarding party removed a welcome supply of boots, flannel shirts, and pea jackets before setting her ablaze. With the twenty-two prisoners from the *Eben Dodge* added to those already on board, the *Sumter's* captive seamen now totaled forty-three. To maintain security, Semmes reluctantly placed half of the men in single wrist irons, alternating each day with the other half. Understanding the situation, the captive sailors submitted without complaint.[25]

For several days the *Sumter* under sail, with her fires banked, continued to struggle eastward in a fitful sea and changing winds. By December 11, dark cumulus clouds were observed building on the horizon, and the barometer began to fall at an alarming rate. Semmes ordered all sails reefed. The top-gallant yards and the jib were quickly hauled down and stowed. Toward evening the howling wind increased its fury from the northeast and drove blinding sheets of rain before it, while the barometer continued to plummet.

As night closed in, an awful scene presented itself, Semmes recalled. *The aspect of the heavens was terrific. The black clouds overhead were advancing and retreating like squadrons of opposing armies, whilst loud peels of thunder and blinding flashes of lightning that would now and then run down the conductor, and hiss as they leaped into the sea, added to the elemental strife. A streaming scud, which you could almost touch with your hand, was meanwhile hurrying past, screeching and screaming like so many demons as it rushed through the rigging. The sea was mountainous, and would now and then strike the little Sumter with such force as to make her tremble in every fiber of her frame. I had remained on deck during most of the first watch, looking anxiously on, to see what sort of weather we were going to make. The ship behaved nobly, but I had no confidence in her strength. ...Seeing the fury of the gale, and that the barometer was still settling, I went below about midnight, and turned in to get a little rest, with many misgivings. I had scarcely fallen into an uneasy slumber, when an old quartermaster, looking himself like the demon of the storm, with his disheveled hair and beard dripping water, and his eyes blinking in the light of his lantern, shook my cot and said, "We've stove in the starboard bow-port, sir, and the gundeck is all afloat with water!" Here was what I feared; unless we could keep the water out of the between-decks, all the upper works, and the masts along with them, would be gone in a trice. I hurried at once to the scene of disaster, but before I could reach it, my energetic and skillful first lieutenant had already, by the aid of some planks and spare spars, erected a barricade that would be likely to answer our purpose.*[26]

After an hour or two, the fury of the storm subsided somewhat, and Semmes was finally able to get some sleep. By 6:00 a.m., the barometer reached its low reading of 29.32, and then began a gradual climb. With the ferocity of the wind reduced to gale force, Semmes ordered the foresail reefed and set the *Sumter's* course east by south. *She scudded as beautifully as she had lain to,* he recorded, *darting ahead like an arrow on the tops of the huge waves that followed her like so many hungry wolves, and shaking the foam and spray from her bows, as if in disdain and contempt of the lately howling storm.*[27]

By December 28, the *Sumter* was near enough to the coast of Spain, that numerous sails began to make their appearance. With Gibraltar and Cadiz being only 500 miles away, Semmes could now afford the expenditure of coal in order to overtake some of the sightings. For the next six days, the *Sumter* overhauled and stopped nineteen vessels, but not one proved to be an American. Several neutral ships did yield a supply of recent newspapers, however. From these, Semmes was heartened to learn that his ship was no longer the lone Confederate cruiser on the high seas. The papers reported that the Northern clipper ship, *Harvey Birch* had been burned by the CSS *Nashville* in the English Channel.[28]

With only four days' supply of coal remaining, and with the pumps having to be manned almost constantly, the *Sumter* arrived in the port of Cadiz, Spain, on the morning of January 4, 1862. With the Confederate flag fluttering proudly from her peak, she steamed slowly and carefully through a throng of international shipping which was anchored in the Spanish port. *A number of the merchant ships of different nations hoisted their flags in honor of the Sumter as she passed,* Semmes related, *and one Yankee ship, there being three or four of them in the harbor, hoisted hers, as much to say, "You see we are not afraid to show it."*[29]

Almost immediately, the United States consul persuaded the military governor to order the *Sumter* to depart within twenty-four hours. Semmes once more sat down in his cabin and composed one of his classic letters, pointing out that in strict conformity to international law, his ship was a commissioned warship, and that he was entitled, therefore, to the rights of a belligerent. He added that, *my ship is in a crippled condition. She is damaged in her hull, is leaking badly, is unseaworthy, and will require to be docked and repaired before it will be possible for her to proceed to sea.* Semmes further reminded the governor that he had 43 Federal prisoners on board and asked permission to turn them over to the American consul. The governor telegraphed Madrid for advice, and within a few hours Semmes received permission to land the prisoners, but it was not until January 12, that the Spanish government gave permission to begin the repairs.

Raising steam, the *Sumter* moved to the Carraca Navy Yard, eight miles east of the city, and within only a few hours, she was standing on the stocks in the government dry dock. Semmes and Kell eagerly examined her bottom. They found that the propeller sleeve was damaged, and a section of the false keel had been knocked off. Semmes was surprised, however, considering the grounding at São Luis, and the pounding she had taken on the Atlantic crossing, that the damage was not more extensive. Small amounts of copper sheathing had peeled away and one plank was indented, but otherwise the hull remained tight. Badgered by the Union consul, Spanish authorities consented to the hull repairs but refused to allow any repairs to the ship's boilers. In addition, the American consul persuaded eight men of the *Sumter's* crew to desert.

Another pressing problem for Semmes was that he was bankrupt. Although he had captured 16 prizes, he had realized only $1,000, and those funds were now exhausted. Semmes telegraphed William L. Yancy, Confederate commissioner in London, for $20,000 to purchase coal and supplies, but as yet, no funds had arrived. On January 17, the repairs to the hull were complete, and the *Sumter* was out of dry dock when Semmes received an order from the governor to depart Spanish waters within six hours. Semmes wrote another letter of protest, and although the governor eventually granted a twenty-four hour extension, a disgusted Semmes, vowing never to enter a Spanish port again, steamed the *Sumter* out to sea without waiting for the reply. The Spanish government, he felt, was too weak and too easily intimidated by the United States government to grant Confederate vessels equal belligerent rights. Henceforth he would enter nothing but French or British ports. With this in mind, and with only one days' supply of coal on board, the *Sumter's* prow was turned toward Gibraltar.[30]

Steaming along the Spanish coast in bright moonlight, the *Sumter* passed the Pillars of Hercules at the entrance to the Straits of Gibraltar, and the Gibraltar light was made at daybreak. Numerous sails dotted the horizon, and soon the telescope revealed two that looked very "American." The first vessel that the *Sumter* approached, was six or seven miles off the coast of Africa and was waiting for the wind to freshen for her run into the Atlantic. Flying Confederate colors, the *Sumter* drew within range, and the pivot gun division fired the usual blank cartridge, which caused the 322-ton bark *Neapolitan,* of Kingston, Massachusetts, to round into the light wind. She was out of Messina for Boston, and was carrying 50 tons of sulfur. Although her papers claimed the British house of Baring Brothers as owners of the cargo, Semmes was convinced that the sulfur was destined for the powder mills of the North, and quickly consigned the *Neapolitan* to the torch. The raging inferno of the Northern bark, fed by the highly flammable sulfur, was viewed with mixed reactions by thousands of spectators on both the African and European coasts.

After transferring the prisoners and setting the *Neapolitan* ablaze, the *Sumter* bounded after the second American vessel. She was the 141-ton bark *Investigator,* of Searsport, Maine, and would prove to be the *Sumter's* 18th and final prize. Her cargo of iron ore carried a legitimate British seal, and she was released under a ransom bond. Semmes collected only $51 from the *Investigator*, and when added to the $86 taken from the *Neapolitan*, constituted all the ready cash in the *Sumter's* cabin safe.

With coal now running dangerously low, and stormy weather setting in, Semmes turned the *Sumter's* head toward the celebrated Rock of Gibraltar. Entering the man-of-war anchorage in the old and famous harbor at 8:00 p.m. on January 18, the *Sumter* dropped her anchor beneath the towering British bastion. As the weary commander sought his bunk for a night of untroubled sleep, while being protected by British guns, little did he realize that the *Sumter's* career as a Confederate cruiser was over.[31]

Repairs to the *Sumter* had to await the arrival of funds from London, and by the time they arrived sixteen days later, so had the United States Navy. The USS *Tuscarora* and the USS *Kearsarge*, which Semmes would get to know very well two years later, arrived and took up stations in the bay. Soon other Federal vessels arrived. There was now no possibility of getting the *Sumter* back out to sea, even if all of the repairs could be accomplished.

Weeks dragged into months, until finally, on April 7, Semmes paid off the remainder of the crew and turned the *Sumter* over to Midshipman Richard E. Armstrong and ten enlisted men.[32]

Semmes, Kell, and most of the *Sumter's* officers sailed for Southampton, for a new and more powerful Confederate warship was nearing completion on the Mersey River near Liverpool. On December 9, 1862, the blockaded *Sumter* was sold at auction to the firm of Melchir G. Klingender & Company, who were secretly representing Fraser,

The *Sumter* capturing her last two prizes, the *Neapolitan* and the *Investigator*, within sight of Gibraltar. The artist has painted what appears to be the Argentine flag flying from the Confederate cruiser.

Trenholm and Company, Confederate agents in Europe. Finally, on the dark night of February 6, 1863, the one time Confederate cruiser, now renamed *Gibraltar* and with a British captain in command, escaped to sea in a howling gale. Taking on a cargo at Liverpool, including two huge 22-ton Blakely guns, she sailed for the Bahamas and then on to Wilmington, North Carolina. Although too slow to be considered for blockade running, she, nevertheless, successfully eluded the Federal warships and safely delivered her precious cargo, entering Wilmington on August 23, 1863. The *Gibraltar* made one additional round trip through the cordon of Union warships surrounding the Confederacy, and was in England undergoing repairs when the war ended. She had served her country well, first as an ocean-going cruiser and later as a blockade runner. Surviving the war, the little *Sumter* eventually foundered and sank during a violent storm in the English Channel several years after the conflict.[33]

During the war, more powerful and more famous Confederate cruisers, with names such as *Alabama*, *Florida*, and *Shenandoah*, roamed the oceans of the world and devastated Union commerce. The frail *Sumter*, however, had led the way. Lieutenant Kell, years after the war, wrote a fitting epitaph for her:

I have always felt that the little Sumter has never had full justice done her, or been accorded her high merit of praise! ... Frail and unseaworthy at best, her career was a marvel. In the hands of a commander as daring as any Viking in seamanship, she swept the waters of the Caribbean Sea as she moved silently on her career of triumph. No ship of her size, her frailness, and her armament ever played such havoc on a powerful foe![34]

Chapter Three

Thunder on the Yazoo

It was midnight when the ghostly shape of the Confederate ironclad CSS *Arkansas* eased up to the landing at Haynes Bluff. Sparks flew from her single stack, while black smoke disappeared into the darkness of the Mississippi night. With throbbing engines and hissing steam, her twin screws churned the muddy waters of the Yazoo River as she strained to pull her anchor lines taut. Soon all was quiet and the crickets and bull-frogs resumed their nightly chants. Confederate soldiers standing guard on the bluff above the river could see light streaming through open gun ports from lanterns hung in her gun deck. Having drilled at the guns for two days and nights, it was now time for her weary officers and crew to rest. Perhaps it was also a time to contemplate what the next twenty-four hours might bring. Some of the men tried to sleep. Others wrote what would become for many, their last letter home. One man, Lieutenant Isaac N. Brown, most likely could not sleep. With the responsibility of this iron monster and her 200 plus men and officers weighing heavily upon him, he may have paused and reflected upon all the work and super-human effort it had taken to get this far.[1]

The *Arkansas* began her life far from this dark landing on the Yazoo River. It was at a hastily constructed shipyard in Memphis, Tennessee, where construction was begun in October 1861, along with a sister ship to be named the *Tennessee*.[2] Due to the scarcity of supplies and the

43

Commander Isaac N. Brown, gallant captain of the CSS *Arkansas* during her run down the Yazoo and Mississippi Rivers. Brown's tireless efforts in completing the *Arkansas* and fighting his way through to Vicksburg won him the respect of his enemies, and the admiration of the entire South.

lack of skilled workers, construction soon fell behind schedule. With the fall of Island Number 10 above Memphis to the Federals on April 7, 1862, and the surrender of New Orleans on April 25, it was painfully evident that the unfinished *Arkansas* had to be moved to a place where she would be safe from the advancing Union forces. After much searching, a refuge was found. With the approach of the enemy's gunboats, the *Tennessee*, not yet able to float, was set afire, and the *Arkansas* was hurriedly towed south down the Mississippi and then northeast up the Yazoo River to the little hamlet of Greenwood, Mississippi. Greenwood was 160 miles up river from Yazoo City, which was itself 50 miles from where the river empties into the Mississippi. Although she was safe from the advancing Federal navy, there were no facilities at Greenwood to enable her completion. It was here at this backwater village that her captain, Isaac N. Brown, found her when he arrived to take command on May 29.[3]

Lieutenant, later commander, Isaac Newton Brown was one of the most capable and energetic naval officers in the Confederate navy. Born in Livingston, Kentucky on May 27, 1817, he was appointed an officer in the U.S. Navy from Tennessee on March 15, 1834. Brown proceeded to establish a reputation for courage and intelligence during his long naval career. He was commended by his superiors for bravery during the Seminole War and ranked first in the entrance exams to the naval school at Philadelphia. (This was prior to the opening of the Naval Academy at Annapolis.) On duty in front of Vera Cruz when it was captured during the Mexican War, Brown returned home from duty on the west coast of Mexico, and was assigned to the Coastal Survey and later to the U.S. Naval Observatory. There he worked closely with famed oceanographer and scientist Matthew Fontaine Maury. After serving at these desk-bound duties for several years, he was assigned as executive officer on the frigate *Susquehanna* and later on the *Niagara*.[4]

By the beginning of the War Between the States, Brown considered himself a resident of Mississippi, and returning home from Japan aboard the *Niagara* in 1861, found his home state had withdrawn from the Union. With no hesitation, the forty-four-year-old career officer resigned his commission from the U.S. Navy after twenty-seven years of service, and immediately offered his services to the new Confederate States of America. His commission of lieutenant in the Confederate navy bore the date of June 6, 1861.[5] (A lieutenant in the navy is equal in rank and pay to a captain in the army.)

While serving at various stations along the Mississippi contracting for and supervising the construction of gunboats, Brown was at Vicksburg when he received a telegram from the Department of the Navy on May 28, 1862. It ordered him to proceed to Greenwood, Mississippi and *assume command of the Confederate gunboat Arkansas, and finish and equip that vessel without regard to the expenditure of men or money.*[6] Leaving immediately on the steamer *Capitol*, Brown hurried up river to Greenwood, arriving the following day. He found the *Arkansas* in deplorable condition. Little had been done to her since she had escaped the Federals and had been towed up the Yazoo. *The vessel was a mere hull,* Brown wrote, *without armor; the engines were apart; guns without carriages were lying about the deck; a portion of the railroad iron intended as armor was at the bottom of the river,* (a barge carrying the iron rails had accidentally sunk) *and the other and far greater part was to be sought for in the interior of the country.* Because of the spring floods, the *Arkansas* was also four miles from dry land![7]

Miraculously finding a diving bell in the backwoods of Mississippi, Brown with his customary energy, and using this device, had all the iron rails lifted from the bottom of the river the day after he took command. With the river falling, he next had the *Arkansas* towed downstream to deeper water at Yazoo City where there were facilities to repair steamboats. Arriving there on June 4, Brown immediately had a log barricade constructed farther down river at Liverpool Landing, where three Confederate gunboats, *Polk, Livingston,* and *Van Dorn,* were anchored below the landing. This should discourage any attempted Federal advance up the river. Organizing a work force of over two hundred men from nearby army units, Brown got to work.[8]

Racing against time, Brown organized the workers into two twelve hour shifts, so that work could continue around the clock. Strict discipline was enforced, and all workers were required to live on board a steamboat tied next to the *Arkansas*. More than a dozen forges, which were requisitioned from nearby plantations, were set up on the river bank while the steamer *Capitol* was tied alongside, and her steam-driven drilling equipment was used to drill the bolt holes in the T-shaped railroad irons. Another concern, in addition to finding and transporting enough iron, was the gun carriages. To solve this problem, executive officer Lieutenant Henry K. Stevens devoted his full attention to the construction of ten carriages at Canton, Mississippi by carpenters who had never seen a heavy naval gun.[9]

By early July, the *Arkansas* was nearing completion. She measured 165 feet in length, 35 feet abeam, and drew 14 feet of water. Her two low pressure-type engines, having been built in Memphis, were new and worked independently, each driving its own screw. The boilers were placed deep in the hull below the water line for added protection from enemy fire. The iron-plated gun box, or casemate, was slanted only fore and aft, the sides being vertical, and was pierced for ten guns.[10] In writing about the necessity of removing the *Arkansas* from the Yazoo, Brown gives an interesting description of his vessel:

We were not a day too soon, for the now rapid fall of the river rendered it necessary for us to assume the offensive without waiting for the apparatus to bend the railway iron to the curve of our quarter deck and stern, and to the angles of our pilot house. Though there was little thought of showing the former, the weakest part, to the enemy, we tacked boilerplate iron over it for appearance sake, and very imperfectly covered the pilot house shield with a double thickness of one-inch bar iron. Our engines' twin screws, one under each quarter, worked up to eight miles an hour in still water, which promised about half that speed

The *Arkansas* nearing completion on the Yazoo River. Workmen on the steamer *Capitol* are swinging one of the ironclad's heavy guns aboard.

Battles and Leaders of the Civil War

when turned against the current of the main river. We had at first some trust in these, not having discovered the way they soon showed of stopping on the center at wrong times and places; and as they never both stopped of themselves at the same time, the effect was, when one did so, to turn the vessel round, despite the rudder. Once, in the presence of the enemy, we made a circle, while trying to make the automatic stopper keep time with its sister screw.

Brown continued: *The Arkansas now appeared as if a small sea-going vessel had been cut down to the water's edge at both ends, leaving a box for guns amidships. The straight sides of the box, a foot in thickness, had over them one layer of railway iron; the ends closed by timber one foot square, planked across by six-inch strips of oak, were then covered by one course of railway iron laid up and down at an angle of thirty-five degrees. These ends deflected overhead all missiles striking at short range, but would have been of little security under a plunging fire.* This shield, flat on top, covered with planking of half-inch iron, was pierced for ten guns, three in each broadside, and two forward and aft. The large smokestack came through the top of the shield, and the pilothouse was raised about one foot above the shield level. Through the latter led a small tin tube by which to convey orders to the pilot.[11]

Her guns, while of various calibers, were nevertheless very formidable. In the bow were two 8-inch Columbiads. The starboard section included one 9-inch Dahlgren, one 6-inch rifle, and one 32 pounder. Her port side also contained one 9-inch Dahlgren, one 6-inch rifle and one 32 pounder. Her stern was protected by two 6-inch rifles. *10 guns in all,* Brown wrote, *which, under officers formerly of the United States service, could be relied on for good work, if we could find the men to load and fire.* In addition, attached to the bow, was a sharp iron ram which would become a trademark of most Confederate ironclads.[12]

Her officers were undoubtedly the *Arkansas'* most valuable asset. Young, intelligent, and eager to strike a blow for their country's independence, they were all career officers of the "old navy," and entered battle with only one thought—to win! The port bow Columbiad and the port 9-inch gun were commanded by Lieutenant George W. Gift from Tennessee, and the starboard bow Columbiad and starboard 9-inch was in charge of Lieutenant John Grimball from South Carolina. The starboard 6-inch rifle and 32 pounder was commanded by Lieutenant Arthur D. Wharton from Alabama, and the port guns of the same caliber were in charge of Lieutenant Alphonso Barbot from Louisiana. Lieutenant Charles W. Read from Mississippi had the stern rifles all to himself. All were under the direct command of the executive officer, First Lieutenant Henry K. Stevens, who was originally from Connecticut, but was appointed from Florida. George W. City was chief engineer, and an impressive array of masters and midshipmen rounded out the list of officers who would take the *Arkansas* into battle.[13]

Lieutenant John Grimball, commander of the starboard bow Columbiad and the starboard 9-inch rifle on the *Arkansas*. Grimball's well-placed shots, along with those from Lieutenant Gift, delivered death and destruction to many of the Federal warships.

Battles and Leaders of the Civil War

Obtaining a good crew of more than two hundred enlisted men was much more difficult. More than one hundred sailors came from the various gunboats that had either taken refuge up the Yazoo or had been destroyed in the battles around Island Number 10, Memphis, and New Orleans. These men knew their business and were fervent in their desire to strike a successful blow at the Northern invader.[14] The remainder of the crew was composed of Captains Harris', Parson's, and McDonald's artillery companies from General M. Jeff Thompson's command, and a few Louisiana artillerists from General Martin L. Smith's command at Vicksburg. The Missouri men had never seen a heavy naval gun before, much less load, aim, and fire one, but they jumped to the task with enthusiasm and learned quickly.[15]

On June 26, Brown took the *Arkansas* down river 25 miles on a trial run to the log and raft barricade at Liverpool Landing. Anchored just below the barrier, and protected by artillery batteries on the high bluff overlooking the river, were three surviving Confederate gunboats: the *Livingston*, the *General Polk*, and the *Van Dorn*. Many of the guns and most of the crew had been stripped from these boats to provide for the *Arkansas*. Nevertheless, Brown had instructed Commander Robert F. Pinkney, commanding the *Livingston* and the *General Polk*, to moor them with their heads downstream, keep steam in the boilers, and be ready to ram any Federal boat that might come prowling up the river. Pinkney failed to do this, and when the two unarmed Union army rams came poking up the river and hove in sight, he panicked and set fire to his boats and fled. They soon burned through their lines and drifted into the *Van Dorn*, and it, too, went up in flames. Arriving with the *Arkansas* above the barrier and seeing the gunboats on fire, Brown sent fire-fighting parties in small boats alongside in a vain attempt to extinguish the flames, but it was too late. The two Federal rams could still be seen watching smugly from a safe distance knowing they had destroyed three "Rebel" boats without firing a shot.[16]

The next day, Brown sent Lieutenant Read and one of the pilots to sound the river at Satarsia Bar, a short distance down river from the barricade. Read found sufficient depth for the *Arkansas*, but the pilot reasoned that in five days, with the river falling at the current rate, there might not be enough water to float her over the bar. The barricade was also a problem. Army engineers told Brown that it would take at least a week to make an opening large enough for the *Arkansas* to pass through. Brown sent Read, along with Lieutenants Gift and Grimball to inspect the barricade the next day. These officers reported that, in their estimation, an opening could be made in the obstructions in less than half an hour. With this information, Brown, on July 4, took the *Arkansas* back to Yazoo City for some last minute repairs.[17]

Brown was in favor of keeping the *Arkansas* in the lower and deeper water of the Yazoo to protect the rich river valley from Federal excursions. He sent Lieutenant Read to Vicksburg, where Read laid his commander's views before the district commander, Major General Earl Van Dorn. Van Dorn, however, had other plans for the *Arkansas*. Fearful that the ironclad would become trapped by the falling water of the river, and also apprehensive that the *Arkansas* would share a fate similar to the gunboats at the barricade, Van Dorn sent Read back with a different message. Brown was to run through the Union fleets that were now besieging Vicksburg and bring his warship to the city. With little understanding of naval warfare or naval vessels, the general even dreamed of sending her down the river, destroying everything Federal on the way, running by New Orleans, and then proceeding on to Mobile to raise the blockade![18]

Before beginning his long return to the *Arkansas* by horseback with Van Dorn's orders, Read was guided by an army officer to a spot on the Mississippi where he could see the Federal fleets. *It was late in the afternoon*, Read wrote, *before we got up abreast with the fleets. The woods were so dense and entangled with vines and briers that we were obliged to dismount and grope our way through the best we could. I had a good field glass, and watched the vessels carefully some time. Farragut's fleet consisted of thirteen heavy sloops-of-war, mounting tremendous batteries, and were anchored in line ahead near the east bank. I was satisfied that none of them had steam up. The fleet of Commodore Davis numbered over thirty iron-clads and six or eight rams. They were moored to the west bank, nearly opposite Farragut's fleet. Below Davis' fleet were about thirty mortar-boats. Davis' vessels appeared to have steam up. While we were making our observations a man-of-war cutter landed near us, but the crew did not suspect our presence.* Read left that night and rode until 2:00 a.m. before stopping to rest at a planter's house. Resuming his ride at daylight, July 11, he finally arrived at Liverpool Landing later that day.[19]

On Saturday, July 12, Brown sent all the mechanics ashore and took his Missourians on board. Amid a cheering crowd of well-wishers, the *Arkansas*, with the Stars and Bars fluttering in the breeze, cast off her lines for the last time at Yazoo City and began her "journey into history."[20] Arriving at the barricade later that afternoon, soldiers quickly removed part of the obstructions and the *Arkansas* eased through, dropping down and anchoring at Satartia Bar. They were now only five hours sailing time from both the Mississippi and all the Federal vessels that Read had so meticulously counted. Brown now gave his executive officer, Lieutenant Stevens, one day to train and organize the men.[21]

Early on Monday morning, July 14, the *Arkansas* eased out into the middle of the river below Satartia Bar and headed downstream. Every man on board now knew, due to Read's careful observations, the tremendous odds which they were about to face. Each must have felt deep in his heart that the chances of successfully passing through that many enemy warships was nearly impossible. Everything proceeded smoothly enough at first. The engines thumped away as the sun rose off the port side, sending its early morning rays through the cottonwoods and reflecting off the placid waters of the Yazoo. It looked as though it was going to be another hot one.[22]

Fifteen miles below Satartia Bar, opposite the mouth of the Sunflower River, one of the gunnery officers brought some distressing news. Brown explained, *...we found that the steam from our imperfect engines and boiler had penetrated our forward magazine and wet the powder so as to render it unfit for use. We were just opposite the site of an old saw-mill, where the opening in the forest, dense everywhere else, admitted the sun's rays. The day was clear and very hot; we made fast to the bank, head down stream, landed our wet powder (expecting the enemy to heave in sight every moment), spread tarpaulins over the old saw-dust and our powder over these. By constant shaking and turning we got it back to the point of ignition before the sun sank below the trees, when, gathering it up, we crowded all that we could of it into the after magazine and resumed our way, guns cast loose and men at quarters, expecting every moment to meet the enemy.*[23]

With darkness now settling on the Yazoo, the *Arkansas* forged ahead trying to make up for lost time. Brown had spent nearly a full day in drying the ship's powder. They had been extremely fortunate that no Union gunboats had come nosing up the river, for if they had, the *Arkansas* would have been almost defenseless. As daylight dwindled, they narrowly escaped the destruction of the smokestack by a low hanging tree. Disaster was averted by quick thinking on the part of Lieutenant Grimball who succeeded in pulling the branches out of the way with a rope. In total darkness now, the big ironclad continued on, being kept in deep water by her experienced Yazoo River pilot, J. H. Shacklett.[24]

The steady thump of her engines and the gentle hissing of steam was a constant reminder to her crew that they were drawing nearer to the enemy. After several more hours, the pilot finally called down to the engine room through the tin speaker tube, for the engineers to slow the engines. Brown had ordered the *Arkansas* stopped in order to allow the crew to get some rest. It was now midnight as Shacklett slowly eased the ironclad up to the landing at Haynes Bluff. The *Arkansas'* first day of glory had just begun.[25]

By 3:00 a.m. on July 15, the soldiers on guard duty at Haynes Bluff could see some movement on board the *Arkansas* anchored at the landing below them. Shadow-like figures could be seen moving about her gun deck; lines were being taken in, and black smoke began to pour from her funnel. Soon the thumping sound of steam engines could be heard above the noise of the chirping katydids. Lifting her anchor, the *Arkansas'* twin screws churned the muddy Yazoo as she glided out into deep water near the middle of the river. Slowly turning her head downstream, she was soon lost in the darkness as she moved away at eight knots. If all went well, they would surprise the Federal fleets at sunrise.[26]

Until now, Flag Officers Davis and Farragut, the Union naval commanders on the Mississippi, had received rumors concerning the *Arkansas* with skepticism. They adamantly refused to believe that the Confederacy had the resources or the know-how to build a warship capable of challenging their massive fleets. Now however, on the night of the 14th, two Confederate deserters stood before them, and both swore that the "Rebel ram" was going to make a run for it the next day. Not wanting to take any chances, Farragut ordered a reconnaissance to leave at daylight. With the first streaks of dawn showing in the eastern sky, three Union vessels pulled away from the remainder of the Federal fleet, turned into the Yazoo, and started up river. Unknown to their commanders as they entered the river, was the fact that ten miles ahead the "Rebel ram" was hard aground. In the darkness, and in spite of the best efforts of her pilot, the *Arkansas* had run aground on a sand bar. After a long struggle and the shifting of the crew from side to side, the *Arkansas* finally broke free. Another hour, however, had been lost.[27]

Inside the *Arkansas* on the gun deck, the lanterns were being extinguished as morning light began to force its way through the open gun ports. Lieutenant Gift wrote of this moment: *As it is now daylight, let me describe the scene on a man-of-war's deck, cleared for action, or at least this man-of-war, on that occasion. Many of the men had stripped off their shirts and were bare to the waists, with handkerchiefs bound round their heads, and some of the officers had removed their coats and stood in their undershirts. The decks had been thoroughly sanded to prevent slipping after the blood should become plentiful. Tourniquets were served out to division officers by the surgeons, with directions for use. The division tubs were filled with water to drink; fire buckets were in place; cutlasses and pistols strapped on; rifles loaded and bayonets fixed; spare breechings for the guns, and other implements made ready. The magazines and shell-rooms forward and aft were open, and the men inspected in their places. Before getting underway, coffee (or an apology thereof) had been served to the crew, and daylight found us a grim, determined set of fellows, grouped about our guns, anxiously waiting to get sight of the enemy.*[28]

Lieutenant Read adds his description of this scene: *Daylight found us seven or eight miles above the mouth of the river. The morning was warm and perfectly calm; the dense volume of black smoke which issued from our funnel, rose high above the trees, and we knew that the enemy would soon be on the lookout for us. ...The men of the Arkansas were now all at their stations, the*

Map of the Yazoo and Mississippi Rivers showing the route taken by the *Arkansas* from Haynes Bluff to Vicksburg.

guns were loaded and cast loose their tackles in the hands of willing seamen ready to train; primers in the vents; locks thrown back and the lanyards in the hands of the gun captains; the decks sprinkled with sand and tourniquets and bandages at hand; tubs filled with fresh water were between the guns, and down below in the berth deck were the surgeons with their bright instruments and lint, while along the passage-ways stood rows of men to pass powder, shell and shot, and all was quiet save the dull thump, thump, of the propellers.[29]

The *Arkansas* was now entering what was locally known as "Old River," which was in reality a small lake formed by a "cutoff" from the Mississippi. Brown, along with his executive officer Lieutenant Stevens, stood on top of the casemate just behind the pilothouse squinting intently into the early morning light. Something in the distance had caught his eye. Using his marine glass he could see them clearly; three ominous plumes of black smoke drifting lazily above the trees several miles downstream. There were no other Confederate vessels in the river, thus it could mean only one thing. The enemy! Descending to the gun deck, Brown called the crew together. *Gentlemen, in seeking combat as we now do, we must win or perish. Should I fall, whoever succeeds to the command will do so with the resolution to go through the enemy's fleet, or go to the bottom. Should they carry us by boarding, the ship must be blown up; on no account must it fall into the hands of the enemy. Go to your guns!*[30]

The three plumes of black smoke that were rapidly drawing closer, emanated from the U.S. Navy ironclad *Carondelet* commanded by Captain Henry Walke, an old friend of Brown's; the "timberclad" *Tyler* commanded by Lieutenant William Gwin; and the army ram *Queen of the West*, with Lieutenant J. M. Hunter commanding. The *Carondelet*, one of the "Cairo" class of Union ironclads, was more than a match for the *Arkansas* with thirteen heavy guns; however, she was slower and lightly armored on the stern. The lighter *Tyler* carried a total of eight guns, and the armored *Queen of the West* (later captured by the Confederates) carried no guns at this time, but would undoubtedly try to maneuver into a position whereby she could ram the *Arkansas*.[31]

While Stevens passed about the gun deck giving encouragement and last minute instructions, Brown returned to the roof of the casemate. The tell-tale smoke was much closer now. There was no need to use the glasses. Suddenly, as the *Arkansas* rounded a bend in the river, there they were. Under a full head of steam, with all their colors snapping in the breeze, they were only a mile or so away and headed straight for the *Arkansas*. The *Carondelet* was in the center and flanked out front on either side by the *Tyler* and the *Queen*. Closing the distance rapidly, the plucky little *Tyler* opened fire first, her well-placed shot slamming into the *Arkansas* and ricocheting off the front of her slanted gun box. The *Carondelet* opened fire next, and more shots disintegrated against the *Arkansas'* railroad iron. With each impact, iron splinters and broken pieces of the Federal's shells were sent spinning and flying over Brown's head, who was still bravely directing her course from atop the gun box. Owing to the slight curve in the river, the *Arkansas'* bow guns could not be brought to bear, and she still had not opened fire.[32]

Lieutenant Gift at the port bow Columbiad, described the opening Federal fire and the *Arkansas'* first casualty: *The gunnery of the enemy was excellent, and his rifle bolts soon began to ring on our iron front, digging into and warping up the bars, but not penetrating. Twice he struck near my port, and still we could not 'see' him. The first blood was drawn from my division. An Irishman, with more curiosity than prudence, stuck his head out the broadside port, and was killed by a heavy bolt which had missed the ship. Stevens was with me at the time; and, fearing that the sight of the mangled corpse and blood might demoralize the guns' crew, sprang forward to throw the body out of the port, and called upon the man nearest him to assist. 'Oh! I can't do it sir,' the poor fellow replied, 'It's my brother!' The body was thrown overboard.*[33]

The *Carondelet* fired again with her three bow guns, all three shots going wild. With the *Arkansas* still pounding toward them, and their shots bouncing harmlessly off her armored front, all three Federal boats backed their engines, turned, and headed downstream. Brown had ordered the pilot to steer for the *Tyler*, and it was finally Gift's moment. When the *Tyler's* stern moved across his sights, Gift yelled, "Fire!" With a pull of the lanyard, the big black Columbiad roared; the *Arkansas* shook and trembled from the recoil; smoke and flames enveloped her bow, while the eight-inch shell with a five-second fuse went screaming toward the *Tyler*. The big shell tore through the *Tyler*, killing the pilot, and with a blinding flash exploded in the engine room killing and wounding more of her crew. Unfortunately, Gift's heavy gun recoiled off its chassis and was out of action for five to ten minutes. *However*, Gift wrote, *Grimball made up for it. He had the best gun captain, Robert McCalla, in the ship, and a superb crew, and his gun seemed to be continually going out and recoiling in again.*[34]

Running ahead of the *Arkansas*, the *Carondelet* and the *Tyler* maintained a brisk fire from their stern guns. With deadly accuracy, heavy solid bolts and explosive shells continued to slam into the *Arkansas'* railway iron, bending and cracking it, but thus far, not penetrating to the interior. The *Arkansas* was closing the distance when the *Queen* began edging to the right as though taking a position to turn and ram. Brown ordered a turn to port and all three starboard guns roared to life sending their missiles of destruction smashing into the *Queen* which now pulled away and ran to "report to the fleet." This left only the *Carondelet* and the *Tyler*, both of whom were suffering greatly from the *Arkansas'* well-placed shots. Gift's Columbiad was now back on its carriage, and along with Grimball's starboard bow gun, was thundering away with a vengeance.

The *Tyler*, keeping pace with the *Carondelet*, was bravely firing her stern guns with surprising accuracy, and her shots were shattering against the *Arkansas* in a shower of sparks. One of the fragments struck Brown on the head causing a nasty wound, ...*but this gave me no concern after I failed to find any brains mixed with the handful of clotted blood which I drew from the wound and examined.*[35] Within a few seconds, a large shell from the *Carondelet* struck the imperfectly armored pilothouse, drove through the iron bars and exploded in a shower of smoke and spinning hot fragments, turning the station into a death trap. Chief Pilot John Hodges was mortally wounded and Pilot Shacklett was disabled. The explosion also blew away the top half of the wheel, and as the two pilots were being carried below, one of them rasped, *Keep in the middle of the river!*[36]

Clearing away the debris, James Brady, a Mississippi River pilot with little knowledge of the Yazoo, took over what was left of the wheel. As the *Arkansas* gained on the two Federals, she moved within musket range and the *Tyler's* upper deck suddenly bristled with sharpshooters who began firing in concentrated volleys. They were aiming for the *Arkansas'* open gun ports and for Brown, who was fully exposed atop the casemate. Minie balls began ricocheting around inside the gun box wounding some of the men, and suddenly Lieutenant Brown

The USS *Carondelet*. She took a beating at the hands of the *Arkansas*, and was left stranded in the willows and mud along the Yazoo River's edge.

was hit: *I was near the hatchway at the moment when a minnie-ball, striking over my left temple, tumbled me down among the guns. I awoke as if from sleep, to find hands helping me to a place among the killed and wounded.* Brown shook off the dizziness, climbed back up the ladder, and again took his station on the roof.[37]

Gift had been concentrating on the *Tyler* but now shifted his attention to the Federal ironclad *...the Carondelet was right ahead of us, distant about one hundred yards, and paddling downstream for dear life. Her armor had been pierced four times by Grimball, and we were running after her to use our ram, having the advantage of speed. Opposite to me a man was standing outside on the port-sill loading the stern chaser. He was so near that I could readily have recognized him had he been an acquaintance. I pointed the Columbiad for that port and pulled the lock-string. I have seen nothing of the man or gun since.*[38]

The *Carondelet* was in trouble. Her interior was shambles from eight 64-pound shells from the *Arkansas'* Columbiads which had torn through her from end to end, smashing everything in their path. Her steering mechanism had been shot away, and listing badly, she ceased to return the *Arkansas'* fire. Brady, who was still at the wheel, shouted to Brown that she was headed for the willows that grew along the eastern bank of the lake, and if the *Arkansas* followed, she would run aground. Brown gave the order, *Hard a-port and depress guns!* Lieutenant Stevens raced along the port side of the gun deck making sure each gun's elevating screw was run all the way up in order to fire down through the *Carondelet's* bottom. Gift, his bow gun now unable to bear on the enemy, was an interested observer: *As we lapped up alongside, and almost touching, we poured in our broadside, which went crashing and plunging through his timbers and bottom. Although his four broadside guns ...one more than we had ...were run out and ready, he did not fire them. We were running near the left or Vicksburg side of the river (we are now in what is called Old River), and, as soon as passed, we headed for the middle of the stream, which gave Read his first opportunity ...and right well did he use it. His rifles 'spoke' to the purpose, for the enemy hauled down his colors.*[39]

The *Carondelet* came to rest grounded in the weeds on the edge of the lake. Brown recalled: *Though I stood within easy pistol-shot, in uniform, uncovered, and evidently the commander of the Arkansas, no more notice was taken of me by the Carondelet than had been taken of my ship when, to escape running into the mud, I had exposed the Arkansas to being raked. Their ports were closed (contrary to Gift's observation), not a man or officer was in view, not a sound or shot was heard. She was apparently 'disabled.'*[40]

Gift was elated: *It was glorious. For it was the first and only square, fair, equal stand-up and knock-down fight between the two navies in which the Confederates came out first best. From the beginning our ship was handled with more pluck, decision, and judgment than theirs (the Tyler excepted); our guns were better fought and better served. Not an officer or man doubted the result from the beginning. We went in to win, and we won.*[41]

It took about an hour for the *Arkansas* to steam the distance from the wreck of the *Carondelet* to the Mississippi. All the while, about 500 yards ahead, the gallant little *Tyler* was paddling for dear life and throwing an occasional shot from her 30-pound stern rifle. With Gift and Grimball replying occasionally, just to keep the *Tyler* moving, Brown now *...had the opportunity of inspecting the engine and fire rooms, where I found engineers and fireman had been suffering under temperatures of 120 to 130 degrees. Lieutenant Stevens had organized a relief party from among the men and rotated them in and out of the engine room every fifteen minutes. The connection (called the breechings) between the furnace and the smokestack had been shot away allowing the flames to enter the gun deck where temperatures were now reaching 120 degrees. With these breechings gone and the stack riddled by fragments and minnie-balls, the furnace was losing its draught and steam pressure in the boilers was dropping alarmingly.* During the chase of the *Carondelet* the engineers were able to keep 120 pounds of pressure, but as they reached the Mississippi there was barely 20 pounds, hardly enough to turn the engines, and her speed was down to less than four knots.[42]

The USS *Tyler*, the plucky Federal gunboat that fought the *Arkansas* down the entire length of the Yazoo River. She had 8 killed and 16 wounded in her running fight with the Confederate ironclad. She was photographed here with her awnings spread, tied to a riverbank.

Chapter Four

Thunder on the Mississippi

As the *Arkansas* glided out into the broad Mississippi at last, not a ship could be seen other than the *Tyler* and the *Queen of the West*. This would soon change. The bright, clear waters sparkled in the early morning sun, and it must have felt splendid to be finally free of the muddy Yazoo. As Brown surveyed the scene from his station atop the casemate, he knew that with her engines barely turning, the *Arkansas* would be more dependent on the current than her own power to take her to Vicksburg.[1] Ten more miles of river separated the *Arkansas* and her men from the safety of the guns above the city. Within these ten miles lay the greatest concentration of enemy guns ever challenged by a lone Confederate warship. Yet, there was no hesitation, no discussion of alternatives, no second thoughts. Duty, honor, and country were not just mere words to men like Brown, Stevens, Gift, Grimball, Read, and others of the *Arkansas*. As professional naval officers, they had been trained to put these values above all others when they were facing the enemy. With these convictions dictating their actions, it is obvious that Brown meant every word when he said that they must ...*go through the enemy's fleet, or go to the bottom*. By their examples and leadership, the *Arkansas'* entire crew, in an incredibly short period of time, had been welded into an efficient, hard-hitting fighting team, and were now eager and determined to get the job done.

In spite of the sounds of heavy firing reaching the two Federal fleets within the last hour, little preparation had been made for battle. Most thought that the firing was from the returning reconnaissance party, and that they were shelling the woods to flush out "Rebel guerrillas." Federal sailors were aghast as the *Tyler* came pounding through their midst, her decks red with blood and her superstructure in shambles. Alarms were sounded and blue-coated tars began rushing for their guns.

The *Arkansas* now rounded Tuscumbia Bend, and there straight ahead, were the waiting enemy warships. Many had no steam pressure in their boilers, but having been warned by the *Tyler*, their guns were manned and ready. *Aided by the current of the Mississippi*, Brown wrote, *we soon approached the Federal fleet; a forest of masts and smokestacks, rams, iron-clads, and other gun-boats on the left side, and ordinary river steamers and bomb-vessels along the right. To any one having a real ram at command the genius of havoc could not have offered a finer view, the panoramic effect of which was intensified by the city of men spread out with innumerable tents opposite on the right bank. We were not yet in sight of Vicksburg, but in every direction, except astern, our eyes rested on enemies.*[2] Lieutenant Gift also described this moment and the reaction of one of his men upon seeing the view ahead: *One of my best men was a tall, athletic young Irishman who had greatly distinguished himself for zeal and courage half an hour before. Putting his eye to the gun he peeped out ahead and saw the immense force assembled to oppose us. In an instant he was overcome, and exclaimed: 'Holy mother, have mercy on us; we'll never get through there!'*[3]

Brown moaned that, *It seemed at a glance as if the whole navy had come to keep me away from the heroic city, ...six or seven rams, four or five iron-clads, without including one accounted for an hour ago, and the fleet of Farragut generally, behind or inside of this fleet.*[4] Farragut's ships included: the flagship *Hartford*, with 24 guns; *Iroquois*, 7 guns; *Richmond*, 21 guns; *Sumter*, 6 guns; *Louisville*, 7 guns; *Oneida*, 9 guns; *Cincinnati*, 13 guns; *Essex*, 5 guns, and the *Sciota*, *Wissahickon*, and *Winona* with 4 guns each.[5] Before the firing began, Brown spotted some of the Federal rams apparently getting up steam behind the protection of these warships with the intent of dashing out among them and smashing into the side of the *Arkansas*. He shouted into the damaged pilothouse, *Brady, shave that line of men-of-war as close as you can, so that the rams will not have room to gather head-way in coming out to strike us!* Of course this made the *Arkansas* a point-blank target for all of Farragut's guns, but better this than to be sliced in half by one of those rams.[6]

They were drawing nearer now. Running with the current, and with a little help from the engines, they advanced toward the gauntlet of waiting guns doing about five knots. Union vessels that had steam in their boilers began to move, some to get out of the way, others maneuvered to positions where they could open fire. *The first vessel which stood out to engage us, Gift wrote, was 'No. 6' (Kineo), against which we had a particular grudge, inspired by Read, who desired us all to handle roughly any sea-going vessel we should see with 'No. 6' on her smoke-stack, as that vessel was engaging the McRae, above Forts Jackson and St. Philip when Lieutenant Commander Huger was killed. Read, who was First Lieutenant under Huger, and devotedly attached to him, saw the 'No. 6' by the flashes of the guns, and had ever since treasured the hope of getting along-side the fellow some day.... I sent my powder boy to Read with a message to come forward, as his friend was in sight. He came leisurely and carelessly, swinging a primer lanyard, and I think I have never looked at a person dis-playing such remarkable coolness and self-possession. On observing the num-bers ahead his eye was as bright and his smile as genuine as if he had been about to join a company of friends instead of enemies. We were now getting close aboard 'No. 6,' and he sheered with his port helm and unmuzzled his eleven-inch pivot gun charged with grape. It was hastily pointed, and the charge fell too low to enter our ports, for which it was intended. This broke the terrible quiet which hung over us like a spell. Every man's nerves were strung up again, and we were ready for the second battle. With a sharp touch of the starboard helm Brady showed me 'No. 6' straight ahead, and I gave him a shell through and through, and as we passed he got the port broadside. He did not follow us up. These two shots opened the engagement.*[7]

The *Arkansas* now became the target for over a hundred guns, and once again shot and shell began to ring against her battered railroad iron. Iron fragments flew in all directions from shells exploding against her sides; giant columns of water rose high into the air from Federal bolts that fell short. The *Arkansas'* ten guns also opened fire. Smoke and flames enveloped each of her gun ports as her explosive shells went hurtling toward the enemy. *It was calm, Brown wrote, and the smoke set-tling over the combatants, our men at times directed their guns at the flashes of those of their opponents. As we advanced, the line of fire seemed to grow into a circle constantly closing. The shock of missiles striking our sides was literally continuous, and as we were now surrounded, without room for anything but pushing ahead, and shrapnel shot were coming on our shield deck twelve pounds at a time, I went below to see how our Missouri backwoodsmen were handling their 100-pounder Columbiads. At this moment I had the most lively realiza-tion of having steamed into a real volcano, the Arkansas from its center firing rapidly to every point of the circumference, without the fear of hitting a friend or missing an enemy. I got below in time to see Read and Scales with their rifled guns blow off the feeble attack of a ram on our stern.*[8]

Another ram began to move out from behind one of Farragut's ships, steaming across in front of the *Arkansas* with the intent of turning and ramming. She was moving slowly, her pressure still coming up in her boilers. Brady shouted to Brown if he should run her down. *Go through him, Brady!*, was the reply. Brady pointed the *Arkansas'* armored prow toward the Federal ram *Lancaster* and called down to the engine room for as much speed as possible.[9] Lieutenant Gift, however, had in his big Columbiad a shell with a five-second fuse that he wanted to dispose of before reaching some of the Federal ironclads. With the *Arkansas* pointed straight for the *Lancaster*, Gift jerked the lanyard and fired, sending the shell crashing into the ram's boiler. The *Lancaster* exploded in a shower of hot steam and scalding water. Her crew came tearing up from below, ripping off their shirts and jumping overboard screaming in agony. The *Lancaster* drifted to one side and the *Arkansas* drove through the mass of humanity struggling in the water.[10] (The commander of the *Lancaster* later reported 18 men killed and 10 wounded by this single shot.)

Brown, who had returned to the roof, now became the target of hundreds of sharpshooters posted on the river's edge. Ignoring the minie balls striking all around him, he continued to direct the course of the *Arkansas* from his exposed position. Twice he was grazed by their bullets and his marine glass was shattered in his hand. Someone shouted that the colors had been shot away. Hearing this, Midshipman Dabney M. Scales, who·was helping Read with the stern rifles, scrambled up the ladder. Racing across the top of the shield through a hurricane of fire, Scales succeeded in knotting the halyards and hoisting the Stars and Bars. They were soon shot away a second time, and when Scales' head appeared at the top of the ladder, Brown ordered him back.[11]

Thus far, other than the minie balls coming through the open gun ports, nothing had penetrated the *Arkansas'* makeshift armor. This, however, was not to last. *We were passing one of the large sloops-of-war, Gift recalled, when a heavy shot struck the side abreast of my bow-gun, the concussion knocking over a man who was engaged in taking a shot from the rack. He rubbed his hip, which had been hurt, and said they would 'hardly strike twice in the same place.' He was mistaken, poor fellow, for immediately a shell entered the breach made by the shot, and bedding itself in the cotton-bale lining on the inside of the bulwark proper, exploded with terrible effect. I found myself standing in a dense, suffocating smoke, with my cap gone and hair and beard singed. The smoke soon cleared away, and I found but one man (Quartermaster Curtis) left. Sixteen were killed and wounded by that shell, and the ship set on fire. Stevens, ever cool and thoughtful, ran to the engine room hatch, seized the hose and dragged it to the aperture. In a few moments the fire was extinguished without an alarm having been created.*[12]

Smoke from the perforated smokestack was seeping into the gun deck, while flames from the furnace (the breechings having been shot away) were raising the temperature to 120 degrees. Still the men of the

The mighty CSS *Arkansas*. A wash drawing by R. G. Skerret done in 1904. The artist incorrectly shows the *Arkansas* with inclined sides to her casemate.

Arkansas labored on, firing as fast as they could load and push the guns out. Gift, with the help of Curtis and a Missouri army captain, was able to get one more round down the barrel of his Columbiad. Before he could fire, though, another round came crashing through the *Arkansas'* side right above his broadside gun. *An eleven-inch shell broke through immediately above the port, bringing with it a shower of iron and wooden splinters, which struck down every man at the gun. My Master's mate, Mr. Wilson, was painfully wounded in the nose, and I had my left arm smashed. Curtis was the only sound man in the division when we mustered the crew at quarters, at Vicksburg. Nor did the mischief of the last shot end with my poor guns' crew. It passed across the deck, through the smoke-stack, and killed and wounded seven men at Scale's gun.*[13]

As fast as they could be moved, the dead and wounded were carried below where the surgeons did what they could, while other crew members swept the iron and wood fragments away from the gun carriages. Shells and powder continued to be passed along the passageways and up to the gun deck where powder boys ran it to the divisions, keeping the *Arkansas'* remaining guns thundering away. *Stationed on the ladder leading to the berth-deck*, wrote Gift, *was a Quartermaster named Eaton. He was assigned the duty of passing shells from the forward shell-room, and also had a kind of superintendence over the boys who came for powder. Eaton was a character. He had thick, red hair, an immense muscular frame, and a will and courage rarely encountered. Nothing daunted him, and the hotter the fight, the fiercer grew Eaton. From his one eye he glared furiously on all who seemed inclined to shirk, and his voice grew louder and more distinct as the shot rattled and crashed upon our mail.*

An artist's concept of the *Arkansas* running the gauntlet of Federal warships above Vicksburg on July 15, 1862.

At one instant you would hear him pass the word down the hatch: 'Nine-inch shell, five-second fuse...here you are, my lad, with your rifle shell, take it and go back quick...what's the matter that you can't get that gun out?' and like a cat, he would spring from his place and throw his weight on the side tackle, and the gun was sure to go out. 'What are you doing here, wounded? Where are you hurt? Go back to your gun, or I'll murder you on the spot...here's your nine-inch shell...mind shipmate (to a wounded man), the ladder is bloody, don't slip, let me help you.'[14]

The Federal ironclad *Benton*, flagship of Rear Admiral Davis, attempted to block the way. Gift sent his last painfully loaded shell slamming into her. Even though the *Arkansas'* engines, with their low steam pressure, were barely turning the screws, Brown ordered the pilot to ram the *Benton*. At the last minute, she moved out of the way and as the *Arkansas* passed by, her starboard guns raked the Federal ship sending their shells crashing through her from rudder to prow. The *Benton* did not reply.[15]

Finally, with Read still hammering away with his stern rifles, the *Arkansas* passed the last of the Union ships. Brown called his officers up to the top of the casemate to take a look at what they had just passed through and to get some fresh air; and *as the little group of heroes closed around me with their friendly words of congratulation, a heavy rifle-shot passed by close over our heads: it was the parting salutation, and if aimed two feet lower would have been to us the most injurious of the battle.*[16] Down below, Gift observed, *A great heap of mangled and ghastly slain lay on the gun deck, with rivulets of blood running away from them. There was a poor fellow torn asunder, another mashed flat, whilst in the 'slaughter-house', brains, hair and blood were all about. Down below fifty or sixty wounded were groaning and complaining, or courageously bearing their ills without a murmur.*[17]

As the *Arkansas* rounded the point above Vicksburg, the city and the high bluffs sparkled in the morning sun. Never had a ship's destination looked so good! Brown and the crew of the *Arkansas* were unprepared for what they saw next. The bluffs above the city, every high building, every piece of high ground which offered a viewing point, was covered with a cheering mass of humanity. With the first sound of the big guns, soldiers and citizens alike had rushed to every vantage point. "The *Arkansas* is coming! The *Arkansas* is coming!" was shouted from person to person until soon, everyone knew what the deep booming sounds meant. They watched with anxious pride as the *Arkansas'* guns flashed through the dense smoke, hoping, praying that she would somehow make it. When the firing stopped and she rounded the point, they simply went wild! Brown and his men could see and hear them now; thousands and thousands of them, each one cheering and screaming at the top of their lungs. Women cried. Men clapped and cheered. Children danced round and round with one another. Flags and old sheets, anything they could get their hands on, were being waved in the morning breeze. This was Vicksburg's moment! Brown and his officers stood on top of the casemate as the battered *Arkansas* glided by and in humble appreciation, acknowledged the cheers of their countrymen. It was an exhilarating moment; a moment in time that none who were there on that bright Tuesday morning, would ever forget![18]

At 8:50 a.m., the still smoking *Arkansas* secured her lines to the wharf below Jackson Street, her flag fluttering from a boat hook which had been thrust up through the roof. Thousands surged through the streets toward the wharf while regimental bands played "Dixie" and "The Bonnie Blue Flag." Some poked their heads through the gun ports to take a look and quickly backed away from the horror they beheld inside. Exhausted gun crews blackened by powder from the waist up, sat around their guns too dazed to move. Wooden splinters and jagged pieces of railway iron covered the grimy gun deck which had been made sticky from the mixture of sand and blood. Gradually, the cleanup began. The dead were carried ashore to be buried, while the wounded were taken to army hospitals. The decks were washed down and the crew sent to breakfast. The tough Missouri artillerists all filed ashore to return to their command, and with the ten killed and fifteen wounded, the *Arkansas'* crew was suddenly diminished to one-half its original number. Carpenters and machinists began working on her damaged casemate while Generals Earl Van Dorn and John C. Brekinridge, both of whom had watched the battle from the dome of the courthouse, rushed on board to congratulate Brown and his men.[19]

Anchored below Vicksburg was the mortar fleet of Federal Admiral Porter, and his gunners had been kept busy lobbing their huge shells into the city for the past month. Many of these mortar crews and their boats fled in panic at the sight of the *Arkansas*, setting fire to one boat that was hard aground. With the realization that the *Arkansas* was stopping at Vicksburg, most of the warships had returned including the heavily armed *Westfield*. Later in the morning, Brown had the *Arkansas* moved down to the coal depot to take on fuel, and the *Westfield* opened fire with her 100-pound parrot gun. Brown reported that, *The Westfield made very fine practice with his 100-pounder rifle gun, occasionally throwing the spray from his shot over our working party, but with the benefit of sprinkling down the coal dust.* The *Arkansas* did not respond, and when her coaling was complete, she moved back out of range to her mooring at the foot of Jackson Street.[20]

While the repair work continued on the *Arkansas*, a mortified and furious Admiral Farragut was tallying his losses:

UNION SHIPS	NUMBER OF HITS	KILLED	WOUNDED
Carondelet	20	5	20
Tyler	14	8	16
Lancaster	1	18	10
Benton	6	1	3
Sumter	12	0	0
Champion	3	0	0
Dickey	3	0	0
Great Western	1	0	0
Miscellaneous Vessels	13	10	20
TOTAL	73	42	69 [21]

Farragut wanted to begin an attack on the *Arkansas* as soon as his fleet could get ready. Admiral Davis, however, pointing out the rashness of a daylight attack under the big guns of the Vicksburg batteries, convinced him to wait until sundown. At dusk they would go down in a double line, ships to the inside, next to the city and gunboats on the outside. Davis' fleet would open fire and engage the attention of the Confederate batteries on the bluffs. *...no one will do wrong, Farragut said, who lays his vessel* *alongside of the enemy or tackles with the ram. The ram must be destroyed.* Farragut's big ships would fire solid bolts, and large anchors were ordered hoisted to the yardarms to be dropped on the "Rebel" ram.[22]

Meanwhile, during the day, the crew and the mechanics worked feverishly to complete temporary repairs and put the *Arkansas* in the best fighting condition possible. Brown knew that the Union commanders would make every effort to reverse the embarrassment and losses they had suffered. After sundown, with the long roll of the drum, the *Arkansas'* weary crew was again called to their guns.

Down they came, Gift remembered, *steaming slowly and steadily, and seemed to be on the lookout for us. But they had miscalculated their time. The darkness which partially shrouded them from the view of our army gunners completely shut us out from their sight, inasmuch as our sides were the color of rust and we lay under a red bank; consequently, the first notice they had of our whereabouts came from our guns as they crossed our line of fire, and then it was too late to attempt to check up and undertake to grapple with us. They came by singly, each to get punished, as our men were again feeling in excellent spirits.*[23] The *Hartford* stood in close and was greeted by a broadside from the *Arkansas'* guns. Aiming at the gun flashes, she unleashed a thunderous salvo of her own, one of which found its mark. The *Arkansas* heaved and shuddered like a wounded animal as a large 11-inch solid shot smashed into her a few inches above the waterline. Careening through the engine room, it cut two men in half, wounded six or eight more, went through the dispensary smashing the ship's medicine supply, and finally imbedded itself in the opposite bulkhead between the woodwork and the armor. The protruding bulge could be seen clearly from the outside the next day. One of the men killed was William Gilmore, one of the pilots, and the heroic James Brady was seriously hurt by being blown overboard. The engines were knocked off their mountings, and the engine room was a shambles of iron fragments and splinters. The *Arkansas'* guns continued to roar, however, shooting at each of the Federals as they passed.[24]

Gift, because of his broken arm, had turned his two guns over to Scales and stood with Brown on top of the casemate. *To be a spectator of such a scene,* he wrote, *was intensely interesting and exciting. The great ships with their towering spars came sweeping by, pouring out broadsides, whilst the batteries from the hills, the mortars from above and below, and the ironclads, kept the air alive with hurtling missiles and the darkness lighted up by burning fuses and bursting shells. On our gun-deck every man and officer worked as though the fate of the nation hung on his individual efforts. Scales was very near, and I could hear his clear voice continually. He coaxed and bullied alternately, and finally, when he saw his object in line, his voice rose as clear as a bell, and his 'Ready! Fire!' rang out like a bugle note.* Finally, the last Federal glided past firing into the darkness.[25]

Weary gunners, numbed by exhaustion, collapsed beside their guns. They had done well, for the Federals had lost 27 (killed and wounded), and the *Winona* was so badly damaged that she had to be run ashore to keep from sinking. Another Federal, the *Sumter*, was holed twice below her armor causing a serious leak. The *Arkansas*, too, had more damage to repair. Her engine room was in shambles, and it would be several days before her screws would again churn the waters of the Mississippi. More bodies and pieces of bodies had to be carried ashore, and more wounded had to be helped to the army hospital.[26]

The next morning, sailors sleeping on top of the casemate were awakened early before daylight by a dull "Boom!" off to the south. Rubbing their eyes and squinting into the faint early morning light, they could see the trail of a sputtering fuse rising from the southern horizon. Slowly, it climbed higher and higher into the dawning sky until finally, it seemed to stop and hang motionless above them. As those who were awake continued to watch in fascination, it began to grow larger in size and then, to their horror, they realized it was falling straight at them! The big 13-inch shell struck the water near by and burst with a thunderous explosion.

Farragut, exasperated and embarrassed by the continual survival of the *Arkansas*, had ordered Porter to sink the ironclad with his big 13-inch mortars. These guns, some above the city and some below, had been playing havoc with the citizens of Vicksburg, and now they were ordered to drop their missiles of destruction on the *Arkansas*. Hitting a large city and hitting a single ship, however, were entirely two different matters. The monsters were able to throw their 200 pound shells a distance of two-and-one-half miles, and while many of the shells came close, sprinkling their iron fragments over the deck, none struck the *Arkansas*.[27] *For seven days and nights, the huge shells were lobbed toward the ironclad, but in time,* Brown observed, *we became accustomed to this shelling, but not to the idea that it was without danger; and I know of no more effective way of curing a man of the weakness of thinking that he is without the feeling of fear, than for him, on a dark night, to watch two or three of these double-fused descending shells, all near each other, and seeming as though they would strike him between the eyes.*[28]

Lieutenant Read wrote of an amusing incident involving a replacement surgeon who came on board. *Both of our surgeons being sick, Captain Brown telegraphed out into the interior of Mississippi for medical volunteers. In a day or two a long, slim doctor came in from Clinton; and as he was well recommended, Captain Brown gave him an acting appointment as surgeon, and directed him to report to Lieutenant Stevens for duty. It was early in the morning when he arrived; the enemy had not commenced their daily pastime of shelling us; the ship's decks had been cleanly washed down, the awnings spread, and everything was neat and orderly. The doctor took break-fast in the ward-room, and seemed delighted with the vessel generally. Before the regular call to morning inspection the officer of the powder division started around below to show the new medical officer his station during action, and the arrangement for disposing of the wounded, etc., etc. In going along the berth-deck the officer remarked to the doctor that in a battle there was plenty to do, as the wounded came down in a steady stream. The 'medico' looked a little incredulous; but a few minutes afterwards, when he perceived the road through which an 11-inch shell had come, his face lengthened perceptibly; and after awhile, when the big shells began to fall around the vessel, he became rather nervous. He would stand on the companion-ladder and watch the smoke rise from the mortar-vessels, and would wait until he heard the whizzing of the shell through the air, when he would make a dive for his state-room. As soon as the shell fell he would go up and watch out for another. Occasionally, when a shell would explode close to us, or fall with a heavy splash alongside, he would be heard to groan, 'Oh! Louisa and the babes!'*[29]

Within three days, the debris in the engine room had been cleaned up and the engines remounted, while carpenters and machinists had patched the two gaping holes in the port side of the gun box and repaired the smokestack. With this completed, the *Arkansas* cast off her lines on 18 July, and headed up river with the intent of giving some of the mortar boats a taste of their own medicine. Seeing her approaching, however, the boats were taken in tow by the ironclads who began steaming upstream. The slower *Arkansas* could not keep up and soon they were out of sight. It didn't matter, for about the same time the Federals were disappearing up the river, one of the *Arkansas'* engines failed, and before she could stop, she had made a complete circle in the middle of the river. With one engine, the help of the current, and lots of opposite rudder, the *Arkansas* finally regained her moorings.[30]

During this period the *Arkansas'* crew was being steadily diminished by fevers and sickness. On the morning of July 22, the 28 men who were left were awakened about 4:00 a.m. by the long roll of the drum calling them to quarters. Looking up river, intense activity could be seen among the upper Federal fleet. The rams and ironclads of Davis' command were all under way, and it looked like an attack was imminent. The indomitable Lieutenant Gift, his broken arm in a sling, described this latest Federal effort to destroy the *Arkansas*: *We were moored to the bank, head up the river, as a matter of course. The fires under the boilers were hastened, and every possible preparation made for resistance. In a few minutes we observed the iron-clad steamer Essex ('Dirty Bill Porter' commanding) steaming around the point and steering for us. The upper battery opened, but she did not reply. Grimball unloosed his Columbiad, but she did not stop. I followed, hitting her fair, but still she persevered in sullen silence.*

Farragut's plan was fór the *Essex* and the *Queen of the West* to attack and ram the *Arkansas*, pushing her into the river bank, and then storm her with boarding parties. Meanwhile, Davis' ironclads and Farragut's men-of-war would engage the army batteries on the bluffs. *On she came,* Gift continued, *like a mad bull, nothing daunted or overawed. As soon as Captain Brown got a fair view of her, followed at a distance by the Queen, he divined her intent, and seeing that she was as square as a flatboat or scow, and we were as sharp as a wedge, he determined at once to foil her tactics. Slacking off the hawser which held our head to the bank, he went ahead on the starboard screw, and thus our sharp prow was turned directly for her to hit against. This disconcerted the enemy and destroyed his plan. A collision would surely cut him down and leave us uninjured. All this time we had not been idle spectators. The two Columbiads had been ringing on his front and piercing him every shot; to which he did not reply until he found that the shoving game was out of the question.* (Porter later claimed that during the encounter, the *Essex* was hit 42 times but only penetrated once.) *Then, and when not more than fifty yards distant, he triced up his three bow port-shutters and poured out his fire. A nine-inch shot struck our armor a few inches forward of the unlucky forward port, and crawling along the side entered. Seven men were killed outright and six wounded. Splinters flew in all directions. In an instant the enemy was alongside, and his momentum was so great that he ran aground a short distance astern of us. As he passed we poured out our port broadside, and as soon as the stern rifles could be cleared of the splinters and broken stanchions and woodwork, which had been driven the whole length of the gun box, we went ahead on our port screw and turned our stern guns on him, and every man (we had but seventeen left) and officer went to them. As he passed he did not fire, nor did he whilst we were riddling him close aboard. His only effort was to get away from us. He backed hard on his engines and finally got off; but getting a shot in his machinery just as he got afloat, he was compelled to float down stream and join the lower fleet, which he accomplished without damage from the batteries on the hills. He fired only the three shots mentioned. But our troubles were not over.*[31]

We had scarcely shook this fellow off before we were called to the other end of the ship—we ran from one gun to another to get ready for a second attack. The Queen was now close to us, evidently determined to ram us. The guns had been fired and were now empty and inboard. Somehow we got them loaded and run out by the time she had commenced to round to. I am not sure, but I think we struck her with the Columbiads as she came down, but at all events the broadside was ready. Captain Brown adopted the plan of turning his head to her also, and thus received her blow glancing. She came into us going at an enormous speed, probably fifteen miles an hour, and I felt pretty sure that our hour had struck. I had hoped to blow her up with the thirty-two-pounder as she passed, but the gun being an old one, with an enlarged vent, the primer drew out without igniting the charge. One of the men, we had no regular gun's crew then, every man was expected to do ten men's duties, replaced it and struck it with a compressor lever; but too late; his boilers were past, and the shot went through his cylinder timbers without disabling him. His blow, though glancing, was a heavy one. His prow, or beak, made a hole through our side and caused the ship to careen, and roll heavily; but we all knew in an instant that no serious damage had been done, and we redoubled our efforts to cripple him so that he could not again attempt the experiment. As did the Essex, so he ran into the bank astern of us, and got the contents of the stern battery; but being more nimble than she, was sooner off into deep water. Returning up stream he got our broadside guns again, and we saw that he had no disposition to engage us further. As he passed the line of fire of the bow guns he got it again, and I distinctly recollect the handsomest shot I ever made was the last at her. He was nearly a mile away, and I bowled at him with the gun level. It ricochetted four or five times before it dropped into his stern. But it dropped there.[32]

Again, the *Arkansas* had damage to repair and more dead and wounded to be carried ashore. But the knowledge was not lost on either side that after eight days and four battles, against unbelievable odds, she was still afloat, her engines were running and all her guns were still capable of hurling their shells at the enemy. In fact, the next day she was seen steaming defiantly up and down the river in front of the Confederate batteries on the bluffs.[33]

On July 25, 1862, a disgusted and disheartened Farragut, his fleet short on fuel, many of his men sick with fever, and his image tarnished by the "Rebel" ram he could not destroy, weighed anchor and led his fleet of warships down the Mississippi toward New Orleans. Six days later, Davis departed north with his ironclads and gunboats. The siege of Vicksburg was over, and considerable credit was given to Brown and the men of the *Arkansas* for making it happen. The Federals would be back with a new leader and a combined army and navy expedition, that would eventually seal the fate of the Confederate Gibraltar on the river. But for now 400 miles of the Mississippi was under Confederate control.[34]

With the Federals now gone, the *Arkansas* would have the time for extensive repairs to be undertaken. Mechanics from Jackson and Memphis descended on Vicksburg to begin the work, while Commander Brown, who had been promoted as of July 15, requested and was granted a four day leave to travel to Grenada, Mississippi to see his family. Turning the *Arkansas* over to his executive officer, Lieutenant Stevens, with orders not to move the ironclad until his return, Brown traveled by rail the 150 miles to Grenada. Totally exhausted from the past three months of feverish activity, he fell ill upon his arrival and was confined to his bed.[35]

While Brown was sick in bed and mechanics were working on the *Arkansas*, Van Dorn decided to send General Breckinridge and 5,000 men south by rail on an expedition to re-capture Baton Rouge, Louisiana. Van Dorn also ordered Stevens to take the *Arkansas* the 300 miles down river to support the attack. With the *Arkansas* still undergoing repairs, and with her commander indisposed in Grenada, Lieutenant Stevens was in a dilemma. Doing what any dutiful subordinate should do, he wired Brown for advice. Telegraphing a reply that reiterated his orders not to move the *Arkansas* until he could get there, Brown had himself carried to the railroad station and placed in the mail car where he could recline on the mail bags. If Stevens could only wait a few more hours, Brown would arrive in time to resume command. Van Dorn, however, was adamant that the *Arkansas* must go. In desperation, caught between conflicting orders, Stevens appealed to Commodore Lynch, district navy commander in Jackson. With no understanding of the condition of the iron-clad, Lynch ordered Stevens to disregard Brown's orders and take the

Major General Earl Van Dorn, Confederate commander at Vicksburg. He and General John C. Breckinridge anxiously watched the progress of the *Arkansas* through Farragut's fleet from the dome of the Vicksburg courthouse. Later, he ordered the ironclad to Baton Rouge, and to her destruction in support of Breckinridge's attack.
Battles and Leaders of the Civil War

Arkansas to Baton Rouge. Hastily gathering enough men to bring the crew up to reasonable strength, the *Arkansas* cast off her lines at 2:00 a.m. Monday morning, August 4, and headed down river.[36]

Unfortunately, one of her most valuable officers was missing as she pounded downstream. Chief Engineer George W. City was flat on his back in a Vicksburg hospital suffering from exhaustion and a high fever. *His care and nursing,* Gift observed, *had kept the machinery in order up to the time of leaving. We soon began to feel his loss. The engineer in charge, a volunteer from the army, had recently joined us, and though a young man of pluck and gallantry, and possessed of great will and determination to make the engines work, yet he was unequal to the task.* Without the skill of Engineer City to coax the engines along, with a deadline of August 6 to be at Baton Rouge, and three hundred miles of twisting Mississippi River to travel, the engines were simply being stressed beyond their limits.[37]

While his ship was beginning her journey down the river, the train carrying the still suffering Commander Brown was pulling into the station at Jackson, Mississippi. Here he learned, via telegraph, that the *Arkansas* had sailed four hours ago. Instead of proceeding on to Vicksburg, an angry and weary Commander Brown, still hoping to join his command in time, now headed for Baton Rouge.[38]

Later, Lieutenant Read wrote about this dash down the river and the unhappy scenes that greeted their eyes: *The Arkansas behaved well, and made with the current about fifteen miles an hour. We steamed on down during all the next day, passing many signs of the wanton and barbarous destruction of property by the enemy. The people on the river banks gathered around their burnt and charred remains of their once happy homes, and hailed with exclamations of delight the sight of their country's flag, and the gallant little Arkansas moving down to chastise the savage foe.*[39]

Passing the mouth of the Red River, the *Arkansas'* engines began to vibrate and hammer badly. Stevens called a council of his officers to discuss whether they should proceed. The young army engineer was called and expressed his opinion that the engines would hold together a while longer, and with this information, Stevens decided to keep moving. Fifteen miles below Port Hudson, and only about eight miles from Baton Rouge, both engines suddenly stopped altogether. Drifting into the right bank, the *Arkansas* was made secure, and the engineers starting working to correct the problem. Gift and Midshipman Bacot were dispatched ashore to a local farmhouse to try to secure information concerning the dispositions of any enemy naval forces around Baton Rouge. Learning that Breckinridge was to attack the Federal works at daylight the next day, and that the only Federal warships present were their old "friend" the *Essex* and a couple of gunboats, they hastened back to the *Arkansas*.[40]

The engineers worked all night on the troublesome engines and by daylight they reported to Stevens that everything was ready to run. In the distance, as the sun rose off the port bow, the rattle of musketry and the booming of cannon could be heard as Breckinridge began his attack. *In feverish haste our lines were cast off and hauled aboard*, wrote Gift, *and once more the good old ship was driving towards the enemy. Like a war-horse she seemed to scent the battle from afar, and in point of speed out did anything we had ever before witnessed. That was a fatal error.*[41]

Rounding a bend in the river, Stevens could see the spires and rooftops of Baton Rouge. In addition, he could see that the Confederate advance had driven the Federals to the riverbank, but Breckinridge's troops were now suffering under a heavy fire from the *Essex*. The call to quarters was sounded, and once more the men of the *Arkansas* rushed to their guns. Suddenly, the starboard engine jammed on dead center, and before the helmsmen could bring her about, her stern had swung downstream, and the bow had wedged itself on some submerged cypress stumps along the river's edge. The engineers frantically went to work again while Stevens and his officers anxiously watched the *Essex* downstream. Throwing some spare railroad iron that was being carried overboard, the *Arkansas* finally floated free of the cypress stumps.[42]

The engineers, Gift recalled, *had pulled the engine to pieces and with files and chisels were as busy as bees, though they had been up constantly then for the greater parts of the two preceding nights.* Near dark, they reported that all was in order once more, and Stevens prepared to steam the *Arkansas* a few hundred yards upstream to take on some coal. They had gone barely a hundred yards when the wrist pin of the starboard engine broke in half. An exasperated Stevens had the ship tied to the riverbank again with her head downstream, and the weary engineers went to work. Fortunately, one of them was a blacksmith, and setting up a forge on deck, he began hammering out a new pin. Because of the makeshift facilities, it took all night to form the new part. By daybreak, August 6, the enemy had become aware of the stranded *Arkansas,* and the *Essex* started up river to investigate.

The Essex led, Gift related, *and came up very slowly, at a rate not to exceed two miles an hour. She had opened on us before the last touch had been given to the pin, but it was finished and the parts thrown together.* Quickly Stevens ordered the *Arkansas* ahead, and once more with black smoke billowing from her stack and her twin screws churning the water, she headed for the enemy.[43]

The USS *Essex.* She attempted to cut the *Arkansas* in half at Vicksburg, and later witnessed the Confederate ironclad's destruction at Baton Rouge. She is shown here loading coal at Baton Rouge in July 1862.

Afterward, Lieutenant Gift, with a heavy heart, wrote about these final moments: *The pleasant sensation of being afloat and in possession of the power of locomotion, was hardly experienced before our last and final disaster came. The port engine this time gave way, broke down and would not move. The engineer was now in despair, he could do nothing, and so reported. The Essex was coming up astern and firing on us. We had run ashore and were a hopeless, immovable mass. Read was returning the fire, but the two ships were scarcely near enough for the shots to tell. We were not struck by the Essex, nor do I think we struck her. An army force was reported by a mounted "home guard" to be coming up the river to cut off our retreat. Stevens did not call a council of war, but himself assumed the responsibility of burning the ship. I recollect the look of anguish he gave me, and the scalding tears running down his cheeks when he announced his determination.*[44]

The destruction of the *Arkansas* five miles above Baton Rouge on August 6, 1862.
Battles and Leaders of the Civil War

While the rest of the crew scrambled out on deck and dropped over the bow to dry land, Stevens, Read, Bacot, Scales, Talbot, and Gunner Travers stayed on board to destroy the ship. Using axes and sledge hammers, they smashed as much of her machinery and fixtures as they could; primers and shells were brought up from below and scattered around the gun deck. Working quickly, they loaded all her guns and ran them out. Cotton mattresses were dragged from the wardroom, piled together and set afire. With the *Essex* drawing closer, and satisfied that the ship would continue to burn, Stevens ordered the remaining officers ashore.[45]

Black smoke billowed up from the depths of the *Arkansas* and soon flames began licking at her gun deck. Ironically, she floated free from where she had grounded, the current turning her around, and the gallant warrior floated downstream pointed toward the *Essex*. As her grief-stricken crew watched from the riverbank, flames began shooting out of her gun ports and the ammunition began to explode. One by one, as the flames reached them, her guns would fire sending their final defiant shots screaming out over the waters of the Mississippi. Unnerved by the sight of the unmanned *Arkansas* charging down upon them with her guns blazing, the *Essex* quickly backed away. Suddenly, with a blinding flash and a thunderous roar, the *Arkansas* was gone. As the debris settled over the river, and burning timbers floated downstream, Commander Brown arrived at the river's edge. He had reached Baton Rouge just minutes too late to see the destruction of the *Arkansas*. Perhaps it was best.[46]

Chapter Five

Captain Fuller and the *J. A. Cotton*

It was a time of tension and anxiety for the owners and operators of steamboats plying the Mississippi out of New Orleans in the spring of 1862. Even though the Federal blockaders had been driven out at the Head of the Passes and into the Gulf the previous October, there were increasing signs of a Union build-up outside the bar. To those familiar with naval affairs, it was evident that this was not just an increase to the blockading fleet, but rather a build-up prior to invasion. Taking advantage of the high water at this time of year, numerous civilian steamboats began to leave New Orleans. Steaming north up the Mississippi, many found their way into the Red River, which flows out of northwestern Louisiana and empties into the Mississippi about 75 miles above Baton Rouge. Just before the Red meets the Father of Waters, the Atchafalaya River branches off from the Red and winds its way southward into the fabled bayou country of southern Louisiana. Spreading its dark muddy waters over the marshy swamplands, so broad in fact that it's known as "The Grand Lake," it finally flows into Berwick Bay. From there it gathers itself together again as a navigable stream, and ultimately breaks through to the Gulf some 90 miles west of New Orleans. Turning into this river, during that spring rush to flee the Crescent City, was the steamboat *J. A. Cotton* under the command of Mississippi riverboat captain, Edward W. Fuller.[1]

Constructed at Jefferson, Indiana, and completed in early 1861, the *J. A. Cotton* was a typical side-wheel steamer of the period, weighing 549 tons, and was built specifically for the passenger and freight trade on the Louisiana bayous. Purchased by the Confederate army in early 1862, she was one of several vessels that arrived in Berwick Bay after the exodus from New Orleans.[2]

Her captain, Ed Fuller, was a civilian, and according to Lieutenant General Richard Taylor, commander of the District of West Louisiana, *was a western steamboat man, and one of the bravest of a bold, daring class.* After a brief stint in command of the armed tug *Music*, which had also escaped the disaster at New Orleans, Fuller approached Major J. L. Brent, Chief

Lieutenant General Richard Taylor, commander of the District of West Louisiana. Taylor's meager forces stubbornly and successfully defended the Louisiana bayou country until the end of the war.

Battles and Leaders of the Civil War

of Artillery and Ordnance on General Taylor's staff, asking for the army's permission and help in converting the *Cotton* into a gunboat. Because of her light construction, Fuller suggested that she be armored with railroad iron for protection of her vital machinery. Brent, on behalf of the army agreed to the proposal, and the conversion commenced.

Heavy timbers, backed by a layer of cotton bales, were fabricated into a partial casemate which was designed to protect her boilers and engines from enemy fire. Once this was in place, a small quantity of railroad iron was tacked on, and a crew was recruited from volunteers among the army units in the area. Two 24-pounder smoothbores and a field piece, supplied by Major Brent, were mounted on the hurricane deck. Captain Fuller's mission, in conjunction with General Taylor's army units, was to protect the rich bayou country from Federal invasion and depredations along the Atchafalaya and Teche Rivers.

The *Cotton* was never a commissioned vessel of the Confederate navy. While owned by the army and commanded by a civilian, there was a strong navy presence on board in the drama that was about to unfold. Several naval officers had been detailed to the "ironclad" to train the army volunteers in the manning of her guns. Among these young officers was Lieutenant Henry K. Stevens, former First Officer and ill-fated temporary commander of the formidable CSS *Arkansas*.[3]

Near the end of October 1862, Union General Weitzel advanced from New Orleans with a force of approximately 4,000 troops. Taken by steamers up the Mississippi to Donaldsonville, 60 miles above New Orleans, his troops disembarked and began pushing south along the north bank of Lafourche River. The only Confederate troops in the area able to offer opposition were 500 men under the immediate command of Colonel Leopold L. Armant. With these troops and a four gun battery, Colonel Armant made his stand along Lafourche.

At the little hamlet of Labadieville, a vicious little fight occurred about ten miles north of the railroad that runs from Algiers opposite New Orleans to Brashear City on Berwick Bay. Overwhelmed by the large Federal force, their ammunition exhausted, and suffering many casualties, the small band of Confederates retreated west along the railroad to Berwick Bay and began crossing over to the village of Berwick City on the western shore.

Brigadier General Alfred Mouton feverishly began concentrating all available troops, including the remnants of Armant's demoralized men, on a line just west of Berwick Bay and astride the Bayou Teche (river). With 1300 men and ten guns assembled, earthworks were thrown up on either side of the Teche with the left flank resting on Grand Lake, and the right on the impassable bayou two thousand yards south of the Teche. Three floating bridges were thrown over the Teche in the rear to facilitate moving troops from one side of the bayou to the other; and to the front, pickets were maintained on the western shore of the bay. It was at this time on Saturday evening, November 1, that Captain Fuller on the *Cotton*, which was anchored in the bay, saw the plumes of black smoke rolling over the trees to the south.[4]

Four Federal gunboats, accompanied by several transports, had departed New Orleans on October 25, under the command, ironically, of Lieutenant Commander Thomas McKean Buchanan, the brother of Admiral Franklin Buchanan, CSN.[5] After much difficulty crossing the bar at the mouth of the Atchafalaya, they finally steamed up the river and arrived at the south end of the bay with the express purpose of destroying the *Cotton* and assisting Weitzel's advance. The four Federal gunboats, whose smoke Fuller could now see, were the *Estrella* with five guns, the *Diana* also with five guns, the *Kinsman* and the *Calhoun*. This was the same *Calhoun* that had flown Confederate colors in the engagement at the Head of the Passes in October of 1861. She had been captured by the tender to the Union frigate *Colorado* on January 23, 1862.[6]

With the Union gunboats rapidly approaching, Fuller quickly gave orders for the steamers *Hart* (towing a barge loaded with sugar), and the *Segar*, along with a steam launch, to get under way. The *Hart* and the *Segar* were both ordered to proceed up the Teche. While the *Hart* obeyed and was safely taken up the bayou, the *Segar*, either through a misunderstanding or by deception, churned up the Atchafalaya, where she was later abandoned and captured. *Launch No. 1*, because of her shallow draft, was ordered to steam up the Atchafalaya and enter Grand Lake where she could not be followed by the deeper draft Union vessels.

With the other boats safely on their way, Captain Fuller turned his attention to the rapidly approaching enemy. Getting the *Cotton* under way, Fuller ordered the pilot, O. S. Burdet, to head for the point where the Atchafalaya River enters the bay from the north. With the engines at full throttle, the Confederate "ironclad" pounded up the bay, while the four pursuing Federals opened fire. Rounding into the Atchafalaya, one of the *Cotton's* guns was brought to bear, and she fired one shot. The good training provided by Lieutenant Stevens and the other naval officers on board was evident as the shell streaked across the bay and struck the *Kinsman* under the port bow.[7]

The Federals, firing from their bow guns, continued their chase, until approaching darkness and the superior speed of the Confederate "ironclad," caused them to give up and return to the bay. Arriving at the mouth of the Teche, and with little space in which to turn around, Fuller rounded to and backed the gunboat into the bayou. *By doing so,* Fuller explained, *we were keeping our teeth to the enemy*. With her large paddle wheels turning slowly in reverse, and trying not to run aground, Fuller continued to back the *Cotton* cautiously up the darkened Teche. Arriving opposite the Fusilier plantation, the improvised "ironclad" was moored for the night.[8]

As daylight broke over the bayou, Fuller received orders to move the *Cotton* above Cornay's bridge, which would put him just to the rear of the Confederate entrenchments. A line of obstructions had been placed in the river at this point, and Fuller was ordered to support the army troops on either side until forced to retire, then retreat to the next bridge, turn the *Cotton* across the bayou, and finally sink her.[9] Fortunately, this Sunday passed quietly, for the Federals were still gathering their forces and ferrying Weitzel's troops across the bay.

On Monday morning, the four Union gunboats advanced up the Teche, and at 1:30 p.m., opened fire on both the *Cotton* and the land batteries on either side of the bayou. Fuller's guns roared in response, and the bayou shook and trembled from the concussion of the heavy guns. The second or third shot from the *Cotton* smashed into the *Estrella* on her port rail, killing two men working a 24-pounder howitzer, wounding another, and cutting away the wheel ropes. The federal boat drifted to one side, and the *Diana* and the *Kinsman* squeezed past. Ignoring, for the moment, the ten artillery pieces on shore which were punching holes in the Union vessels with almost every shot, the

Federals concentrated their fire on the *Cotton*. Solid shot and explosive shells literally rained on her makeshift armor. Bravely her navy trained and directed army gunners stood to their guns, sending their heavy shells screaming down the bayou and crashing into the Federal boats.[10]

The *Diana*, fouling her bow pivot rifle, stopped and the *Kinsman* took the lead. Pressing up to the obstructions within a few hundred yards of the *Cotton*, the *Kinsman* opened fire. Turning broadside, she raked the land batteries with grape-shot, causing the artillerists to limber up their guns and pull out. With the field artillery gone, the *Kinsman* and the *Cotton* proceeded to slam shot after shot into one another. While the *Cotton* deflected most of the incoming shells, the Federal boat was not so fortunate. Fuller's gunners sent three solid shots in quick succession, plunging through her starboard side near the waterline.[11] The *Kinsman* was leaking badly and listing to one side which prevented her from effectively training her guns on the Confederate "ironclad." One of the *Cotton's* solid bolts had gone through her shell room and magazine, killing two sailors and wounding four more.

The *Calhoun* now moved up to take her place, and Fuller's gunners shifted their attention to their former friend. For twenty minutes the two fought it out at close range, the *Cotton* sending eight shots slamming into the *Calhoun*. Finally, with no infantry support on either side of the Teche, Fuller ordered the *Cotton* to begin slowly backing up the bayou while maintaining her fire. At that moment, Gunner F. G. Burbank reported that he had run out of powder cartridges and had no cloth to make more. In desperation, and thinking quickly, Fuller ordered the trouser legs of some of the gunners cut off, and with these, hastily fashioned more cartridge bags to keep the *Cotton's* guns thundering away. Slowly, with the big paddle wheels turning in reverse, the *Cotton* moved up the bayou until, at length, she backed around a bend in the Teche and both sides ceased firing.

As the navy and army men slumped by their still smoking guns on the hurricane deck, Captain Fuller took stock of the damage. *We had to morn the loss,* he reported, *of one brave soldier killed by an accidental discharge of his gun, which severely wounded another. Another was accidentally wounded at another gun by the recoil of the carriage and has since died. One man was wounded by a piece of the enemy's shell. These are all the casualties that occurred. The boat sustained no perceptible damage.*[12]

The Federals, not wanting to spend the night in the narrow bayou where the Confederates could fire on them from the banks of the river, retreated back to Berwick Bay. The *Kinsman* had been hit 54 times and had two killed and five wounded. The *Estrella* was hit three times and had two killed and one wounded, while the *Calhoun* was struck eight times. The hapless *Diana* had her stern "blown off" by three shots and had to be towed out. One "ironclad" Confederate steamboat and ten artillery pieces had met and bested four of the United States Navy's finest armed gunboats.[13]

Early the next morning, the *Cotton* resumed her position above the obstructions. During the night, additional iron rails had been located and positioned on her battered casemate to further shield the engines. All day, while Fuller anxiously paced the deck, the men of the *Cotton* watched and waited by their guns. By sundown, there was still no sign of the Federals. No Union forces advanced up the Teche this day,

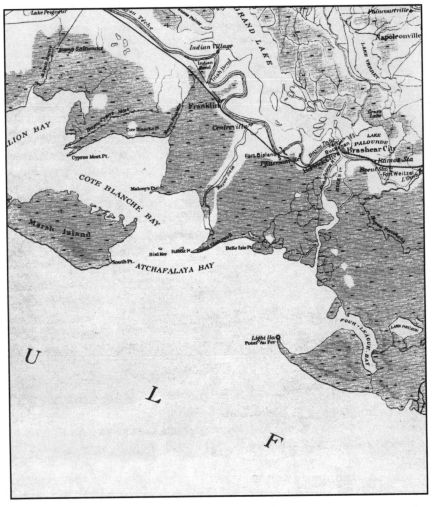

Map of Louisiana bayou country showing Atchafalaya Bay and the Bayou Teche flowing down from the northwest.

Official Records

because they were still down in the bay hastily making repairs to their boats. The *Cotton* had earned the grudging respect of Commander Buchanan who reported that, *The Cotton made some excellent firing.* For some reason, through the reports of deserters and contrabands, the Federals had developed the impression that the *Cotton* was an iron-clad almost as formidable as the *Virginia* or the *Arkansas.*

On Wednesday, the 5th instant, Captain Fuller wrote in his report, *the enemy again opened fire upon us with four boats at about 10:30 o'clock.* (The log of the *Calhoun* shows that only the *Calhoun* and the *Estrella* went up on Wednesday; the others still undergoing repairs.) *They fired from behind a point out of our range for about twenty minutes; then two of them steamed up into sight. We then immediately returned their fire, and with such effect that the enemy retired and abandoned the contest in fifty-five minutes from firing the first shot. The two boats that came into sight were badly damaged and their loss heavy; ours nothing, the only damage being a trifling break in the cabin roof. This day victory was clearly outs. The enemy retired from action badly discouraged, with severe loss. We were unhurt.*[14]

The *Cotton's* guns had, indeed, worsted the Federals. The *Calhoun's* log reported that at *11:30 a raking shot struck us, taking off the forward truck of (the) gun carriage of (the) 30-pounder, killing 2 seamen and slightly wounding 1.*

On Thursday, November 6, the Federals opened fire again on the *Cotton*, this time from long range while remaining out of sight. Captain Fuller and his gunners did not reply. The Union forces now contented themselves with consolidating their hold on Berwick Bay while awaiting reinforcements from New Orleans. As the months of November and December slipped away, the *Cotton* continued to retain control of the Teche and the surrounding bayou country. As the new year rapidly approached, General Taylor was writing to Secretary of State Judah P. Benjamin that *something might be done for Fuller. He certainly deserves it. He defeated four of the enemy's gunboats.*[15] Early in January of 1863, Ed Fuller's nomination to the rank of lieutenant in the Confederate navy was forwarded to the War Department.

General Weitzel, whose force had now been increased to 4,500, began a combined army and navy advance up the Teche on January 13, 1863. With the *Kinsman*, the *Estrella*, the *Calhoun*, and the *Diana* advancing up the bayou, Weitzel assembled his command in line of battle, and moved his force to a point just below the obstructions, where they bivouacked for the night.

Fuller, with the *Cotton* in her same position as the previous November, must have wondered, as he watched the glowing Union camp fires that night, how much longer he could hold out against such numbers. Of major concern, was the vulnerability of the *Cotton* to attack by riflemen who might gain the shoreline opposite her. If this happened, combined with fire from the Union gunboats, Lieutenant Stevens' army crew might be driven from their guns. To guard against such an attack, numerous rifle pits had been dug on both sides of the bayou below the obstructions and emplacements built for the ten artillery pieces. With the Confederate troops, who were now increased to nearly 2,000 men, manning these, Fuller hoped that General Mouton would be able to halt the combined Union advance, and protect the *Cotton*.

At 8:00 a.m. the next morning, Fuller could see, through a drizzling rain, four plumes of dense black smoke drifting lazily up toward the low hanging clouds. The Federals were coming. Lieutenant Stevens rushed about the hurricane deck giving advice and encouragement, while making sure everything was ready. In the engine room, coal heavers shoveled coal into the furnace, while the engineer watched the rising pressure on the steam gauge. Advancing slowly, so as to stay in line with the infantry, the *Kinsman* and the *Estrella* opened fire at 9:00 a.m., their heavy rifled shots whistling over the *Cotton*. Fuller held his fire, for his guns were smoothbores and could not yet reach the Federals.

As soon as the first Union boat, the *Kinsman*, came within range, Fuller's gunners opened fire, sending their shots screaming down the bayou. The army batteries on shore now joined in, the bark of their field pieces easily discernible above the roar of the heavy naval guns. As the *Kinsman* and the *Estrella* reached the obstructions, Confederate

The *J. A. Cotton* battles Union gunboats in Bayou Teche, Louisiana, January 14, 1863. In this Federal drawing, the *Cotton* is depicted beyond the trees to the right, with the Confederate flag flying from her stern.

muskets unleashed a tremendous volley which riddled the Federal boats, killing and wounding many of the Federal sailors, and sending wooden splinters flying in all directions. Smoke, held low by the drizzling rain, drifted quickly away before a brisk southeast wind. The roar of musketry and heavy guns was continuous, obliterating all other sounds and making it impossible to hear shouted commands. The *Kinsman* began firing grape and canister into the Confederate rifle pits, while continuing to engage the *Cotton*. The *Cotton's* navy training was evident, again, as she sent five shots crashing into the *Kinsman*.[16]

Somewhere on shore, in one of the Confederate rifle pits, a soldier touched two wires to the terminals on a galvanic battery, and a tremendous explosion erupted under the *Kinsman's* stern. The Union boat backed away, only slightly damaged by the exploded torpedo, but riddled and listing badly from the plunging shots hurled at her by the *Cotton* and the batteries on shore. The *Calhoun* moved up behind the *Estrella* to take her place.

The *Cotton* continued to hammer away at the *Estrella* and now the *Calhoun*. Fuller had made sure that he had enough powder bags this time. Lieutenant Stevens paced the hurricane deck shouting instructions and encouragement to the sweating army gunners. Roughly one hour had gone by, and while the *Cotton* had been struck numerous times, miraculously, she still had not been severely damaged. Looking below the smoke and fire surrounding the Union vessels, however, Captain Fuller could see what he feared most.

Long lines of blue infantry were spread out on both sides of the bayou and were steadily advancing toward the Confederate rifle pits. Federal artillery began playing on the Confederate positions when suddenly, on the *Calhoun*, Federal Commander Buchanan fell heavily to the deck. He had been killed instantly by a Confederate musket ball that had pierced his head.[17]

As Fuller anxiously watched, blue-clad infantry began to push the ragged Confederates out of their rifle pits. Some of the artillery crews, fearful of loosing their guns, were now working frantically trying to limber up their pieces, while struggling to control their frightened horses. Soon the gray troops on both sides of the Teche began to waiver and break under the constant pressure of twice their numbers.

While the *Cotton's* guns continued to engage the Federal boats, Fuller called down to the engine room to begin backing the boat. The gunboat's paddle wheels had hardly begun to turn, when she was struck by a storm of musket volleys fired at close range. Hand-picked Union sharpshooters, sixty on each side of the bayou, had raced ahead of their comrades and were now opposite the *Cotton* and pouring death and destruction onto her decks. Her gunners dropped and began to crawl away seeking any place of shelter they could find. Some who were painfully wounded, dragged themselves to safety, while others who fell remained where they lay, their lives ebbing away in little rivulets of blood that spread along the deck. Among these still forms, lying quietly on the *Cotton's* hurricane deck, was the lifeless body of the brave navy lieutenant from the *Arkansas*, Henry K. Stevens. Struck by the first volley, Lieutenant Stevens was killed instantly.[18]

With her guns now silent, the sharpshooters doubled their fire and sent volley after volley crashing into the *Cotton's* sides. Shells from the *Estrella* and *Calhoun* continued to smash into her iron casemate sending chunks of wood and iron fragments flying in all directions. With her paddle wheels revolving, the *Cotton* was now beginning to move astern when another volley of musketry rattled against her pilothouse. Federal minie balls punched through the thin wood and smashed into Fuller, tearing and ripping painful wounds in both arms. Cut and bleeding, his arms dangling uselessly at his sides, Fuller gamely used his feet on the wheel to steer the boat and continued backing the *Cotton* up the bayou.[19]

As Fuller tortuously continued to back the *Cotton*, the welcome sound of Confederate field pieces was heard above the roar of the Federal guns. The Union riflemen, who had been delivering their deathly volleys into the *Cotton*, were diving for cover. Confederate shells began to explode among them and screaming loads of canister came ripping through their ranks. The devastating fire was from a six-gun battery commanded by Lieutenant B. F. Winchester. Seeing the blue riflemen assailing the *Cotton*, the young army lieutenant had whipped his teams into a gallop and charged down the bayou road. Quickly turning the guns around and unlimbering, he opened fire. Now, with the Federal sharpshooters hugging the ground in a desperate attempt to escape this murderous fire, Fuller was able to back the *Cotton* out of range and behind the reformed Confederate battle lines.[20]

While the *Cotton's* machinery was undamaged, her hurricane deck was in shambles. Splintered pieces of wood along with jagged iron fragments lay scattered about. Lifeless bodies still lay in their final grotesque positions, while below, the wounded groaned in pain or suffered in silence. Lieutenant E. T. King assumed command and ordered all the dead and wounded, including Captain Fuller, to be removed and carried aboard the steamer *Gossamer*. The steamer was then ordered to get under way and proceed up the Teche to the town of Franklin, where a temporary field hospital had been established.

With the dead and wounded removed, King gamely took the *Cotton* back down the bayou to support the struggling Confederate troops. Again the guns of the battered *Cotton* roared their defiance at the Union gunboats. Suddenly, several concealed batteries of Federal artillery opened fire on her, smashing her already damaged superstructure with their well-aimed shots. More wood and iron began to fly, and her army gunners were forced to scurry for cover. With her side-wheels again turning in reverse, King began backing the *Cotton* up the bayou for the last time.

Arriving at the landing where he had unloaded the wounded, Lieutenant King had the *Cotton* tied to the bank. While her engines and machinery, which had been protected by the makeshift casemate, still worked, the rest of the gunboat was a floating wreck. With the *Cotton* now out of range and Mouton's exhausted troops formed again in their front, the Federals halted. Still unable to pass the obstructions with their gunboats, the Union forces slackened their fire, and soon nightfall put an end to the carnage. Lieutenant Stevens, a corporal, and three privates from the *Cotton's* gun crews were dead, while nine wounded, including Captain Fuller, had been carried aboard the steamer *Gossamer*. Many more of her exhausted crew members sat around the deck nursing minor cuts and bruises.[21]

At 5:00 a.m. the next morning, a large red glow lit up the pre-dawn sky over the Louisiana bayous. The sunken *J. A. Cotton*, her battered hulk stretched across the Teche, lay engulfed in roaring flames. General Mouton, determining that his small force was too weak to stop the Federals, had during the night, ordered the "ironclad" gunboat turned across the bayou, scuttled and burned. When General Weitzel discovered the *Cotton* burning at daylight, he reasoned that his immediate objective had been accomplished, and he began preparations for returning his Federal command to Berwick Bay.[22]

As she had done when her guns roared from her hurricane deck, the now sunken and blackened wreck of the *Cotton* still barred the way to the rich bayou country of western Louisiana.

Ed Fuller eventually recovered from his painful wounds. In April 1863, while still awaiting the arrival of his commission from Richmond, he was in command of the Confederate *Queen of the West* when the Federals advanced up the Atchafalaya River. Hit by a Federal shell, the *Queen* caught fire, and before Fuller, who had been injured again, could make his escape, he was captured. Unable to walk because of his wounds, Fuller was carried aboard the Federal steamer *Maple Leaf*, and transported north to the bleak prison on Johnson's Island. There, far from his beloved Louisiana bayous, Captain Fuller died on July 25, 1863.[23]

Chapter Six

Fast Ships and Dark Nights

No naval activity during the War Between the States has been more glamorized and romanticized than the exploits of the swift, gray-colored steamers and their dashing captains that challenged the Federal blockade off the Confederate coast. Indeed, many of the specially built steamers, with their folding stacks and hinged masts, were extremely fast for their day, and some of their captains fell neatly into the Hollywood image of that gallant and debonair hero of *Gone with the Wind*, Rhett Butler. But the story of blockade running during the war is more than the tale of romantic captains, fast ships, and swooning Southern belles. It is the narrative of ordinary but dedicated officers and men, some civilian, some Confederate navy, and some state navy, who willingly placed their lives in harm's way for their country—and for profit.

It is estimated that just approximately 300 steamers tested the Federal blockade during the war; of these, 136 were captured and 85 were destroyed. The majority of those destroyed was not by enemy action, but from running afoul of the numerous shoals along the ragged Southern coast. These 300 steamers made approximately 1,300 attempts of which over 1,000 were successful. With this volume of activity, civilian captains such as Robert Smith, James Carlin, Louis Coxetter, and the gallant Lockwood brothers, Thomas and Robert, all became well known in the households of the South during the war. Their exploits in such vessels as *Margaret and Jessie, Kate, Colonel Lamb,* and *Cecile* were closely followed via the newspapers of the day. The ships that they piloted were owned and operated by many of the importing and exporting firms that shipped cotton out of the Confederate States and sold it on the European markets. The proceeds from these sales were used to purchase the ships, pay the crew, and acquire the arms and materials that were transported back to the struggling Confederacy. It was risky business; however, statistics show that the average runner needed to be successful on only one or two runs in order to totally repay the owner's investment. All runs successfully made after that were pure profit.[1]

To better control the amount of war material versus civilian goods being transported on the steamers running the blockade, the Confederate government realized the necessity of owning its own line of blockade runners. Many of the sleek, fast steel-hulled ships built in England and in Scotland were purchased directly by the government and operated by the Ordnance Bureau or Treasury Department. These ships, the *Lady Davis,* the *Phantom,* the *Robert E. Lee,* the *Atlanta* and the *Flora,* to name only a few, were captained by regular Confederate naval officers. Again, such officers as John Wilkinson, Mike Usina, Joseph Fry, Richard N. Gayle, J. M. Burroughs, and John Newland Maffitt became well known for their daring and successful exploits.

Another important area of blockade-running operations, but less known than the civilian and Confederate-owned blockade runners, were those vessels owned and operated directly by the states, with North Carolina being the most active. In July of 1862, North Carolina's Adjutant General James G. Martin, "began to shiver with apprehension" with the notion that he would be unable to find enough uniform material to clothe the 67,000 North Carolinians under arms.[2] The people and government of North Carolina were determined that their state's soldiers would not have to depend on the Confederate government for their needs. As a result of this herculean effort, North Carolina was the only state during the war to fully clothe and arm her own troops in the field. But Martin saw that local supplies would soon be exhausted, and so proposed to outgoing Governor Henry T. Clark that the state purchase a steamer to bring in the needed raw materials from England. Clark felt he did not have the authority, but newly elected Zebulon Vance, who took office in September of 1862, was convinced by Martin, and ordered the operation to proceed.

The state issued $1,500,000 in cotton bonds, and Vance dispatched to England, John White and Lieutenant Thomas M. Crossan of the North Carolina navy, with instructions to purchase material, especially shoes and blankets for the North Carolina troops, and a vessel to transport the supplies to the Confederacy. The North Carolina bonds carried by White and Crossan, paid seven percent annually, beginning July 1, 1863. This interest would be collected in Manchester, England. If the bond holder wished to cash in his bonds, they could be redeemed for cotton in North Carolina. To acquire the cotton, a bond holder was required to give a sixty-day notice to the North Carolina commissioners in England, who in turn would arrange for the cotton to be shipped from the interior of the state to the port at Wilmington. A £100 bond was worth approximately twelve bales of cotton, with each bale weighing 400 pounds. The exchange was a better deal than the Confederate cotton bonds.[3]

Vance had chosen his agents well. John White, an established dry goods merchant in North Carolina, took charge of all purchasing and shipping of supplies for the state. Shortly after arriving in England, White entered into a partnership with the prominent London firm of Alexander Collie & Company, which was already well established in the blockade-running business and had dedicated representatives in Wilmington. Collie would continue to broker the North Carolina bonds in England, and purchase and ship military hardware to North Carolina right up to the very end of the war.[4]

Lieutenant Crossan's instructions were to locate and purchase a steamer for the state that would be able to outrun anything that the Federals might have on blockade duty. Thomas M. Crossan was northern born and a former lieutenant in the United States Navy. Prior to the war, he had met and married a North Carolina girl, and upon the secession of that state, he resigned his commission and hurried to Raleigh to offer his services to the Old North State. Appointed a lieutenant in the North Carolina navy, he had been given command of the first armed vessel in the state's fledgling navy, the NCS *Winslow*. The state of North Carolina, as well as most other Southern states, formed their own navy upon their state's secession from the Union. Before the fall of 1861 (records are not clear), the ships and most of the personnel had been transferred to Confederate service.[5]

Crossan's first command, the *Winslow*, was formerly the *J. E. Coffee*, a side-wheel steamer of 207 tons, which had plied the waters between Norfolk, Virginia and the eastern shore of Virginia. She had been purchased by North Carolina and armed with a 32-pounder gun and a six-pounder brass rifle. (Some accounts list the *Winslow* as having had only one gun.) Acting under orders from Governor Clark, Crossan had steamed to Pamlico Sound with the *Winslow*, and had begun preying on Northern shipping outside Ocracoke Inlet, off Cape Hatteras. Beginning in May of 1861, the *Winslow* had intercepted and captured eight enemy merchant ships, one of which, the sailing brig *Hannah Balch*, was in the hands of a Federal prize crew. The *Hannah Balch* had been captured a few days before by the USS *Flag*, as she attempted to run the blockade into Savannah, and now Crossan had the pleasure of escorting her into a Confederate port. It appears, from what few records survived, that Lieutenant Crossan had remained in the North Carolina navy when most of that service's ships and personnel had been transferred to Confederate service.[6]

Now, by the beginning of 1863, Crossan was about to perform his greatest contribution to his adopted state. He found the vessel that, unknown to him at the time, would almost single-handedly supply all North Carolina soldiers with their arms, uniforms, and accouterments. She was the *Load Clyde*, an iron side-wheeler that had been traversing the route between Glasgow and Dublin. The price of the sleek vessel, plus extra fittings and equipment, cost the state of North Carolina $170,972.30, but she would prove to be worth every penny.[7] Newly built by Caird and Company of Glasgow, she was 236 feet long, 26 feet abeam, and drew 10 feet of water when fully loaded to 902 tons. Two oscillating steam cylinders of 63-inch bore and 78-inch stroke turned her giant thirty-foot paddle wheels. With steam pressure in her boilers at twenty pounds per square inch, these powerful engines drove her forward at seventeen knots, and with pressure increased to thirty pounds, she clicked off twenty knots without difficulty, a phenomenal speed for that era. Crossan proudly rechristened her, *Advance*.[8]

Within a month, with Englishman Joannes Wylie signed on as her sailing master, Crossan had the *Advance* plowing her way across the North Atlantic toward the Confederacy. In her cavernous hold were tons of gray cloth for uniforms and cotton cards for the looms of the dedicated women of North Carolina. On June 28, 1863, with the red, white, and blue banner of North Carolina whipping from her mast, she steamed majestically up the Cape Fear River and docked at the quarantine station approximately fifteen miles below the port of Wilmington. Throughout the city, the news was out, "the *Advance* had arrived!"

Lieutenant Crossan telegraphed Raleigh, and Governor Vance was on the next train for Wilmington. The fiery governor was extremely proud of "his" blockade runner, and Purser James Sprunt, NCN, narrated an amusing description of the governor's arrival: ...*the next day, Sunday, (Vance) went down on one of the river steamers with a number of his friends to the ship. ... After spending several hours on board examining the ship and partaking of the hospitalities of its officers, it was determined to take her up to the city without waiting for a permit from the health officers, as it was assumed the governor's presence on board would be justification for the violation of quarantine regulations. Accordingly, steam was raised, and she came up to the city and was made fast to the wharf in front of the custom house.*

All incoming vessels were required to stay at the quarantine station until they were certified free from yellow fever, a process that usually consumed fifteen days. Vance had already obtained a waiver for the vessel, and the officers and crew had been examined and declared free of the dreaded disease. Sprunt continued: *Scarcely had the ship been secured to the wharf when a military gentleman in full uniform* (Lieutenant Colonel Charles E. Thorburn) *made his appearance, and though he was told that the vessel belonged to the state, and that the governor was on board, he seized the occasion to make a display of his authority and to magnify his own importance. With the manner of a Sir Oracle, and in a loud and commanding tone of voice, he peremptorily declared that no one should leave the ship, and ordered her immediate return to (the) quarantine station down the river. Governor Vance happened to be standing near the gangway, heard distinctly the rude speech of the military satrap and noticed his offensive manner; and his crest rose on the instant.*[9]

Zebulon Vance, who had been colonel of the 26th North Carolina regiment prior to his election as governor, had no use for General William Whiting, commander of the Wilmington district, whom he considered a despot and a drunk. But that feeling was trivial compared to the fierce emotions the petty Whiting's underling provoked in the hot-tempered governor standing on "his" blockade runner. Not only was this pompous Thorburn rude and arrogant, he was also a Virginian! *With flashing eyes he turned upon him,* Sprunt recalled, *and in a voice of concentrated passion exclaimed: "Do you dare to say, sir, that the governor of the state shall not leave the deck of his own ship?"*

The North Carolina blockade runner *A. D. Advance* photographed at Nassau, Bahamas in 1863. Note the Confederate first national flag aft, and her feathering port paddle wheel.

A damaged portrait of Governor Zebulon B. Vance of North Carolina taken at the time of his inauguration. Vance was extremely proud of the accomplishments of the *Advance*.

Thorburn shouted back, "I shall let no one off this ship, be he Governor Vance or Governor Jesus Christ!" The lieutenant colonel ordered a detachment of soldiers nearby to shoot anyone who attempted to disembark. Vance had to be restrained. With members of his staff surrounding him, the Governor was "convinced" that he should retire to Crossan's cabin, where the passion of his anger could be allowed to cool. Here was North Carolina's ship crammed to the gunwales with urgently needed supplies for her state's soldiers in the field, and this fool wanted to hold it in quarantine for two weeks with the state's governor pacing the quarterdeck! It was more than Vance could bear. Fortunately, someone had the good sense to send for the proper official.[10]

In the meantime, Sprunt continued, *the Chairman of the Board of Commissioners of Navigation, P. W. Fanning, ...arrived upon the scene and promptly settled the matter by giving his permit for the ship to remain where she was, and the immediate landing of all who desired to do so. The Governor was the first to step upon the gangway, and as he passed down he stopped for a moment, respectfully saluted Mr. Fanning, and in a ringing voice exclaimed: "No man is more prompt to obey the civil authority than myself, but I will not be ridden over by epaulettes or bayonets!" The large crowd which had assembled gave him three cheers as he disappeared from view, and added three more for the gallant ship Advance, from whose masts and yards innumerable flags were flying in the breeze.*[11]

The quiet historic town of Wilmington, North Carolina became the most frequented port for the sleek blockade runners during the war. Situated twenty-eight miles from the mouth of the Cape Fear River, Wilmington, in 1860, was North Carolina's largest city. With a population of just under 10,000, the deep-water port was noted for its beautiful churches and impressive mansions, and even boasted a theater in the town hall operated by the local Thalian Association. But the emergence of Wilmington as the Confederacy's chief blockade-running port brought extensive changes to the quaint old city on the Cape Fear. First Lieutenant John Wilkinson, CSN, recalled those days: *The staid old town of Wilmington was turned "topsy turvy" during the war. Here resorted the speculators from all parts of the South, to attend the weekly auctions of imported cargoes; and the town was infested with rogues and desperadoes, who made a livelihood by robbery and murder. It was unsafe to venture into the suburbs at night, and even in daylight, there were frequent conflicts in the public streets between the crews of the steamers in port and the soldiers stationed in the town, in which knives and pistols would be freely used; and not infrequently a dead body would rise to the surface of the water in one of the docks with marks of violence upon it.*[12]

Early on the evening of July 24, 1863, just twenty-six days after the arrival of the *Advance*, Lieutenant Crossan carefully eased the big steamer down the Cape Fear to New Inlet just opposite Fort Fisher. Her voluminous hold was crammed with bales of valuable North Carolina cotton, and her mostly British crew, along with all her Southern officers, were on deck straining to catch a glimpse of the Union blockaders in the fading light. Crossan, too, studied the dark silhouettes and formulated his plans. Later, after the moon had set, the crew took up their assigned stations, and orders were whispered down to the engine room. Firemen swung shovels of clean-burning anthracite coal into the roaring furnace, and the engineer watched as steam pressure inched toward thirty pounds. At a given signal, with all lights extinguished, save a small hooded light over the compass, the *Advance* bounded forward, and within minutes her sharply pointed bow was parting the dark ocean swells as she raced unnoticed past the Federal ships. The muffled throb of her powerful engines and the splashing of her paddles failed to reveal her presence, and quickly she disappeared into the dark Atlantic—destination, Bermuda.

The *Advance* proved to be one of the most successful blockade runners, and for more than a year her arrivals and departures at Wilmington could be predicted with almost clock-like precision. Most of her inbound trips originated in Bermuda, with only two runs being made from Nassau. Lieutenant Crossan piloted her eighteen times through the ring of enemy vessels surrounding the Confederate coast, and for the most part, every trip was fraught with danger and excitement.

In October of 1863, the Reverend Moses D. Hoge of Richmond, Virginia was returning home to the Confederacy as a passenger on board the *Advance*. The minister had been in Europe and was transporting a large shipment of Bibles, testaments, and tracts back to the Southern states, which were to be distributed to the soldiers. Even though he was returning to his beloved Virginia, the journey was a particularly sad one for him, for while in England, he had been notified of the death of his eldest son. Reverend Hoge kept a journal of his voyage to the Confederacy, and reading it 130 some years later, with a little imagination, one can almost feel the throb of the powerful engines and hear the splash of the paddles:

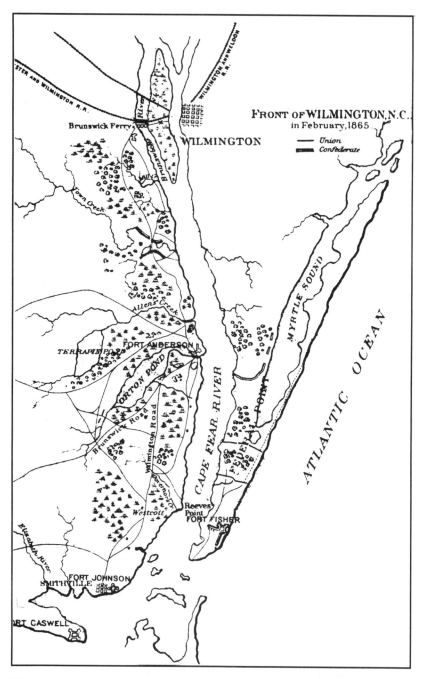

The entrance to the Cape Fear River leading to Wilmington, North Carolina.
Confederate Military History, Vol. 4

Bermuda, Wednesday, October 8, 1863. — At 12 o'clock I went on board the Advance. My fellow passengers are Rev. Mr. Terry, Mrs. Pender, Messrs. Burrton, Walker and Regnault. Got off at 10 o'clock; beautiful view of Bermuda as we rapidly sped along. The Advance is a fine vessel. Hoge listed the ship's officers: Lieutenant Crossan, captain; Joannes Wylie, sailing master (Hoge referred to Wylie as the "English captain"); Doctor Swan, surgeon; Mr. Flanner, purser; Mr. Smith, signal officer; James F. Taylor, petty officer; and James MaGlenn, chief engineer. Hoge's journal continues: *...We have taken no state rooms on the Advance, although there are a great number of unoccupied ones, but our little company of passengers all stay in the saloon at night. The fare is rather rough, but that is nothing when we have a good ship homeward bound.*[13]

The first day out of Bermuda, problems arose: *We have been in much trouble on the ship today. The coal, which was thought to be very good (Welsh coal, Cardiff) is found to be of very bad quality. This morning we could not get up steam as usual. The serious question is discussed whether we had better return to Bermuda. After running fourteen knots we dropped down to five. It is thought useless to go on toward the blockaders to ensure a capture. We put the vessel about and sailed a while due east, but after a little while the draft increased and the paddles made their former revolutions of from twenty to twenty-three per minute.*

The difficulty was (that) there was a mixture of something like kelp and sand, which melted on the bars of the grates and choked the draft, making a deposit they called slag. It was terribly hard on the fireman to keep them clear.

October 9, 1863. —I am now on board the Advance, about 100 miles from the North Carolina coast. It is 4 o'clock, p.m., and I am sitting on the bottom step of the paddle box, from which I can look down directly into the water and see how beautifully it divides before the bow of the steamer, darting through at a noble speed. This is one of the most pleasant days as to temperature I ever felt, clear, coolish, without being cool and something life-giving in the air.[14]

It took approximately three days to steam the 674 miles from St. George's to Wilmington. As more warships were added to the Federal blockading fleet, additional vessels were made available for far-reaching patrols along the route between Bermuda and Wilmington. A steamer headed for the Confederacy, therefore, was never really safe nor out of danger, for at any moment a fast, black-hulled enemy warship could appear on the distant horizon. As the rakish *Advance* sped on, Reverend Hoge pondered the dangers and the chances that they must take:

It is a day for thought, a time for review and anticipation. Tonight we will know our fate, whether it is to be the bottom of the sea, a northern prison, or Richmond. I am not apprehensive, but I know the risks. We have heard nothing from Wilmington. No steamers came out while we were in Bermuda, though several were expected. We may be running into a trap — as we know not what progress the Federals may have made in the way of excluding blockade-runners. We may be damaged by the fire of the fleet, even if we succeed in running the gauntlet and although I do not repent coming, and notwithstanding the uncertainty, I have no desire to turn back, yet I know we may be disappointed just on the happy eve of getting home and indeed may never reach it at all. I have spent much time this morning in prayer, in solemn consecration of myself to God, and in supplication for a spirit of submission to His will. I try to commit myself and my dear family and church to His holy keeping.

They were drawing closer now. The constant beat of the engines, the gentile hissing of steam, the monotonous splashing of the paddles, all were constant reminders that they were approaching the area of maximum danger.

We have been mustered on deck and had our places in the boats assigned to us, in case we have to abandon the steamer tonight. I go with Captain Crossan and Mrs. Pender, and the rest of our boat's crew are firemen and sailors. Terry, Burton, Walker and Regnault go in the other lifeboats, the rest of the crew in the two aft boats. This looks like business. It is the purpose to destroy the Advance and take to the boats if we are intercepted. I should dread capture on my dear wife's account. It would almost break her heart, after our long separation and the sorrow she has borne.[15]

It was rare that a blockade runner would attempt to run through the entire Federal fleet in broad daylight, but as Lieutenant Crossan was about to demonstrate,—sometimes there was little choice. The weather had evidently deteriorated and with no horizon and heavy clouds hiding the sun, it was impossible to accurately plot the speeding steamer's position. Although both Crossan and Wylie attempted to take observations before darkness set in, the thick overcast and poor visibility prevented them from establishing the *Advance's* location. Unknown to them, the powerful current of the Gulf Stream had swept them far to the north.

About 9 o'clock at night we saw a light and the dim outline of land. At first it was thought to be the signal light near fort Fisher, and Mr. Smith wanted to make signals, but after long inspection, discovered that it was a lighthouse. We then changed our course southward and ran along the shore, all night in doubt as to where we were. Captain Crossan once thought we might be south of the entrance to Wilmington and running toward Charleston. This shows how completely at sea we were! When it grew light enough to see the coast more plainly, our officers recognized certain localities on Masonboro Sound, the salt works etc., and we ascertained we had just made the land north of Cape Lookout, 80 miles from the point we expected to strike.

With Masonboro Sound being only twenty-five miles north of New Inlet, which was the entrance to the Cape Fear River, and with daylight breaking, Crossan now had a desperate decision to make. They could either turn around and race for the open sea, with considerable likelihood that they would be spotted by the ring of warships surrounding

Wilmington, or they could continue to hug the coast and trust to the superior speed of the *Advance* to carry them close enough to be protected by the guns of Fort Fisher before being cut off by a Federal warship. Crossan called a hurried conference of his officers, including the pilot Kit Moss, to determine what was to be done. Assured by Engineer MaGlenn that the engines were running perfectly and producing full power, he chose to forge ahead to make a run for the bar at New Inlet. If ever there was a time that the *Advance* needed to make twenty knots, it was now.

Reverend Hoge was astounded that they continued to race ahead: *Captain Crossan prepared to run up near enough to see which blockaders were within view and I supposed he would then stand out to sea and lie off until night and then run in at his leisure, but to my astonishment, although it was about 8 o'clock in the morning, the sun shining brilliantly and the sea level as a floor and three blockaders guarding the entrance, he steamed straight on toward Fort Fisher. The blockaders seemed confused for a few moments by the audacity of the movement, but presently they came about and all three struck for the shore, intending to cut us off. They came on very speedily, but finding that we were running so swiftly they opened upon us with shrapnel, shell and solid shot.*[16]

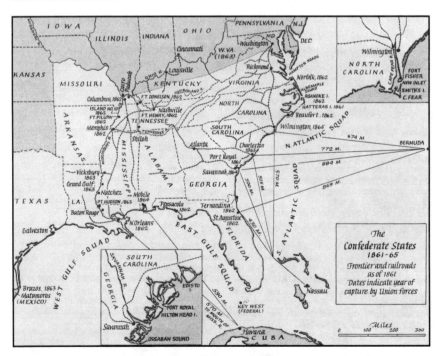

Map showing the distances from the Bahamas, Bermuda, and Havana, Cuba, to various Confederate ports.

It was a scene of intense excitement. We could see people on the shore, watching the result. ...the shells were ploughing up the water and tearing up the sand on the shore, bursting over and around us, and yet not one struck us. It was almost a miracle. Two or three of their shells struck the sand just at the edge of the water and directly opposite to us and the wonder was how the balls could get there without passing through us. Captain Crossan certainly made a hazardous experiment. Had the mist near the coast not veiled us somewhat from the view of the enemy as we approached, and had he seen us in time to make chase ten minutes sooner, he would have headed us off and driven us ashore, or had one of his shots penetrated our boilers, we would have been blown to fragments. Had we been compelled to take to our boats, we would have still been in great danger, for we would have been under fire perhaps an hour, when the smooth sea made it as easy to fire accurately from the deck as (though) from the walls of a fort.

As it was, by the favor of a good Providence, we escaped unharmed and very soon ran by Fort Fisher, when the guns of that fort opened on the block-aders and a pretty little fight took place between them, the vessels quickly withdrawing, however, one of them having been struck. As we passed the fort our crew cheered heartily, (and) we ran up our Confederate flag.[17]

During the winter of 1863–1864, the *Advance* continued her regular runs to and from Bermuda. Enemy warships were not the only hazard that Crossan and his vessel had to face, for the gray Atlantic can be a stormy place during the winter months. Chief Engineer MaGlenn recalled one of these stormy passages:

On one occasion there were four steamers leaving St. George's, Bermuda, including the Advance, for Wilmington. But two of these arrived in Wilmington. One put back to Bermuda badly disabled; the other was lost in the gale. On this occasion I was limited to twelve revolutions per minute for thirty-six hours, or during the severest of the gale, which was just enough for the ship to mind the helm, being head to the gale all this time and water increasing in the hold to such an extent that it got within six inches of the grate-bars. In fact, I thought our time had come, and I informed Captain Crossan how matters were in the engine and fire room, and that "we could not hold out this way much longer." I suggested to him the importance of turning the ship around and running before the wind, to enable me to get the water out by working the engines faster. He remonstrated by saying that "to attempt such a thing in a night like this would be certain destruction to the ship and all on board, but do the best you can until morning and when the worst comes, I may attempt it in daylight, but I feel confident we will have a change for the better by morning. The barometer has commenced to rise and is going up rapidly. It is the first time it has made a movement in that direction for two days."

Strange to say, by 8 o'clock the next morning, it was perfectly calm, but a tremendous sea was rolling, which knocked us about considerably. This was

Lieutenant Thomas M. Crossan, NCN (left), captain of the steamer *Advance*, and his able assistant, Chief Engineer James MaGlenn, NCN.

North Carolina Regiments, 1861–1865

the heaviest gale we had ever experienced. On arrival in Wilmington, we made some improvements in bilge and other pumps, which was actually necessary to make her seaworthy in anything like heavy weather.[18]

By the summer of 1864, the *Advance* was badly in need of repairs. She had been constantly on the move since June of the previous year, and it was absolutely necessary that her engines and machinery undergo a complete overhaul. During May and June, she was in Liverpool, England where these repairs were finally accomplished. By July 29, however, she was plowing her way back to Wilmington with another load of vital supplies for North Carolina's troops. By this time the *Advance* had been joined by three other steamers in which North Carolina and Alexander Collie & Company were joint owners. They were the *Don*, which made ten successful runs through the blockade; the *Hansa*, which ran the gauntlet twenty times; and the *Annie*, which made thirteen successful trips. In spite of their accomplishments, all of North Carolina's steamers, including the *Advance*, were ultimately captured in 1864.[19]

Late in the day on September 9, 1864, Crossan steamed slowly down the Cape Fear and anchored just inside New Inlet for the last time. The *Advance's* hold was packed with North Carolina cotton bales, with additional bales lashed to the deck fore and aft. Clearly visible through the inlet were at least twenty-five to thirty Federal blockaders. Many years after the war, Engineer MaGlenn wrote sadly of this last voyage: *Although the night was not altogether favorable, we started as soon as the tide would permit. Of course smoke, sparks and flames from the stack had to be kept down. This was very difficult to do, as our last shovelful of good coal was used shortly after crossing the bar and in plain sight of some of the fleet. Those that could see us would throw rockets, indicating the direction we were going. Then the dodging on our part (began), and the frequent change of the ship's course to keep from running into them. The excitement at this time was very great. Yet all was as quiet as the grave on board and every man was at his post and doing his duty faithfully. The rocket firing and shooting were very heavy, and nothing but good management on the part of our officers could have pulled us safely through the fleet that night.*[20]

By daybreak, the *Advance* was clear of the inner ring of blockaders, but telltale plumes of black smoke were pouring from her twin stacks. Vance would bitterly claim that the capture of the *Advance* was caused by the confiscation of all the anthracite coal at Wilmington by Secretary Mallory for use in two Confederate commerce raiders. Mallory, however, vehemently denied that the Confederate navy had "stolen" the *Advance's* coal. Surviving records show that the navy did seize coal at Wilmington for their ships; however, it was two weeks <u>after</u> the capture of the *Advance*. It is still unclear why the *Advance* was burning inferior coal that morning, but the result was lower speed, and two distinctive smoke plumes that could be seen for miles.[21]

At sunrise there was nothing in sight, MaGlenn continued, yet our black smoke was giving us away. Some of the fleet were following it and about 8 o'clock a vessel was discovered chasing us and appeared to be gaining (USS Santiago de Cuba). Everything possible was done to increase the speed of the Advance, but the steaming qualities of the coal were against us. ...We were in hopes we could evade the pursuing steamer in the darkness of the night, but in our present condition, she was too fast for us and was able to throw some shot over us some time before sundown, which caused us to stop the ship and surrender.[22]

The captured *Advance* was taken north, her cargo of cotton auctioned off, and the vessel transferred to the United States Navy. She was renamed the USS *Frolic*, armed with a few guns, and ironically, participated in the final great bombardment of Fort Fisher by the Federal fleet in January of 1865. She remained in Federal service until October 1, 1877, at which time she was sold to private interests.[23]

It is unfortunate that there are no surviving documented statistics to illustrate the success of North Carolina's blockade-running program. That it was a success, however, cannot be questioned. Vance spoke often of the program in speeches after the war, and he always remained especially proud of the accomplishments of the *Advance*. The figures he quoted were mostly estimates, but even with a reasonable margin for error, they are still very impressive. In an address before the Maryland Line, delivered in Baltimore on February 23, 1885, he recalled:

By the general industry and thrift of our people and by the use of a number of blockade-running steamers, carrying out cotton and bringing in supplies from

Europe, I had collected and distributed from time to time, as near as can be gathered from the records of the Quartermaster's Department, the following stores: *Large quantities of machinery supplies; 60,000 pairs of hand cards; 10,000 grain scythes; 200 barrels of blue stone for wheat growers; leather and shoes to 250,000 pairs; 50,000 blankets; gray wool cloth for at least 250,000 suits of uniforms; 12,000 overcoats ready-made; 2,000 best Enfield rifles, with 100 rounds of fixed ammunition; 100,000 pounds of bacon; 500 sacks of coffee for hospital use; $50,000 worth of medicines at gold prices, large quantities of lubrication oils, besides minor supplies of various kinds for the charitable institutions of the state. Not only was the supply of shoes, blankets and clothing more than sufficient for the supply of North Carolina troops, but large quantities were turned over to the Confederate government for the troops of other states.*[24]

The speedy *Advance* and her brave commander, Lieutenant Thomas M. Crossan, played a significant role in this success story, and they were sorely missed after their capture. No better epitaph for the *Advance* and her gallant captain could be written than that by General D. H. Hill in his two-volume work, *Bethel to Sharpsburg,* when he related that it was tragic that the *Advance*, which "had contributed so much to the welfare of the war-harassed state and was regarded in an affectionate personal way by a half-million people, was compelled to strike her colors." In reporting her loss to the North Carolina legislature, Governor Vance wrote that she was the "pride of the state and the benefactor of our soldiers and people."[25]

A wash drawing of the *Advance* under a full head of steam. This accurate illustration was sketched by R. G. Skerrett in 1899.

Chapter Seven

The *Georgia* Is Loose

For a few brief days in the early summer of 1863, five Confederate warships prowled the lonely expanse of gray Atlantic waters. From the dark coast of Brazil to the night shores of New England, the distant glow of their blazing handiwork spread fear and panic among the sea-going commerce of the United States. Prompted by the ravings of such Northern statesmen as Navy Secretary Gideon Welles, Secretary of State Henry Seward, and others in the Lincoln government, the Northern press called them "pirates." But according to international law, "pirates" they were not. They were simply courageous and dedicated Southern officers and their crews, making legitimate war on the maritime commerce of a cruel and invading foe.

The most famous and successful of these five Confederate commerce raiders was the CSS *Alabama* under the command of the renowned Captain Raphael Semmes. The *Alabama* had recently departed Bahia, Brazil, and was now in the south Atlantic almost opposite Rio de Janeiro. Not too far away over the horizon was the second Confederate cruiser, the recently commissioned CSS *Tuscaloosa*, under the command of Lieutenant John Low. A sailing brig, she only recently had been a captive prize of the *Alabama*, but now armed with two brass 12-pounders, she, too, was searching the vast Atlantic for enemy sails.

Hundreds of miles to the north, in the mid-Atlantic east of the upper coast of South America, the third Confederate warship, the CSS

Florida, under Commander John Newland Maffitt, was filling the balmy June nights with the orange-red glow of her blazing victims. As was the *Alabama,* she was the product of that redoubtable Confederate naval agent in England, James D. Bulloch. Analogous to Semmes of the *Alabama,* Maffitt had also commissioned a captured vessel as a Confederate cruiser. Lieutenant Charles W. Read had destroyed that vessel and commissioned another, and now had the Stars and Bars flying from the fourth commerce raider on the high seas, the sailing brig CSS *Tacony.* During this period in June, the citizens of Massachusetts could stand on the beach at night and count the number of Northern ships destroyed by the glow of their burning hulls.

The fifth Confederate warship scouring the horizons for Northern vessels in June, was near the island of Trinidad off the coast of Venezuela. With few surviving records to tell her story, the exploits of the CSS *Georgia* are little known today. She was under the captaincy of Commander William L. Maury, and as her sister cruisers *Alabama* and *Florida,* had been spirited out of England, disguised as a British merchant ship. But unlike her sisters, she was not the product of Bulloch's clandestine efforts, but of the illustrious and diplomatic "Pathfinder of the Seas," Commander Matthew Fontaine Maury.

Maury had gained world-wide acclaim prior to the war for his scientific accomplishments concerning the winds and currents of the oceans around the globe. Little has been written, however, concerning Maury's mission to England on behalf of the Confederate navy. Some of this can be attributed to a Confederate government that generally looked upon Maury as an eccentric and a trouble maker. Much can also be attributed to the man himself, who did have a thorny personality, and even in the old navy, held unpopular views and seemed to disagree with everyone. None of this should detract, however, from his very real accomplishments on behalf of the Confederacy.[1]

Commander William L. Maury. A native of Virginia, he served as captain of the CSS *Georgia.* Commander Maury was a distant cousin to Matthew Fontaine Maury who arranged for the purchase of the *Georgia* in England.

Born near Fredericksburg, Virginia in 1806, Maury spent his child-hood in Tennessee before being appointed a midshipman in the U.S. Navy at the age of nineteen. With little formal education, he was, nev-ertheless, intrigued by the effects of winds and currents during a cruise aboard the USS *Vincennes*, when he began devoting all his energies to the study of navigation. Restricted to shore duty because of a crippling stagecoach accident, Maury was appointed superintendent of the navy's Depot of Charts and Instruments, in July of 1842. Two years later he also assumed the superintendency of the new Naval Observa-tory in Washington, D.C. The inquisitive Maury began searching through the musty files of his agencies, reading everything he could find pertaining to old naval voyages, some of which dated back to the eighteenth century. His fertile mind concluded that there were sea-sonal patterns to the winds and currents of the principal oceans of the world, and that they could be predicted with almost certain accuracy. By knowing the patterns, navigators of vessels could take advantage of favorable winds and currents, and avoid areas particularly suscep-tible to storms during dangerous seasons of the year.[2]

In 1847, Maury published his *Wind and Current Chart of the North Atlantic*, and the following year, *Explanations and Sailing Directions to Accompany the Wind and Sailing Charts*. By the middle of the nineteenth century, no ocean-going vessel dared to leave port without Maury's references on board.

While Maury found great acceptance of his theories and much praise from the naval circles of Europe, where he formed the International Maritime Meteorological Conference in Brussels, he experienced only jealousy from his contemporaries at home. Many naval officers looked upon him as an inept, self-proclaimed scientist and considered him un-fit for the title because of his lack of a formal education. The proud com-mander never forgot or forgave those who slighted him, and was ex-tremely vocal in his pronouncements of bitterness. This antagonism to-ward such individuals as Jefferson Davis, Judah P. Benjamin, and Stephen R. Mallory, who one day would become his superiors in the Confederate government, would dog Maury for the rest of his life.[3]

Upon the secession of Tennessee from the Union, Maury resigned his commission in the United States Navy and offered his services to the new Confederate States. Appointed a commander in the Confeder-ate navy, he labored for fourteen months attempting to build wooden gunboats on the James River below Richmond, while at the same time, working diligently to develop and perfect the electric torpedo.

Maury had been experimenting with containers filled with gunpow-der which were designed to float beneath the surface of the water, and could be detonated by closing an electrical circuit connected to a bulky

Wollaston battery. His experiments were ridiculed by Mallory and many others in the government, who also felt that exploding a torpedo or mine under an unsuspecting enemy was an act of barbarism. Maury fought back with his usual prickly comments, accusing the naval secretary of mismanagement and complaining about the lack of funding for his torpedoes. On October 12, 1862, an embittered Maury, his 13-year-old son, and Midshipman James Morris Morgan, who was acting as the commander's aide, sailed from Charleston aboard the blockade runner *Herald* bound for Bermuda.[4] From St. George's he would proceed via Halifax to Liverpool, England. In Maury's pocket were written orders from the Navy Department assigning him to Europe on "secret service" to develop and perfect his torpedoes and to purchase and put to sea, a vessel to cruise against the commerce of the United States. Whether for political reasons or just to be rid of him, Mallory could not have chosen a more distinguished and respected representative to the naval and financial circles of England than Commander Maury.[5]

Arriving in Liverpool on November 23, Maury went directly to the offices of Fraser, Trenholm and Company to arrange financing for his mission. While there, he met Bulloch for the first time, and doubtless, outlined for the Confederate naval agent, his instructions from Mallory. Assured by Trenholm of financial backing for his experiments, Maury and his son rented an inexpensive third-floor flat in London. Almost immediately he was besieged by many admirers from his Brussels' days including scientists, naval officers and friends, one of whom was Captain Marin H. Jansen of the Royal Netherlands Navy. Jansen, who had maintained a warm correspondence with Maury since their first meeting in 1853, happened to be in London on business, when he learned that Maury, too, was there. Wasting little time, he rushed to see his old friend and offered to use his influence to help Maury in any way possible.[6]

The British government had neutrality laws which prohibited the direct sale of warships to a belligerent, and various legal maneuvers had to be devised by Confederate agents to circumvent this. Prompted by a letter received from Mallory pertaining to the acquisition of vessels in England that could be armed and sent to raid Union commerce, Maury wrote to his friend Jansen in December of 1862:

Let me be frank and friendly and to the point, with the condition if you don't like this proposition, that you will commit this to the flames and oblivion.

You are visiting for your own information the building yards.... Will you not visit all of them? And in your mind note every vessel that they have in progress — from the frames to completion, her size and draft and fitness for armaments. She should be not over 15 ft. draft, good under canvas, fast under steam, with the ability to keep the sea for a year using steam only when necessary....

Also note any gunboats or ironclads that you may come across. In short make a note of all that comes under your observation upon a subject which you know is a hobby with me. As soon as you find one which you think would interest me particularly and fulfill certain conditions, please drop me a line.[7]

While Maury continued his research into the development of the electric torpedo and lobbied the British government for intervention, Jansen discreetly scanned the many shipyards in England and Scotland looking for suitable ships on Maury's behalf. In January of 1863, Maury received a letter from his friend detailing several potential vessels which, in Jansen's judgment, could easily be converted into commerce raiders. All that was needed in order to proceed were the necessary funds and authorization from Secretary Mallory. Both arrived in early February 1863, at the commander's London residence in the dispatch case of Maury's cousin, First Lieutenant William L. Maury.[8]

Now that he had the necessary funds, Maury was excited at the prospect of getting a cruiser to sea. *Lewis Maury brought me $1,500,000 cotton certificates,* Maury wrote to his friend R. D. Minor. *He arrived about 1st February. This was the first ... pounds I could lay hands on since leaving Richmond. These certificates require the signature of Mr. Mason.* James Mason, Confederate agent to Great Britain, was reluctant to sign the certificates, lest it have a negative impact on the $15,000,000 Erlanger loan being negotiated by agent John Slidell in Paris. Maury emphasized the need for haste, and *after awhile he* (Mason) *agreed to sign them on condition I would not put them on the market for 60 days....So I took them and raised money on them for 60 days by depositing them in a bank for 60 days as collateral and in six weeks had a fine cruiser out to sea under Lewis Maury.* Compared to the trials and tribulations that Bulloch went through to launch the *Florida* and *Alabama*, Maury's accomplishment seemed extremely simple.[9]

One of the ships which seemed to satisfy Maury's requirements had been spotted by his good friend and was nearing completion in the shipyard of Denny Brothers at Dumbarton, Scotland. She had the dockyard name of *Japan* and was intended to be a "fast merchant steamer." Jansen appreciated her possibilities as a warship, but failed to take into account her limited coal capacity and the fact that her sails were intended as auxiliary sails only. This would mean that if launched as a Confederate warship, she would not be able to cruise the oceans under sail alone, and would spend most of her time looking for a port in which she could replenish her coal supply. Nevertheless, Maury felt she had possibilities, and through another cousin, Thomas Bold of Liverpool, purchased the nearly completed *Japan*.

The *Japan*, soon to become the CSS *Georgia*, was an iron-hulled steamer of approximately 600 tons. She was 212 feet long, and 27 feet abeam. Her engines of 200 horsepower drove a single screw, but unlike the *Alabama* and *Florida*, she had no lifting device to raise it when under sail. Mechanical problems plagued Maury's cruiser, particularly her engines and the gears to her propeller shaft. In addition, reports would later indicate that her best speed was only about nine knots. Maury never went near the shipyard where the *Japan* was being constructed, leaving all the details to Jansen. By the end of March, Jansen had the steamer ready to sail, and to the Dutch captain Maury wrote: *A thousand thanks to my good friend for going ahead with such vision. I am charmed with the prospects of your being ready so early. I shall give the passengers notice.*[10]

The "passengers" were the officers selected by Bulloch who would serve under Commander William L. Maury (Maury had been promoted on February 17) on board the soon to be CSS *Georgia* (see Appendix D). Lieutenant Maury was from Virginia, and upon the secession of his home state, had resigned from the United States Navy on April 20, 1861. Accepting an appointment as a commander in the Virginia navy, he later was commissioned a First Lieutenant in the Confederate navy on June 10, 1861. During the remainder of 1861 and for most of 1862, he commanded a naval battery at Sewell's Point, Virginia, and assisted in the placement of torpedoes and electric mines in the James River for the defense of Richmond. Additional assignments included service at the Charlotte Naval Station, and at Charleston from which he sailed for England carrying orders and funds for his cousin Matthew Maury. First Lieutenant Robert T. Chapman from Alabama was executive officer, and First Lieutenant William E. Evans from South Carolina was the *Georgia's* next ranking officer.[11]

Because the *Japan* could not be armed in English waters without violating British neutrality, Commander Maury purchased heavy naval guns, small arms, munitions, and supplies in London, and chartered the small tug *Alar*, with instructions to her captain to rendezvous with the *Japan* at the tiny French Isle d'Ouessant off the coast of Brittany. The *Alar* was a small vessel regularly engaged in ferrying passengers between New Haven in England to the channel islands off the coast of France; therefore, her departure would not arouse any undue suspicions. On Saturday, April 4, about twenty men, carrying their supplies and baggage, arrived at the dock where the *Alar* was loading. The British collector of customs noted that they seemed to be supervised by "a man, rather lame, . . ." It is likely that it was Matthew Maury, and if so, it was the only time that he went near any operation that could connect him with his cruiser.[12]

Lewis Maury and his officers sailed on board the *Alar* as "passengers," along with the complement of British sailors who had been recruited for a "trading voyage." Meanwhile, on April 1, 1863, the *Japan* had steamed out of Scotland's Clyde River, having been inspected, cleared, and approved as an ordinary merchant vessel, and her course was set for the south channel rendezvous. With surprising ease, Maury had spirited a new steamer out of England, and had done so in a surprisingly short period of time.[13]

When the *Japan* and the *Alar* arrived off the Ushant Light on the Isle d'Ouessant, the two ships moved to a protective cove, and the transfer of guns, arms, and equipment began. Accounts vary as to the exact armament carried by the *Georgia*. The first reference is by the U.S. consul in Glasgow who reported that: "Her battery consisted of two 100-pounders, two 24-pounders, and one 32-pounder, all Whitworth guns." Scharf, in his *History of the Confederate States Navy*, repeats this description, and even the naval *Official Records* list the *Georgia's* armaments as such. It seems likely, however, that the reference to "100-pounders" is either a mistake or a misprint. Midshipman Morgan, who served throughout the cruise, was the only member of the *Georgia's* crew to leave a written record of his experiences. Time and again in his *Recollections of a Rebel Reefer*, printed in 1917, he refers to the *Georgia's* battery as two small 10-pounder Whitworth guns ("pop-guns" he called them), which were mounted on the quarterdeck, two 24-pounders mounted on the forecastle, and a 32-pounder Blakely rifle mounted in pivot forward of the main mast. (This is the same type of pivot rifle carried by the CSS *Alabama*.) Although written many years after the war, it still seems reasonable to assume that Morgan's description is the more accurate.[14]

With the men working feverishly, the two small 10-pounders and the two 24-pounders were successfully swung aboard. But even in the cove, the rough seas prevented the transfer of the heavy Blakely. Commander Maury ordered the two ships to a sheltered location along the French mainland near Brest, and finally the large pivot rifle was hauled on board. By the end of the fifth day, everything had been transferred, and Maury steamed the *Japan* to just outside the French three-mile limit. Here, on the evening of April 9, 1863, the Stars and Bars were slowly hoisted to the peak, and Commander Maury read his orders from the Navy Department. With this concluded, the *Japan* was formally commissioned as the CSS *Georgia*.

Maury now faced the sailors who had sailed from England on the *Alar* and requested all those willing to sign the Articles of Enlistment in the Confederate navy for three years or the war, to step forward. One man only, of the sixty odd sailors, shuffled to the front, and announced that he was a spokesman for the rest. The men, he reported, were demanding higher wages because of the added risks involved and would not enlist unless their demands were met. Maury explained that a Confederate sailor's wages were fixed by law, and that he had no authority to increase them, whereupon every man scrambled over the side and boarded the *Alar*. Fortunately, nine sailors who had come out on the *Japan* volunteered to ship on the cruiser, and they were quickly accepted. Although shorthanded, Maury ordered the warship's course set to the southeast, and with her fires extinguished to conserve coal, the *Georgia* sailed quietly out into the black Atlantic. Matthew Fontaine Maury's persistence, hard work, and connections with influential friends had paid off, and now the *Georgia* was loose.[15]

Midshipman Morgan described the *Georgia* as she struck out across the dark and lonely Atlantic: *It was the 9th of April, 1863, when this little friendless ship of only about five hundred and fifty tons started on her long and hazardous cruise. She was as absolutely unfitted for the work as any vessel could conceivably be: she lay very low in the water and was very long for her beam; her engines were gear engines, that is a large wheel fitted with lignumvitæ cogs turned the iron cogs on the shaft, and frequently the wooden cogs would break. When they did, it was worse than if a shrapnel shell had burst in the engine room, as they flew in every direction, endangering the lives of everyone within reach. Her sail power was insufficient, and owing to her length, it was impossible to put her about under canvas. She was slow under either sail or steam, or both together.*

Commander Matthew Fontaine Maury, famous "Pathfinder of the Seas." Through his many friends and contacts, Maury was able to successfully purchase the *Georgia* and have her spirited out of England.

The next day found the new Confederate cruiser sailing leisurely on a heading of south-by-west. Much work still remained to be done on board, for the transfer of the stores from the *Alar* was accomplished rather hurriedly because of the proximity of the French coast. (In fact, a French frigate had been dispatched to investigate the supposed violation of French neutrality, but when she arrived, the *Georgia* was gone.) Various boxes and containers were strewn about the deck, and even the guns still lay in their wooden crates. Before the *Georgia* could hope to fulfill her role as a Confederate cruiser, these guns had to be mounted.

The morning of the 10th of April dawned fair, with light breezes and a comparatively smooth sea, Morgan wrote, *and the officers and men set to work fastening to the deck iron traverses for our pivot gun. Then came a most difficult job, shorthanded as we were, that of mounting the guns on their carriages; and to add to our troubles the sea commenced to rise. With all the most intricate and ingenious tackles our seaman-like first lieutenant* (Robert T. Chapman) *could devise, it was an awful strain upon us, as the heavy gun swung back and forth with the roll of the ship. However, by almost superhuman exertions we succeeded in getting the guns into their places on the carriages; then we felt very man-of-warish indeed.*[17]

For the next three weeks, the *Georgia*, her auxiliary sails proving woefully insufficient, plodded along on a southwesterly course. By April 20, eleven days after her departure from Isle d'Ouessant, she was only 1,350 miles from her starting point which meant that under sail, she was averaging about four knots. On the evening of April 20, a disappointed Maury ordered Engineer Pearson to light the fires and raise steam. Later that night, the power of the throbbing propeller was added to the meager sails. The next day, Maury exercised the crew at the guns, firing several blank cartridges and one live round from each cannon. The results of this exercise, no doubt, impressed upon Commander Maury the absolute necessity for more gunnery practice for his merchant sailors.[18]

On April 25, several ships were sighted and stopped, however, all proved to be neutral. At around 4:15 p.m., the cry "Sail ho!" resounded from the masthead, and soon a large full-rigged ship with long tapering spars, a sure sign of an American, could be seen from the main deck. The distant merchant vessel unfurled all her remaining sails in an attempt to escape, but with the cruiser's engines pounding away, the *Georgia* slowly began to gain on her. The British colors were flying from the *Georgia's* mast, but shortly after 5:00 p.m., they were hauled down, and the red and white Confederate ensign was run up the halyards. Soon a shot from the Blakely went bounding over the water just in front of the quarry, and immediately she hauled into the wind and began furling her sails, while the United States flag was run up to her peak. Maury ordered a boat lowered, and Lieutenant Evans, Midshipman Morgan, and a prize crew rowed over to what proved to be the *Dictator* of New York. She was laden with four thousand tons of American coal and was out of Liverpool bound for Hong Kong. Because the *Dictator* contained a large supply of provisions which were needed on board the *Georgia*, Maury ordered that the captured ship's officers and crew, a total of 31 men, be brought on board the Confederate cruiser, and for Evans and his prize crew to lay off the *Georgia* until morning. The *Dictator's* sailors were brought aboard the *Georgia* one at a time, clasped in double irons and hustled below. Maury did not want the Northern sailors to discover the fact that they outnumbered his entire crew.[19]

The CSS *Georgia*. Under steam alone, her top speed was only nine knots. Broken wooden cogs in her gearing created a hazard in her engine room and resulted in numerous breakdowns.

The next morning, strenuous attempts were made to transfer coal and some provisions from the prize, but a rising sea soon made it impossible. With great reluctance, Maury ordered the torch applied, and with her good English coal fueling the flames, the *Dictator* quickly became a raging inferno. While the Northern vessel burned, the ever-exciting cry of "Sail ho!" was shouted from the masthead, and the *Georgia* quickly gave chase, only to find that the sighting proved to be an English bark.

The *Georgia* continued on her southwesterly course sighting an occasional sail, all of which proved to be neutral. On April 28, Maury made an embarrassing discovery. Morgan wrote that they ...*chased a paddle-wheeled bark-rigged steamer; it seemed rather strange that we should overtake her so rapidly, but when we got near to her we discovered that her engines were disconnected and that her paddles were being turned by her momentum through the water. We had the British flag proudly flying at our peak, and suddenly we made another discovery; she was a man-of-war! Suddenly, she broke out her ensign and there we saw the British Union Jack! The way that British flag came down from our peak and was replaced by the Confederate flag looked like legerdemain. The Englishman then dipped his colors to us—a courtesy that we very much appreciated and which we returned with great satisfaction, as it was the first salute of any kind we had received.*[20]

On April 29, the cruiser passed between the islands of San Antonio and St. Vincent, which is part of the Cape Verdes group that is approximately 500 miles off the western coast of the continent of Africa. Maury intended on entering the little harbor of one of the islands to replenish his supplies and was rapidly approaching the entrance, born along by the wind whistling between the two islands which was now blowing at almost gale force. *We shot by a promontory,* Morgan recorded, *and there before our eyes we saw the town and harbor of Porto Grande, and there also we saw lying peacefully at her anchor a sloop-of-war, with the Stars and Stripes fluttering from her peak! Instantly everybody on our ship was in a state of excitement and commotion. The officer of the deck gave the order "Hard-a-port!" quickly followed in rapid succession through his speaking-trumpet by "Main clew garnets and buntlines!"—"Haul taut!"—"Up courses!"—"T'gallant and topsail halyards!"—"Let go!"—"Haul down!"— "Clew up!"—"All hands furl sail!"—and officers and men rushed aloft, and working like Trojans, soon had her under bare poles. Four bells were rung for full speed ahead, and the little ship gallantly breasted the high sea in the face of the half-gale of wind; but patent log nor the old-fashioned chip-and-line could be persuaded to show more than four knots.*

Captain Maury was evidently very anxious and sent for the English chief engineer and asked him if that was the best he could do. The chief said he thought it was. Captain Maury then told him that if the American man-of-

war was the Mohican, as he thought she was, he had served on board of her and she could make seven knots an hour easily against that sea and wind, and significantly added, "You know that being caught means hanging with us according to Mr. Lincoln's proclamation!"

The chief disappeared below and in a few minutes our improvement in speed was remarkable.[21]

Maury directed the *Georgia* around to the far side of the small island, and finding a sheltered cove, ordered the anchor dropped. Sending one of his young lieutenants ashore to climb a prominent hill, Maury instructed him to keep a sharp lookout with his marine glass, and let him know the moment the Federal vessel left port. Soon the panting lieutenant came scampering back to report that the Union ship was indeed steaming out to sea, but headed in the opposite direction from their little secluded cove. Evidently the Federal vessel had failed to notice the Confederate cruiser as she steamed by the mouth of the harbor.

That night, without landing any of his prisoners or acquiring any supplies, Maury ordered the anchor raised, and the *Georgia* continued on her course. For the next two weeks she meandered south under sail alone, with her fires banked and her course set toward the east coast of Brazil. Numerous vessels were spotted and some were stopped; however, they all proved to be under legitimate neutral flags. While the *Georgia* continued on her course, one-by-one, the prisoners from the *Dictator* asked for an interview with Lieutenant Chapman. Although fed the same rations as the Confederate sailors, and brought up on deck each day for exercise, many were becoming tired of their confinement in irons and offered to sign the Articles of Enlistment in the Confederate navy. In all, according to Morgan, the second and third mates and twenty-seven Northern seamen from the *Dictator's* crew joined the *Georgia's* ranks, and they would prove to be some of the finest sailors any Confederate cruiser ever had.[22]

The *Georgia* was now entering an area that old sailors referred to as the "doldrums." This was the wide expanse of Atlantic Ocean that extended approximately ten degrees above and ten degrees below the equator. Here winds were constantly shifting from one point of the compass to another, and then suddenly, there would not be enough breeze to even stir the sails. Storms were frequent, and giant water spouts were a constant threat to the unwary mariner. Only Maury, and perhaps Chapman, knew the cruiser's exact position and their destination, but the old salts among the crew had a good idea where they were. *One night, in the morning watch just before daylight,* Morgan wrote, *an old sailor said to me, "We are near land, sir." I asked him how he knew and he told me to feel how wet the deck was with dew; and although the sea was smooth, the stars shining brightly, and the ship becalmed, I found the deck as*

First Lieutenant Robert T. Chapman, executive officer of the *Georgia.* After the cruise, Chapman returned to the Confederacy in October of 1864, carrying the Great Seal of the Confederate States. This same seal is now on display at the Museum of Confederacy in Richmond, Virginia.

wet as though water had been poured over it. The old "shellback" then informed me that dew never extended more than thirty miles from land. This was news to me, but I found that the Jack Tar was right.[23]

It was a dark, moonless night on May 13–14, when the *Georgia* eased her way into All Saint's Bay and dropped anchor in front of the picturesque Brazilian city of Bahia (present day Salvador). In spite of the darkness, many vessels could be seen riding at anchor, and Chapman and Evans were sure that two of them were warships, but of what nationality, they could not discern.

There was little sleep on the Georgia the night of our arrival, Morgan remembered. *Day broke and we found ourselves very near the two men-of-war. What was their nationality? It seemed an age before the hour for colors arrived, but when it did, to our great delight, the most rakish-looking of the two warships broke out the Stars and Bars! "It is the Alabama!" we gasped, and commenced to dance with delight. The officers hugged one another, each embracing a man of his own rank, except the captain and myself. Like the commander, I was the only one of my rank aboard, so I hugged myself.*[24]

Raphael Semmes, commander of the famous CSS *Alabama*, and Commander Maury had been shipmates in the old navy. In addition, two of the *Georgia's* lieutenants, Evans and Chapman, had served under Semmes and his first lieutenant, Kell, on board the CSS *Sumter* in 1861. These officers were eager to visit the *Alabama* and renew their old friendships. Knowing that Semmes was the ranking officer between the two ships, Maury ordered his gig lowered and was rowed to the side of the jaunty *Alabama*, where he paid his respects to his old shipmate. Soon all the officers of both cruisers were mingling together seeking news of friends and relatives and asking what each had heard about the course of the war that was raging across their homeland. The crews of both ships were given liberty, and Bahia was rocked by the intoxicated and carousing celebrations of the seamen from the *Georgia* and the *Alabama*.

Because most of the crew of the *Dictator* had joined the Confederate service, the only remaining prisoners left on board were the *Dictator's* captain and the first mate, who were quickly sent ashore in custody of the American consul. Despite the protest of the local governor, who was evidently very nervous with two Confederate warships in his harbor, the *Georgia* began taking on coal from the English bark *Castor*, which had been chartered to deliver the precious fuel to the Maury's cruiser. Meanwhile a wealthy Englishman living in Brazil invited the officers of both cruisers on a train excursion over the road that he was building into the interior. Midshipman Morgan left a vivid description of this brief interlude away from the trials and cares of a devastating war: *The country through which we passed was rich and beautiful, and at the end of the finished line our officers were regaled with all sorts of good things to eat and drink. On returning to Bahia he invited us to a dance to be given at his residence that night, and naturally as many of the officers as could be spared from duty accepted. The ball was quite a swell affair; all the British colony were there of course, and many Brazilian ladies; they came from curiosity, but nothing could induce them to risk dancing with the "Corsairos." This, of course, made us youngsters imagine that we looked rather formidable.*[25]

Raphael Semmes was greatly esteemed by his men, but he remained very detached and separated from them. Other than his first lieutenant, he rarely spoke even to his officers except to give some command in regard to the working of the ship. This distancing and aloofness, while lonely for him, enhanced his image in the eyes of the officers and men, and caused them to respect him as the absolute and unquestionable supreme commander. With this image of Semmes in mind, it is understandable why Morgan was so amused by an incident which occurred when the officers returned to their respective ships.

Shortly after midnight we said good-night to our host and hostess and such of the guests as were not afraid to speak to us, and proceeded to the quay where Captain Semmes' gig was waiting for him. The cutters from the Alabama and Georgia, which were to take the officers to their respective ships, had not yet come for us, and we thought we saw before us a long wait; but Captain Semmes very kindly invited us to crowd into his gig, saying that after she put him aboard the Alabama, she would take those of us belonging to the Georgia to our ship. On our way to the Alabama, Midshipman Anderson, the captain's personal aide, who had had a rather strenuous day of it, fell asleep. He was seated alongside his commanding officer and his head fell on the captain's shoulder. Lieutenant Armstrong, who was seated opposite him, was about to reach over and awaken Anderson, but Captain Semmes by a gesture stopped him, saying, "Let the boy sleep; he is tired out." Had Anderson been awake he would rather have dropped his head in the ship's furnace than on Captain Semmes' shoulder, for the captain was not a man with whom anyone would care to take liberties. As it was, however, Ned had the honor of being the only man who ever made a pillow out of "Old Beeswax" as Semmes was called behind his back.[26]

After being supplied with 528 pounds of powder from the *Georgia's* magazine, the *Alabama* sailed from Bahia on May 21, 1863. By the next day, all coal and provisions were on board the *Georgia*, and even the former crew members of the *Dictator*, though bleary-eyed from too much rum, were all present and accounted for. With the *Georgia's* slow speed, it was imperative that she depart after dark because Federal warships might be lurking outside the harbor. Late in the day, intense preparations were evident on deck as officers and men scurried about performing last minute duties in preparation for putting to sea. At sundown, all boats were hoisted in and secured, and the fires were started in the engine room. Coal heavers continued to shovel the black fuel into the blazing furnace, and by 8:30 p.m., enough steam pressure had been built to start the engines. Engineer Pearson cautiously opened the valves leading to the cylinders, and the big flywheels with their wooden cogs began to turn as steam cracked and hissed through the maze of lines and valves leading from the boilers to the engines. With her propeller turning, the anchor was quickly raised, and gaining headway, the *Georgia* eased slowly toward the open sea. The gong in the engine room clanged four times, calling for full speed, and as the welcome swells of the dark Atlantic greeted the accelerating cruiser, sailors rushed into the rigging to unfurl her diminutive sails. Soon the darkened *Georgia*, with no lights showing, save a hooded one over the binnacle, was pounding over the building waves with her head pointed east by north. The second leg of her search for enemy merchant vessels had begun.[27]

Chapter Eight

Requiem for a Cruiser

For the next week the CSS *Georgia* cruised under sail with her fires banked approximately 250 miles off the coast of Brazil. Only one vessel was intercepted during this period, and she proved to be a Dutch bark. Aware that by this time the word had spread of the presence of the two Confederate cruisers, and that most Northern merchant vessels were avoiding the area, Commander William L. Maury ordered the *Georgia's* magnetic course set for 180 degrees, which would take her deeper into the South Atlantic. Soon many vessels began to appear, and some were stopped and boarded, but all proved to be neutral.[1]

Finally, on June 8, 1863, not far outside the harbor of Rio de Janeiro, a splendid large clipper ship hove into view from the masthead. She was making for the anchorage at Rio, and her long slender masts and sails, which were as white as snow, gave a positive indication that she was American. Again, the engine room gong rang four times, and the *Georgia* bounded after the racing clipper. It was close. She was near the marine league; however, and Lieutenant Ingraham, the youthful navigator, took his sightings and pronounced her to be still within international waters. Quickly the guns were cast loose, and within a few minutes a shot from the Blakely pivot rifle whistled across her bow. The rakish clipper hoisted the U.S. flag and lost no time in hauling around into the wind and furling her sails. Soon the

117

Georgia, with the Confederate ensign whipping in the breeze, was alongside. The graceful clipper ship proved to be the *George Griswold* of New York. While she was of American registry, the *Georgia's* boarding party determined that her cargo was properly documented as belonging to a neutral party; therefore, Maury released her on a $100,000 bond.[2] A ransom bond was a contract signed by the master of a captured vessel, obligating the owners of the ship to pay the bonded amount to the Confederate States six months after the ratification of peace. The total collapse of the Confederacy, of course, made these bonds null and void.

Maury reported the *Georgia's* position when the *George Griswold* was captured, as "23° 10' south latitude, 41° 36' west longitude with Cape Frio bearing northwest by west at a distance of nineteen miles." Midshipman Morgan, however, recalled that great plumes of black smoke were plainly visible in the Brazilian port of Rio from warships, as they prepared to investigate the sound of the *Georgia's* guns. The Confederate cruiser lost no time in departing the area, and it was not until after nightfall that they lost sight of the trailing Brazilian warships.[3]

On June 13, after a long chase and the firing of a blank cartridge, the bark *Good Hope* out of Boston, bound for Cape Town, was captured. Her cargo consisted of various commercial goods,—and one brine-filled casket containing the body of her dead captain. It seemed that the captain had died shortly after leaving Boston, and his son had taken command. With no one on board to conduct the funeral ritual, and not wishing to bury his father at sea without a

Midshipman James Morris Morgan, of the *Georgia*. Morgan, resplendent in his Confederate uniform at age 17, posed for this photograph in 1863, and later wrote of his adventures aboard the cruiser in *Recollections of a Rebel Reefer*.

proper service, he had made special efforts to preserve the body until they could return to Boston. After transferring needed provisions from the prize, and bringing the crew of twenty on board, Maury, at the earnest request of the deceased captain's son, agreed to transfer the coffin to the deck of the *Georgia*. *This was no easy thing to do in a small boat with the sea running quite high,* Morgan wrote, *but the feat was accomplished and it was safely hoisted out of the boat by means of a "whip" sent down from our main yard, and reverently placed on two carpenter's "horses" which awaited it just in front of the entrance to the cabin. Here it was covered with the Stars and Stripes, the flag the dead man had sailed under, and which we were told he loved so well in life.*

The next day, June 14, a solemn service was held on the deck of the *Georgia*, and Morgan remembered it well: *Several of our heaviest projectiles were made fast to the foot of the coffin, and when all was ready, the ship's bell was tolled for divine service, the prisoners were relieved of their irons, and all hands were summoned to bury the dead. The prisoners and our crew mingled together as they gathered around the coffin, at the head of which stood Captain Maury, prayer book in hand, with the son of the dead man standing beside him, while our officers reverently took their places behind. Captain Maury then read the beautiful ritual of the Episcopal Church for the burial of the dead at sea.*[4]

It was a bright sunny morning, and while the devotional service continued, thick black smoke rose hundreds of feet into the clear sky as the *Good Hope* blazed fiercely nearby. Before Maury had concluded the reading from the prayer book, the lookout at the *Georgia's* masthead interrupted the service with the call, "Sail ho!" Paying no attention to the cry, the Confederate commander never hesitated, but continued with his service. Morgan tiptoed forward and scrambled up the mast to see for himself, and sure enough, a stranger was rapidly approaching. As the distant vessel drew nearer, Morgan could see that her sails were snowy white, a sure sign of an American, and he could just barely make out what appeared to be a man-of-war pennant flying from her topmast. Presently, much to his alarm, the Stars and Stripes broke out from behind her sails!

I waited no longer, he wrote, *but scampered from aloft, and softly stealing up behind Captain Maury, who was still reading from his prayer book, said in a whisper, "American man-of-war bearing down on us rapidly, sir!" Never a muscle did he move, nor was there the slightest change in his solemn voice until he had finished, and the prisoners had lifted the coffin and committed the body to the care of the deep blue sea. Then he ordered me to beat to quarters and cast loose the guns.*[5]

The American ship was rapidly closing, and while the gun crews stood ready with lanyards in hand, the gun captains kept the pieces pointed at the approaching vessel. Young Morgan, however, had been mistaken. Fortunately she was not a warship, but a Northern merchant bark, and she hove to only a hundred and fifty yards away. A boat was lowered from her deck, and the stranger's captain rowed quickly to the *Georgia's* side. Morgan remembered the amazing and somewhat amusing scene that followed:

We lowered a Jacob's ladder over the side, and the captain of the bark, jumping out of his boat, ran up it like the true sailor he was. As he leaped onto our deck he exclaimed, "This is dreadful! Can I be of any assistance? — How did it happen?" Captain Maury stepped forward and told him the Good Hope had been burned by his orders. The man for a moment looked aghast, and then an expression of indignation passed over his features as he asked, "Are you a pirate?" Captain Maury replied, "That is what your people call me." He then took the skipper into his cabin and heard his story.

He (the Northern skipper) had sailed from the United States before the war had begun, and had made the long voyage around Cape Horn into the Pacific, where he had wandered about until he had got as far north as the Bering Sea. On his return he had stopped at one of the South Sea islands, overhauled and painted his ship, whitewashed his sails, and had then hoisted a homeward-bound pennant. He was well on his way when, that morning, he had seen a dense column of smoke which he felt sure could come only from some unfortunate ship that had caught fire in the middle of the South Atlantic, and had at once left his course to go to her assistance. The first lieutenant of the Georgia went on board the bark, whose name was the J. W. Seaver, and searched her, finding many old newspapers, but none of a later date than October, 1860. Although her cargo was American, Captain Maury let him go, saying that he would stand a court martial before he would burn the ship of a man who had come on an errand of mercy to help fellow seamen in distress. We put our prisoners, as many as wanted to go, on board the Seaver; we also put sufficient of the provisions we had taken from the Good Hope to last them for the voyage. There were not many of them, as most of the crew expressed a desire to ship with us, and they proved to be among the best men we had.[6]

After the encounter with the *J. W. Seaver*, Maury sailed the cruiser due east, away from the coast of South America. Only one ship was sighted, and she proved to be a French brig bound from Bordeaux to Buenos Aires. On June 18, the *Georgia's* lookout sighted the barren island of Trindade, which lies in the middle of the South Atlantic approximately twenty degrees south of the equator. Finding a secluded cove, Maury ordered the anchor dropped, and instructed the lookout to keep a sharp eye for passing ships. Trindade is only about six miles in circumference, and its rocky terrain rises to a height of more than 800 feet above the desolate Atlantic waters. Most northern-bound merchant vessels used it as a sighting to check their position on their long voyage to Europe and North America. Maury's plan was to wait at Trindade, watch for passing vessels, and pounce on the first American they might see.[7]

For several days the *Georgia* lay at Trindade, with only non-American vessels plodding by the island. Finally, on the morning of June 25, the lookout reported what appeared to be an American sail on the horizon. The fires had been banked, but firemen rushed to the engine room, and soon the *Georgia* was bounding across the waves in pursuit. Not wanting to waste precious coal, Maury ordered a blank cartridge fired as a signal to heave to, but the loud report of the Blakely had no effect on the fleeing vessel. As the *Georgia* drew nearer, the big Blakely boomed again, sending a solid shot whistling across her bow. Still the stranger did not stop. With the *Georgia* finally drawing alongside, the American captain reasoned that he had no chance of escape, and he immediately surrendered to his fate. The vessel was the *Constitution*, a large full-rigged ship bound from Philadelphia to Shanghai with a cargo of coal and a crew of twenty-six men. The *Constitution* also had a large number of passengers on board, including a group of missionaries who were returning to their respective stations in China. Midshipman Morgan was selected to be a member of Lieutenant Evan's prize crew, which was quickly dispatched on board. Long after the war, his harrowing experience was still fresh in his mind:

Half a dozen of us were put on board the prize, and as there were several other sails in sight, the Georgia went off in chase, leaving us to work the big Constitution to the island where we expected our cruiser to rejoin us. The wind was very light and we made but slow progress. In the mean while the Georgia had disappeared below the horizon and we began to feel very lonesome. For safety's sake we placed one half of the crew in irons and put them down below; the other half we kept on deck, making them work the ship for us until night came and then confined them all on the lower deck.

The wind died completely at sunset, and the *Constitution* never made it to the island. Evans and his eight-man crew secured the vessel as best they could, and patiently awaited the *Georgia's* return. The next morning dawned calm and fair, but there was still no sign of the Confederate cruiser. Evans ordered the missionaries and passengers to remain aft of the main mast, while communication with their crew, who were kept in irons below deck, was strictly forbidden. All day the prize crew watched and waited. Night came, and still the *Georgia* had not reappeared. The prisoners, who were now all confined below, were becoming restless, and Evans threatened to cover the hatches with tarpaulins if they did not quiet down. An armed guard was stationed at each ladder leading to the lower deck with orders to shoot the first head that appeared above the combing.

The night was very dark, Morgan continued, *and the rising sea caused the ship to roll more than ever. Toward midnight a large vase became loosened from its fastenings and fell to the deck with a crash; then pandemonium broke loose. The women, screaming that the pirates were going to murder them,*

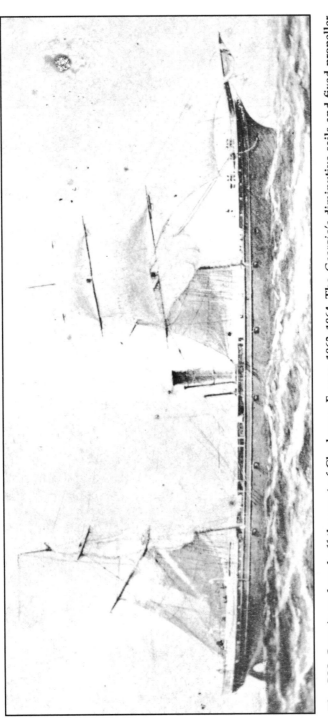

The CSS *Georgia* anchored off the coast of Cherbourg, France, 1863–1864. The *Georgia's* diminutive sails and fixed propeller were a handicap when it came to cruising under canvas alone.

rushed out of their rooms in their night-clothes and prostrated themselves on the deck, begging for mercy. Just then—to add to the terrors of the situation— the cries of the women were drowned by the boom of a cannon and the shriek- ing of a rifled shell as it passed over us. I rushed on deck and through the speaking trumpet shouted to our unseen foe, "Ship ahoy! Don't fire, we sur- render!"—A hail came out of the darkness, asking what ship we were. I was going to answer that it was the United States ship Constitution, a prize of the Georgia, but as the words "United States" came out of my mouth there was some more banging of the great guns. Things were too serious for further conversation, so hastily ordering a boat lowered, I rowed over to the strange craft and found her to be the Georgia!

The *Georgia* had chased after several vessels, all of whom proved neutral, and as happened all too often, several wooden cogs in her gears had broken causing her to be laid up for a day while the engi- neers struggled to make repairs. Returning to the island in the black- ness of night, the officer of the deck swore that he heard commands coming out of the darkness such as would be given to a gun crew preparing for action. He also thought he heard Morgan say that they were the "United States sloop-of-war *Niagara*." Fortunately, none of the *Georgia's* shells had found their target.[8]

The *Georgia* continued to lie in the tiny desolate anchorage, and when not chasing a reported sail, the crew tediously transferred coal from the *Constitution* to the cruiser in buckets. On June 27, a neutral was boarded which carried the ill news of the death of "Stonewall" Jackson, and the flag of the *Georgia* was sadly lowered to half-mast. The next day, the American ship *City of Bath* was captured, and Maury quickly bonded her and transferred all his unhappy passengers and crew from the *Constitution* to her. By July 8, it was time to move on. The *Georgia* had scoured the waters around Trindade for almost three weeks, and Federal warships could possibly be drawing near. Before leaving, however, the *Constitution* had to be destroyed, so her cable was slipped and she was set on fire. While the prize burned, Maury ordered the guns cast loose, and the captains to exercise their crews at the guns. After several rounds were fired by each gun crew, it was plainly evident why the *Constitution* was not hit on that dark night when Morgan was on board. The midshipmen recalled that they proved to be "mighty poor range-finders and gun-pointers."[9]

Maury ordered the *Georgia's* course set due east, and with all her sails unfurled, her engines running perfectly, for the moment, the Con- federate cruiser turned her head toward the fabled continent of Africa.

Throughout the rest of July and into the month of August, the *Geor- gia* cruised slowly eastward over the desolate expanse of the vast South Atlantic. Many vessels were stopped and some were boarded, but all proved to be neutrals with the exception of the *Prince of Wales*. She was an American vessel out of Bath, Maine, and was captured on July 16, 1863. Although the ship was American, the boarding party determined that her cargo was properly documented as belonging to a neutral, and she was released on a $40,000 ransom bond. For the next several weeks, the *Georgia* plodded along in the vast expanse of the South Atlantic where there was little or no traffic. Not until reaching the northbound track of vessels that had sailed around the Cape of Good Hope, did the cry "Sail ho!" again echo from the masthead. Within the space of three days, August 13, 14, 15, eight merchant ships were stopped, but only one, a British vessel, was boarded. On August 16, with picturesque Table Mountain looming in the background, the *Georgia*, with her coal running dangerously low, dropped anchor in Simon's Bay, at Simon's Town, South Africa.[10]

Almost immediately, a British official boarded the *Georgia* and informed Maury, that in accordance with the Queen's policy toward the belligerents, the cruiser would be allowed to stay only twenty-four hours. The English colony's attitude had cooled somewhat toward the Confederacy, caused in part by several captures made by the *Alabama* in disputed waters. In fact, the *Alabama* had only recently departed Simon's Town after a lengthy stay, and the officials were reluctant to grant another Confederate warship the same privileges. Maury explained that the decks were leaking badly because they needed to be re-caulked, the engines had broken down just as they entered port, and he needed to re-coal. (Morgan wrote that it was the "habit" of the engines to "break down" just as they came to anchor in order to obtain a stay of more than 24 hours.) Maury added that the ship's hull was fouled with a growth of sea grass from eight to twelve inches long that needed to be removed. After a thorough inspection, British officials consented to an extended stay, but only to accomplish repairs that were "absolutely necessary."[11]

The crew, such as those who were not on duty or assigned to the coaling operation, were given liberty. Many of the officers obtained horses and rode the twenty-mile distance over the dusty road to Cape Town. On August 28, the British troop ship H.M.S. *Himalaya* arrived in Simon's Bay with a regiment of Highlanders on board bound for India. Morgan recounted an interesting meeting with the Highlanders: *One day, while returning from shore in one of our cutters, I steered her very close to the troopship. The band was playing on the quarter-deck, and as we approached the band struck up "Dixie," and I stood up in the boat and took off my cap. The Himalaya's crew and the soldiers raised a cheer which was quickly suppressed, and I afterwards heard that the bandmaster and the officers who had instigated him to play "Dixie" had been reprimanded.*

Later that evening, the *Georgia's* officers were invited to dinner on board the *Himalaya*. *The dinner was a very picturesque affair,* Morgan recalled, *the gay uniforms of the officers with their gold lace and the beautiful attire of their wives and daughters; the scene was not one to be easily forgotten. The Highlander pipers playing their bagpipes marched three times around the table, and a more awful screeching noise than they made it had never before been my misfortune to hear. A Scotch officer greatly embarrassed me by asking if I did not think it delightful music. When the table was cleared of all the good things, the colonel arose and said, "Gentlemen, will you fill your glasses?" This having been done, he again arose, and solemnly proposed the toast which consisted of only two words, "The Queen!" The glasses were emptied, and the function was at an end.*[12]

The following day, August 29, 1863, revealed a scene of intense activity on board the *Georgia*, as it was Maury's intention to put to sea that evening. While the *Georgia's* bunkers were overflowing with coal, and her deck seams were freshly caulked, lack of time had prevented the cleaning of her hull, and the long algae clinging to her bottom would reduce her already slow speed to no more than five knots. Several of the original nine English crew members that had come out in the *Japan* could not be found among the bars and brothels of Simon's Town, and it was assumed they had deserted. The majority of the *Georgia's* crew was now composed of the volunteers from the *Dictator* and the *Constitution*. The *Georgia* would have the dubious distinction of being the only Confederate cruiser to be commanded by Southern-born officers and crewed by Northern-born sailors.[13]

By 8:00 p.m., steam was hissing in the boilers, and the order was given to raise the anchor. Passing out of the bay, the *Georgia* steered a southwest course, and by 4:00 a.m., she was some twenty miles distant from the Cape of Good Hope. As light began to spread over the horizon, numerous sails could be discerned, which, fortunately, were heading straight toward the Confederate cruiser. They were confirmed as Indian merchant ships loaded with silks and tea from the Orient, but not one was American. *We had changed our course,* Morgan wrote, *and accompanied them until evening of the next day when we found ourselves under the shadow of Table Mountain. The sun was setting when suddenly we saw a great paddle-wheel steamer, her double walking beam engines making her nationality unmistakable. She was headed for Table Bay, her course taking her across our bow and she soon was only about five miles away.*

Captain Maury ordered all hands to assemble at the mast and said to them, "Men, that steamer is the Vanderbilt* (USS Vanderbilt: 3,360 tons, 11 heavy guns); *she can outrun us and she can whip us after she catches us. I am going to lay you alongside of her and you had far better follow me aboard her and die like men fighting for your lives than to tamely allow yourselves to be hung from her yardarms. Go to your guns!"* To the great relief of the *Georgia's* "boarders," the mighty *Vanderbilt* never noticed the diminutive Confederate cruiser.[14]

Near midnight on August 30, with the soft lights of Cape Town twinkling in the distance, the American merchant ship *John Watts* was overhauled and seized. The *Georgia's* log recorded the capture as occurring at longitude 34° 3' south, and latitude 18° 6' east, but Morgan wrote that, *I fear that we were perilously near that sacred limit called the "marine league" within which captures were unlawful.* The *John Watts* was out of Maulmain bound for Falmouth, England, and her papers documented her cargo as belonging to a neutral. By 3:00 a.m., Maury had the American vessel bonded for $30,000 and allowed her to proceed. After the *John Watts* had disappeared over the early morning horizon, Maury ordered the cruiser's course set northward toward the area along the equator known as the "doldrums." Perhaps here, in a region of light winds and calms, the *Georgia* with her encrusted bottom could still find and overhaul a Northern merchant vessel.[15]

It took the slow *Georgia* nearly a month to reach the equator, 3,150 miles to the north. Maury tarried in the area of the doldrums for four or five days during the latter part of September, and while a few ships were intercepted and examined, none were American. With the *Alabama*, the *Florida*, and the *Georgia* prowling the northern and southern waters of the Atlantic Ocean, United States' shipping everywhere was rapidly being sold to other nations rather than chance an encounter with the "Rebel pirates." Maury would have been gratified if he could have seen the scores of American vessels all over the world that were rotting at their wharves, because they were unable to obtain cargoes. In the United States, bowing to the clamor being raised by wealthy shippers and an irate public, more and more warships were being diverted from blockade duty along the Southern coast and sent on elusive and fruitless searches for the Confederate cruisers.

The *Georgia* had been at sea for over six months, and not once had she entered a port where adequate facilities existed to accomplish proper repairs. Her bottom was fouled with sea growth, and she was desperately in need of an overhaul, which could only be accomplished in dry dock. On his departure from England in April, Maury had determined that France might hold a more liberal attitude than England toward Confederate warships seeking repairs, and with this hope, he turned the *Georgia's* prow northward.

During the trek northward from the equator, and when approximately 200 miles due west of the African principality of Morocco, on October 9, 1863, an excited "Sail ho!" was shouted by the lookout. The vessel was obviously American, and almost immediately the signal gong clanged four times in the *Georgia's* engine room. Putting on all the speed that her fouled bottom would allow, the Confederate cruiser hurried after the Northern vessel. With only a light breeze to fill the quarry's sails, the *Georgia* gained rapidly, and soon the deep boom of her pivot rifle echoed across the water. Slowly the American vessel came about, and resigned herself to her fate. Her papers verified that she was the *Bold Hunter* of Boston, and was bound from Dundee, Scotland to Calcutta with a cargo of English coal. Unknown to Commander Maury at the time, she would also be the *Georgia's* last prize. With darkness approaching, the Confederate cruiser hove to leeward, and her captain and crew were brought over to the deck of the *Georgia*. As was Maury's practice, the crew was manacled in single irons and sent below, while the captain was invited to share his cabin.[16]

There was no question concerning the neutrality of the *Bold Hunter's* cargo, and early the next morning the *Georgia's* boats were plying back and forth between the two vessels bringing all the supplies and provisions they could carry. As always the *Georgia* was running low on coal, and Maury wanted very much to transfer the *Bold Hunter's* cargo to his bunkers, but as misfortune would have it, the wind now began to pick up and the sea to build. Attempting to transfer coal utilizing small boats in a turbulent and rising sea, proved to be an extremely dangerous task. After approximately half a dozen trips in which several boats were almost lost, Maury gave it up, and ordered the operation abandoned. Reluctantly, Maury signaled the prize crew to set fire to the *Bold Hunter*, and return to the *Georgia*.[17]

We had hardly finished hoisting our boats to the davits, Morgan wrote, *when a great cloud of smoke burst from the hatches of the Bold Hunter coming from the thousands of tons of burning coal in her hold. The wind had by this time increased to a gale and the sea was running very high. ....The wind was very light when we captured the ship and she hove to with all her sails set, even to the royals. The flames leaped from her deck to her tarry rigging and raced up the shrouds and backstays and burned away her braces—her yards swung around, her sails filled, and the floating inferno, like a mad bull, bore down on us at full speed, rushing through the water as though she was bent on having her revenge. To avoid a collision, the order was given on the Georgia to go ahead at full speed. The gong in the engine room sounded, the engine turned the screw, and the screw began to churn the water under our stern. The engine made two or three revolutions—then there was a crash—followed by yells as the engineers and oilers rushed on to the deck accompanied by a shower of lignum-vitæ cogs and broken glass from the engine room windows. The order to make sail was instantly given, but before the gaskets which confined the furled sails to the yardarms could be cast off, the burning ship was upon us. She had come for us with such directness that one could easily have imagined that she was being steered by some demon who had come out of the inferno which was raging in her hold.*

With the failure of the engines and lack of time to unfurl the sails, the approaching *Bold Hunter*, engulfed in a mass of flames, conveyed a scene of imminent disaster. One can imagine the feeling of horror and helplessness as the blazing inferno bore down upon them. *We stood with bated breath,* Morgan continued, *awaiting the catastrophe which seemingly was about to overtake us. The Bold hunter was rated at over three thousand tons and had inside her a burning cargo of coal of even greater weight—the Georgia was scarcely one sixth her size. Onward rushed the blazing ship, presenting an awesome spectacle with the flames leaping about her sails and rigging while a huge mass of black smoke rolled out of her hatches. High above our heads her long, flying jibboom passed over our poop deck as she rose on a great wave and came down on our port quarter, her cutwater cleaving through the Georgia's fragile plates as cleanly as though they had been made out of cheese.*

The force of the impact pushed the Georgia ahead and for a moment we congratulated ourselves that we had escaped from the fiery demon whose breath was scorching us. But the Bold Hunter was not yet satisfied with the injuries she had inflicted. Recovering from the recoil, she again gathered way and struck us near the place she had previously damaged, but fortunately this was a glancing blow which had the effect only of wrenching off our port quarter davits and reducing the boat which was slung to them to kindling wood. Not yet satisfied, the apparently infuriated inanimate object made a third attempt to destroy the Georgia, this time, fortunately, missing her mark and passing a few yards to leeward of us. Her sails having burned, she soon lost headway and helplessly lay wallowing in the trough of the sea while the fire ate through her sides, and her tall masts, one after the other, fell with a great splash into the sea. Before she went down surrounded by a cloud of steam we had a good view through the great holes burned in her sides of the fire raging inside her. I imagine it was a very realistic imitation of what hell looks like when the forced drafts are turned on in honor of the arrival of a distinguished sinner.[18]

The *Georgia* now definitely needed repairs. She was leaking badly from the effects of the collision with the *Bold Hunter,* and only by the supreme efforts of the ship's carpenter was she enabled to stay afloat. Her engine room was a shambles, and it took several days of tedious rebuilding of the wooden teeth in the flywheels before her weary engineers could start the engines again. Maury ordered the cruiser's course set for the island of Tenerife and the little port of Santa Cruz in the Canary Islands.

After replenishing his supplies and releasing the prisoners from the *Bold Hunter,* Maury intended on sailing to a French port where he could put the *Georgia* in dry dock. The Confederate cruiser was now approaching the European shipping lanes and numerous vessels were beginning to be sighted. If the wind was light, the cruiser gave chase, and she even overhauled and boarded a few. However, all proved to be neutral.[19]

As the Confederate cruiser continued to make her way slowly northward, Midshipman Morgan, while standing the late night watch on

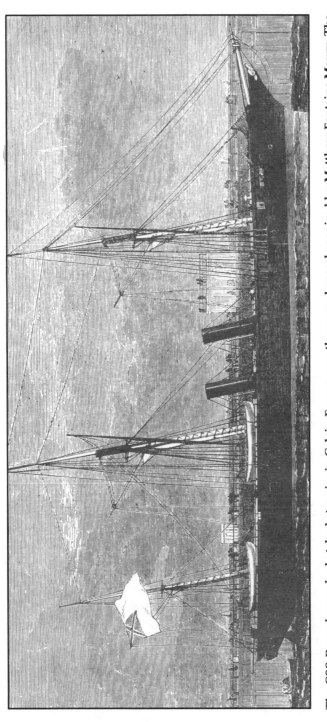

The CSS *Rappahannock*, sketched at a pier in Calais, France, was the second vessel acquired by Matthew Fontaine Maury. The *Georgia* waited five weeks off the coast of Africa for her, but the *Rappahannock* was detained by French authorities.

October 13–14, encountered a frightening phenomenon: *The night was starlit and the sea was smooth—the only air stirring being that made by the slow progress of the steamer. ... Four bells (2 a.m.) had just struck, when the stillness of the night was broken by a frightened "Land ho!" from the lookout. Instantly the officer of the deck asked, "Where away?" and the lookout answered, "Dead ahead, sir!"—and added in what was a frightened wail, "For God's sake, stop her, sir!" By this time the officer of the deck had seen the cause of alarm and had signaled the engineer to stop and then to go astern at full speed.*

The sudden reversing of the engines woke the entire crew, and they came scrambling up on deck to see what was wrong. *One look was enough—there, not a ship's length ahead, was land which towered up into the darkness. It looked as though it would be impossible to stop our headway before we should be dashed to pieces on it. Captain Maury and all his officers were gathered on the poop deck. It was the only time I ever saw the captain show any excitability. He rather peremptorily demanded an explanation from the navigator, who insisted that his calculations were right and that the nearest land to us was the Canary Islands, distant more than one hundred miles. The captain pointed to the land, a cable's length or less away, an unanswerable argument. The navigator could only shake his head doubtfully and reiterate that, despite all appearances being against him, he was sure his work was correct. The captain went into his room and together they went over the calculations, but no error could be discovered. Then the captain came forward and looked long and intently at the obstacle which barred our further progress, apparently. Suddenly, I was surprised to hear him laugh in his usual gentle way, and then I almost jumped out of my boots as I heard him give the order to go ahead at full speed. As he passed me on his way back to his cabin he simply said, "Mirage!"...Through the rest of my watch it seemed to me that the next revolution of the engine must necessarily plunge our flying jibboom into those phantom rocks. The mirage faded away before daylight, and that morning at a distance of a hundred and ten miles we plainly saw the Peak of Tenerife towering above the clouds.*[20]

The *Georgia* entered Santa Cruz on the morning of October 15. The Canary Islands were a favorite hunting ground for American whalers, and the Lincoln government had sent warships to the area to protect them. Islanders reported that a Federal man-of-war had departed Santa Cruz only the day before the arrival of the Confederate cruiser. The prisoners were landed, essential repairs were made, and taking on a few extra provisions, the *Georgia* sailed out to sea on October 18.

As the Confederate cruiser approached the continent of Europe, she was almost constantly within sight of numerous sails. Some were obviously non-American, but others had to be stopped and boarded, their papers examined, and then allowed to proceed. The *Georgia's* log records, that during the ten days spent sailing from Tenerife to

Cherbourg, thirty vessels were either "spoken to" or boarded. None, however, proved to be Northern-owned or carried American-owned cargo.[21] While at Simon's Town in South Africa, Maury had received letters reporting that, because of the advancing Union armies, his wife and children had become refugees, and he was now justifiably worried about their safety. By now, the commander's health had begun to fail, and Morgan reported that he became very melancholy and rarely appeared on deck. In addition, the discipline of the ship was beginning to exhibit the absence of the iron hand of Lieutenant Chapman, the executive officer. Chapman had asked to be transferred back to England while the cruiser was at Simon's Town, and Maury had granted his request. Lieutenant Chapman had been a strict disciplinarian, but Lieutenant Evans, who replaced him, while an excellent officer, did not have the same influence over the men.

Things had gone from bad to worse than bad, wrote Morgan, *until one day some of the stokers discovered that a coal bunker was only separated from the spirit room, where their grog rations were stored, by a thin bulkhead; this they bored through. They must have known the location of a particular barrel of whiskey, for they bored through the head of that also, and inserting a piece of lead pipe into the hole, they got all the liquor they (temporarily) wanted. This they distributed among the crew and soon there was a battle royal going on on the berth deck which the master-at-arms was unable to stop.*

Lieutenant Evans and several other officers went below and persuaded the mutineers to assemble on the main deck. After subduing the loudest of the drunken sailors, the rest meekly submitted to being placed in irons, and were hustled below to sleep it off. In reading Morgan's account, it appeared that the *Georgia* needed to make port for more reasons than just repairs. Finally, at 2:15 a.m., on October 28, 1863, the Confederate cruiser entered the man-of-war harbor at Cherbourg, France, and dropped her anchor.[22]

She had been at sea for seven long months, and during that time, had destroyed or bonded nine Northern vessels. While not an enviable record compared to the more famous Confederate cruisers, she had, in conjunction with her sister raiders, contributed to the practical elimination of all American commerce in the Atlantic Ocean. Her adventures, however, were not over.

One of the first actions taken by Commander Maury after arriving at Cherbourg, was to request permission to accomplish the needed repairs on the *Georgia*. Permission was granted, and during the next three months, the Confederate cruiser underwent the necessary overhaul. One sad note to the arrival of the *Georgia* in France, were two letters waiting for Midshipman Morgan. They informed him of the death of his two brothers, Captain George Morgan, First Louisiana Infantry, and Thomas G. Morgan, a captain in the Seventh Louisiana. Both of these units were part of the old "Stonewall" Brigade.[23]

Maury journeyed to Paris to meet with Flag Officer Samuel Barron, the supreme Confederate naval commander in Europe. In addition to outlining the many limitations of the *Georgia* as an effective cruiser, Maury also asked to be relieved for reasons of health. Barron granted his request, and telegraphed orders for Lieutenant Evans to assume command. Barron had new plans for the *Georgia*. Another ship had been purchased and spirited out of England by Matthew Fountain Maury. Commissioned the CSS *Rappahannock*, she was now at Calais undergoing overhaul and refitting. Barron and other senior naval officers in Europe concluded that, because of the *Georgia's* slow speed and her limited coal capacity, her armament should be transferred to the *Rappahannock*, and the *Georgia* would then be decommissioned and sold.

Evans received orders to effect a rendezvous with the *Rappahannock* off the coast of Morocco, and transfer all stores, armament, and ammunition from the *Georgia* to her. In the meantime, the USS *Kearsarge*, learning of the presence of the *Georgia* at Cherbourg, had begun patrolling the channel waters just outside of the three mile limit. On a dark night in the middle of February 1864, the anchor was quietly raised, and the *Georgia* proceeded out into the English Channel with no sign of the *Kearsarge*. With a clean hull and overhauled engines, she raced down the channel and was soon pounding over the swells of the broad Atlantic. After a voyage of several days, Evans ordered the *Georgia* stopped, and she dropped anchor about one mile off a deserted Moroccan beach forty miles south of Mogador.

We could see no signs of vegetable or other life on the desolate looking land, Morgan wrote, *with the exception of some bushes at the foot of the mountains. Day after day we lay there lazily rolling on the swell of the sea, the monotony only broken occasionally by watching camel caravans to or from Magador come along the beach and wind their way around the mountains, disappearing in the apparently limitless and glaring desert waste.*[24]

For almost five weeks the *Georgia* lay immobile under the burning sun, off the coast of Morocco. It was becoming evident to Evans that the *Rappahannock* was not going to show. French authorities, unknown to him, had been threatened by U.S. officials, stating that claims would be brought against France if the *Rappahannock* were allowed to sail. The emperor's detention order had reached the *Rappahannock* just hours before the *Georgia* sailed. The *Rappahannock* would never get to sea, but would spend the remainder of the war serving as a receiving ship for the many Confederate naval officers, who were sent to Europe to man Bulloch's projected ironclads. Realizing by now that something must have happened to the *Rappahannock*, Evans weighed anchor and steamed back toward France, arriving at Bordeaux on March 25.

The *Georgia* was still slated for decommissioning, but Bullock felt it advisable to bring her to England to accomplish this. Again, with several Federal warships patrolling outside the harbor, Evans successfully stole out of Bordeaux on April 30, and arrived at Liverpool two days later. With her armament removed, the *Georgia* was sold on June 1, 1864, for £15,000 to an Englishman who converted her into a peaceful merchant vessel. In spite of her legitimate sale and her British registry, she was captured on her first voyage by the USS *Niagara*, and sent to the United States to be adjudicated by a prize court.[25]

Once again I saw the Georgia, Morgan concluded,—*in 1866. On this occasion she was lying at a wharf in Charleston Harbor being loaded with cotton. I don't believe she had been painted since I left her in Liverpool and she looked like any other dirty old tramp steamer. I asked her mate if the wooded cogs ever gave him any trouble, and he replied, "Only when she gets us in a tight place in bad weather, or we are trying to avoid a collision."* Ex-Midshipman Morgan could certainly relate to that![26]

The valiant former CSS *Georgia* was wrecked on the rocky coast of the Gulf of St. Lawrence in 1867. The *Georgia* will always be overshadowed by her more famous Confederate sisters, but she and her captain, Commander William L. Maury, fulfilled their duty well on the vast gray waters of the Atlantic Ocean.

Chapter *Nine*

" . . . You Had Better Surrender"

Early morning light was just beginning to force its way over the eastern Alabama horizon. It was a little before 6:00 a.m., and overhead squealing seagulls wheeled and darted as they searched for an early morning meal. The day was Friday, August 5, 1864, and out over the still dark Gulf of Mexico not a cloud marred the wide expanse of southern sky. As the men of the Confederate ironclad CSS *Tennessee* sipped their early morning coffee, Admiral Franklin Buchanan, "Old Buck" to them, paced the upper deck of the casemate and intently watched the black smoke rising on the southern horizon. Since the first glimmer of daylight, observers at Fort Morgan had also been watching the ominous build-up of Union vessels out in the gulf. Buchanan, too, could see them now—long lines of enemy sloops-of-war with smaller gunboats lashed to their port sides, and on their starboard quarter steamed a row of ugly and sinister-looking ironclad monitors. They were moving slowly, aiming for the 800 yard-wide channel that leads into the bay. During the night, the blockade runner *Red Gauntlet* had successfully avoided the Federal fleet, slipped through this same channel, and delivered her valuable cargo to the wharves at Mobile. Suddenly, the shrill cry of the boatswain's pipe pierced the morning air, the long roll of the drum was heard, and bells began clanging in the engine room. The men of the *Tennessee* threw their coffee overboard, and with the shouted commands of officers audible

134

above the commotion, began scrambling to their stations. The long-awaited battle of Mobile Bay was about to begin.

By the beginning of the war, Mobile, Alabama was one of the most important deep water ports in the South. Second only to New Orleans in the number of vessels clearing her harbor for the Gulf of Mexico, the city prospered prior to the war as a center for trade and commerce. The state of Alabama was the second largest cotton producer behind Mississippi, and the majority of this cotton was exported abroad through the port of Mobile. When Farragut's Union fleet captured New Orleans on April 25, 1862, Mobile took on an added importance to the Confederacy as the primary port on the Gulf for the exportation of cotton and the importation of essential war materials. The Army of Tennessee and other armies in the deep south depended heavily upon

Admiral Franklin Buchanan, who directed the small Confederate squadron at Mobile, Alabama. The crusty old flag officer flew his command pennant from the *Tennessee*, and was painfully wounded in the engagement.

the tenuous string of blockade runners carrying supplies from Havana, Cuba to Mobile. Early in the conflict, and especially after the fall of New Orleans, Confederate officials realized the strategic importance of the Alabama gulf city and began taking steps to protect it.[1]

The city of Mobile is situated thirty miles from the Gulf at the northern end of Mobile Bay. With two major rivers, the Tombigbee and the Alabama, flowing into it from the north, the bay varies in width from 15 miles at the lower end to 6 miles at its northern or upper end. The principal entrance to the bay from the Gulf of Mexico is via the Main Shipping Channel which runs at an angle toward the northeast. Mobile Point, a thin spit of sand that juts out from the mainland to the east of the channel, reaches to within 300 yards of the deep water passage which runs along the sandy beaches off the point. Dauphin Island, which is the easternmost island in the chain that borders Mississippi Sound, is situated on the other side of the channel and is three miles west of Mobile Point. A smaller second channel, known as Grant's Pass, skirts the north coast of Dauphin Island and connects Mississippi Sound with Mobile Bay. This entrance was used mostly by coastal vessels traveling between New Orleans and Mobile.

Guarding the Main Shipping Channel to the east on Mobile Point was the brick and masonry structure of Fort Morgan. By the time the Federals attacked, the pentagonal-shaped fort, completed in 1834, was garrisoned by 640 men consisting of a portion of the 1st Alabama Battalion of Artillery, one company of the 21st Alabama Regiment, and the 1st Tennessee Regiment, all under the command of Brigadier General Richard L. Page. By the summer of 1864, the fort mounted seven 10-inch, three 8-inch, and twenty-two 32-pounder smoothbore guns, along with two 6.5-inch and four 5.6-inch rifled cannons. Page constructed a formidable water battery consisting of 29 more guns, most of which were 10-inch Columbiads.

Three miles across the channel on the eastern tip of Dauphin Island, and similar to the solid brick structure of Fort Morgan, stood Fort Gaines. Commanded by Colonel Charles D. Anderson, its force of 854 officers and men included six companies of the 21st Alabama, two companies of the 1st Alabama Battalion of Artillery, the Pelham Cadets, some reserves, and Companies D and F of the C.S. Marine Corps. Although the fort mounted 27 guns, because of the distance from the Main Shipping Channel, its role would be of secondary importance in the defense of Mobile Bay.[2]

Situated on Tower Island, a small sand-covered shell bank at the mouth of Grant's Pass, stood the unfinished work named Fort Powell. Commanded by Lieutenant Colonel James W. Williams, the fort's 140 men, two companies of the 21st Alabama, and a part of Culpepper's South Carolina Battery, served an 8-inch and a 10-inch Columbiad, along with five smaller rifled guns. Fort Powell, too, would play only a minor role in the forthcoming battle.[3]

Stretching eastward from Fort Gaines to the edge of the Main Shipping Channel, 800 feet from Fort Morgan, was a series of piles and underwater obstructions laced with torpedoes and designed to force all shipping under the guns of Fort Morgan. All Confederate land forces in the area were under the command of Major General Dabney H. Maury, and though the forts were formidable, Maury knew that the cooperation of a strong naval force would be absolutely essential in turning back any Federal attempt to force their way into the bay. That naval force, in spite of the usual shortages of materials and skilled workers, had been building slowly since the fall of New Orleans.

On May 1, 1862, Confederate authorities entered into a contract with Henry D. Bassett, a Mobile shipbuilder, for the construction of two ironclad floating batteries. The small city of Selma, located about 160 miles up the winding Alabama River, was chosen by Bassett as the construction site. Selma was distant enough inland to be safe from Federal excursions, yet far enough down river to enable the ironclads to be floated to Mobile for final preparations. Another factor which probably influenced Bassett's choice of Selma, was Colin McRae's iron foundry. McRae had opened the foundry on a bluff overlooking the river adjacent to the town in 1861, and he promised to deliver guns, boilers, and even armor plating for the vessels. Using the products of this foundry, Basset optimistically committed to the completion of the *Tuscaloosa* by July 1, and the *Huntsville*, 30 days later.

As the war dragged on, Secretary Mallory commandeered the foundry for the navy and assigned Catesby ap R. Jones, late of the CSS *Virginia*, as its superintendent. The Selma Ordnance Works cast and machined Brooke rifles of superior quality during the war, with some calibers measuring as large as ten inches.[4]

In October of 1862, the keel was laid for a third ironclad at the expanded shipyard next to the foundry. She was destined to be the CSS *Tennessee*, and would prove to be one of the most powerful warships ever constructed in the Confederacy. The timber used for her hull and frame came from the surrounding Alabama countryside, and the iron for her armor was mined at nearby Brierfield.[5]

On August 21, 1862, Franklin Buchanan was promoted to the rank of admiral for his "gallant and meritorious conduct" while commanding the *Virginia* in the engagements at Hampton Roads. Later that month, though still limping from his wound received in Virginia, he was given command of all Confederate naval forces in the Mobile area.

Buchanan's primary responsibility, upon taking command, was to hasten the building of the ironclads at Selma. Commander Charles H. McBlair was given the task of overseeing the progress on the *Tuscaloosa* and *Huntsville*, while Buchanan concentrated on the *Tennessee*. With the crusty old admiral controlling the flow of materials to the navy yard, the *Tennessee* progressed smoothly while progress on the other two vessels fell behind. Although McRae had received funds from the Navy Department for the erection of a rolling mill at his foundry, skilled machinists to build the necessary equipment could not be found. With McRae unable to roll the needed plates, Buchanan turned to the Shelby Iron Works, which was about 60 miles away. From Shelby a small supply of plates for the *Tuscaloosa* and the *Huntsville* began to arrive, but the majority of the iron, including all of the plates for the *Tennessee*, was later produced at the Schofield and Markham Works in Atlanta.[6]

As winter approached, the big ironclad on the bluff high above the Alabama River began to take shape. She was, indeed, large. Commander James D. Johnston, who would later serve as her captain, described the basic construction: *She was 209 feet in length and 48 feet in breadth of beam. The shield for the protection of her battery and crew was 78 feet 8 inches long and 8 feet high above the deck, which at each end of the shield was only about 18 inches above the surface of the water when the vessel had been prepared for service. Sponsons of heavy timber projected about five feet from the sides in a*

Commander James D. Johnston. As commander of the CSS *Tennessee*, Johnston faced the painful duty of surrendering the battered ironclad to the surrounding Federal forces.

line with the deck, extending seven feet below it, the lower edge of the shield covering the outer angle or apex of the sponsons. The sides of the shield were of yellow pine and white oak, 23 inches thick, placed at an angle of 33 degrees with the deck.[7] (Other sources have placed the angle of the shield at 45 degrees and the thickness as 25 inches.)

Wanting to take advantage of the high water in the river, Buchanan convinced the builders to launch the *Tennessee* early, even though she was only a covered shell. On Sunday, February 8, 1863, one of the most powerful ironclads built in the Confederacy, slid rapidly down the steep slope into the Alabama River, —and had her first "engagement." Johnston described her launching: *About midday, there was heard the sound of a gun, and immediately afterward the Tennessee was shot into the swift current like an arrow, and the water had risen to such a height that she struck in her course the corner of a brick warehouse, situated on an adjoining bluff and demolishing it. This was her first and only experience as a ram.*[8]

Buchanan had ordered Johnston to take two steamers up river and to tow the *Tennessee* to Mobile as soon as she was launched. It took more than a week for the two steamers, with the *Tennessee* in tow, to make the long trip down the twisting Alabama. The captain of one of these steamers, the splendid *Southern Republic,* alleviated the boredom of the tedious trip by announcing their arrival at each town along the way with several rousing stanzas of "Dixie" played on the ship's ornate calliope.

After arriving at Mobile, the *Tennessee* spent the remainder of the year and into 1864 having her armor, engines, and machinery installed. The iron plates, which were rapidly arriving from Atlanta, were two inches thick, seven inches wide, and twenty-one feet long. Three layers of these plates were attached to the end and sides of the forward part of the casemate, to just aft of the pilothouse. From that point to the aft end of the shield, two layers of two-inch and one layer of one-inch iron plate was secured to the shield. The iron extended two feet below the waterline and then angled back to meet the hull, thus forming a knuckle to protect against enemy rammings. Even the deck, where it was not covered by the casemate, was overlaid with two inches of iron plate. One and one-quarter inch diameter bolts running through to the interior of the casemate, secured the five-to-six inches of iron to the twenty-five inches of wood backing. Nuts and washers secured the bolts on the inside. These would become deadly missiles and cause serious injury to some of the crew when they would be stripped off from the violent concussions of pounding solid shot.[9]

While the iron plates were being laid on the *Tennessee's* shield, her engines and armament arrived. The ironclad's engines most likely came from the river gunboat *Alonzo Child,* which had become stranded up the Yazoo River. Transported overland to the Tombigbee River, they were then floated downstream to Mobile. Since the *Alonzo Child* was a side-wheel steamer, the engines had to be modified to propel the *Tennessee* through a series of gears and shafts. With the shortage of iron a persistent problem, some of the propeller shaft gears were fabricated from wood. The fourteen foot draft and 1,273 ton weight of the ironclad, coupled with the complicated gearing to the propeller, resulted in a top speed of only six knots which was not enough to operate effectively as a ram.[10]

While her engines may have been weak, her armament certainly was not. The *Tennessee's* casemate was pierced with ten gunports, which accommodated six guns. Two 7-inch Brooke rifles, cast by Catesby Jones at the Naval Gun Factory at Selma, were installed in the forward and aft pivot positions. In addition to their field of fire over the bow and stern, they could also be turned to fire out the forward and aft broad-side ports on each side. With the great demand being placed on the gun factory at Selma for Brooke rifles, Jones was unable to supply the broadside guns for the *Tennessee.* In January of 1864, Jones wrote Buchanan informing him of the cause for further delay: *We had an accident which may have been very serious. An explosion took place whilst attempting to cast the bottom section of a gun pit. The foundry took fire, but was promptly extinguished. Fortunately, but two of the molds were burned. I had a narrow escape; my hat, coat, and pants were burned. Quite a loss in these times, with our depreciated currency and fixed salaries. As a large casting is never made without my being present, I consider my life in greater danger here than if I were in command of the Tennessee.*[11]

Four 6.4-inch Brooke rifles, which were cast in Atlanta, were eventually mounted as broadside guns. Each gun port was equipped with wrought iron sliding shutters that were five inches thick and could be opened and closed by a system of chains and pulleys. While these shutters looked good in design, they would prove to be easily jammed after being struck by a shot during battle, rendering the gun at that port completely useless.

Another design problem which soon became evident, was the exposed positioning of the rudder chains which ran along the top of

One of the *Tennessee's* 7-inch Brooke rifles now on display at the Washington Navy Yard, Washington, D.C. The two guns in the background are also from the *Tennessee*.

Author's Collection

the after deck. Buchanan recognized this danger and attempted to hide their presence by having 1-inch sheet iron channels tacked on over them. Still, one shot striking a channel could jam the rudder permanently.[12]

She had taken a long time to complete, and had cost $883,880, but by the end of January, the big ironclad was all but complete. At 9:00 a.m. on the morning of February 16, 1864, she was officially commissioned the CSS *Tennessee*, and her officers were assigned and ordered aboard.[13]

While Buchanan flew his flag from the *Tennessee* as commander of the Confederate Mobile Squadron, the ironclad's actual captain was Commander James D. Johnston of Kentucky. Johnston had resigned from the U.S. Navy on April 10, 1861, and after seeing service at New Orleans, had been given command of the iron and cottonclad steamer *Baltic* at Mobile. By February of 1863, the *Baltic* had been declared unfit for service, and Buchanan, much impressed by Johnston's abilities, ordered him to command the *Tennessee*. Johnston's executive officer was Lieutenant William L. Bradford from Alabama, who had also seen service at New Orleans aboard the gunboats *Jackson* and *Ivy*. Arthur D. Wharton, also from Alabama, was the second lieutenant, and Edward J. McDermett of Texas was third lieutenant. Wharton had earned an excellent record

in Confederate service having served on the *Arkansas* during her courageous fight through the middle of the combined Federal fleets above
Vicksburg. McDermett had been on board the *Louisiana* at the Battle of
New Orleans, and had served on the ram *W. H. Webb* on the Red River.
Destined to be taken prisoner when the *Tennessee* surrendered, he escaped his captors in New Orleans, only to be killed in a minor engagement at Lake Maurepas in the last weeks of the war.[14]

While there were some exceptions, Buchanan complained constantly
about his lack of experienced officers. In a letter to Jones on May 7,
1864, he grumbled that he had *...but few officers, and many of them are
inefficient, and all inexperienced. ...I have neither flag-captain nor flag-lieu-
tenant, nor midshipmen for aide(s); consequently, I have all the various duties
to attend to from the grade of midshipmen up.* Buchanan tried persistently
to get Jones transferred to his command, but Secretary Mallory felt
Jones' service was indispensable at the Selma Gun Factory.[15]

Finding capable seamen to man the vessels of the squadron was an
even greater problem. After countless letters from Buchanan to the government in Richmond asking to have men detailed from the army, 150
men from a Tennessee unit were finally transferred to the ironclad. "Ole
Buck" was not impressed by these men either: *There are on board...these
vessels some of the greatest vagabonds you will ever read of. One or two such
hung during this time would have a wonderful effect.* After the Battle of Mobile Bay, Buchanan would have nothing but praise for his "vagabonds."[16]

In addition to the *Tennessee*, three small gunboats comprised the
Mobile Squadron. They were the *Selma*, a side-wheel steamer armed
with four guns and commanded by First Lieutenant Peter U. Murphey;
the *Gaines*, also a side-wheeler with six guns and commanded by First
Lieutenant John W. Bennett; and the *Morgan*, a side-wheeler with six
guns under the command of Commander George W. Harrison. The
four vessels of the Mobile Squadron, with 22 guns and 470 officers and
men, were destined to face the Federal fleet of Admiral Farragut consisting of 18 warships, mounting 160 guns, and manned by approximately 3,000 officers and men.[18]

Once the *Tennessee* was commissioned, the problem of reaching the
deep water in the lower part of the bay was the major concern of
Buchanan and Johnston. *But as the draught of the vessel was over thirteen
feet,* Johnston wrote, *and there was only nine feet of water on the Dog River
Bar, at the mouth of the Mobile River, it became a serious problem to solve as
to the means of floating her over this bar. Sidney D. Porter, a naval architect,
conceived the idea of building heavy camels or floats, to be made fast to the
sides of the ram; the surfaces in contact with the ram to conform to the model
of the hull; and the camels were to contain a sufficient weight of water to
counter-balance in part the weight of the vessel.*[19]

Because of her deep draft, the *Tennessee* was towed up the Mobile
River, into the Spanish River, and then down to the bar. Workmen

The CSS *Tennessee* prior to the Battle of Mobile Bay. She is accurately depicted here in a wash drawing by artist F. Muller.

began attaching the camels, or caissons, to the sides of the vessel using heavy chains, and when they were finished, the pumping operations began. Unfortunately, the caissons proved to be too small for the heavy ironclad, for she was lifted less than two feet. Writing to Captain John K. Mitchell, chief of the Bureau of Orders and Detail, Buchanan lamented that, *I am doing all I can to get the Tennessee over the bar. ...What folly to build vessels up our rivers which cannot cross the bars at the mouths.* The admiral complained that he would have to go nearly twenty miles down the bay before adequately deep water would be found.[20]

Undaunted by the failure of the caissons to lift the *Tennessee* over the bar, Buchanan ordered Porter to construct six new ones of a larger type. These were almost completed, when at about midnight on April 3, they caught fire, and three were totally destroyed and the others heavily damaged. With grim determination, the workers began building more caissons to replace those that were lost, and with this delay, the *Tennessee* raised anchor on April 5, and steamed back to Mobile. It would be another month before the larger caissons were ready.

By May 17, the *Tennessee* was back at the bar and the larger caissons were chained tightly to her sides. The pumping operation began anew. Slowly the massive ironclad began to rise until, finally, with two steamers towing and her own propeller churning the muddy bottom, the *Tennessee* passed safely over the bar.[21]

With the vessel now in the lower part of the bay, Buchanan hoisted his admiral's flag on the ironclad on May 22 and held a general inspection of the squadron. With the *Tennessee* operational, and counting on the element of surprise, he was determined to attack the Union blockading fleet off the mouth of the channel. President Davis, in fact, had been urging him "to strike the enemy before he establishes himself on the Bay with his land forces."

At sundown on May 23, Johnston mustered the crew on the quarterdeck where the admiral's fighting order was read to them. With enthusiasm for a battle in the squadron at fever pitch, steam was raised during the night, and before daybreak the *Selma*, the *Morgan*, the *Gaines*, the *Tennessee*, and even the leaky old *Baltic*, were under way and headed for the channel. When within three-quarters of a mile of Fort Morgan, the pilots reported that because of the bad weather, the waters of the Gulf appeared to be too rough, and Buchanan was forced to postpone the attack to the following night.

On the following evening when the anchor was raised, it was discovered that, because of the low tide, the ironclad was hard aground. When the Federals discovered the *Tennessee* in the lower bay the next day, the attack was called off.[22]

For the next two months, Buchanan waited, hoping that the additional ironclads would soon be completed. The *Nashville*, which had been built at Montgomery and floated down to Mobile, was nearly ready, but she was ponderously slow with vulnerable side-wheels and was still without her armor. To provide some measure of protection, workmen began stripping the iron plates from the decrepit *Baltic* and attaching them to the *Nashville*. The *Tuscaloosa* and the *Huntsville*, which were no more than floating batteries, were unarmored, and three vessels being built up the Tombigbee were not yet complete. If Farragut chose to attack, Buchanan would have only the *Tennessee* and the three small gunboats with which to challenge the Union fleet.[23]

While watching and waiting for the next two months, the crew was kept busy drilling at the guns and lending what support they could to an occasional blockade runner. The *Tennessee's* log states that on May 26, an unidentified steamer passed by rapidly heading for the Main Shipping Channel and the Gulf. The *Morgan* fired a gun, whereupon the runner *Denbigh* flashed a coded light and proceeded safely to sea. By June 7, she was back from her round trip to Havana, and with heavy firing reported, she sped through the cordon of Union ships undamaged and dropped her anchor off Fort Morgan. The *Denbigh* made one more round trip to Havana, and on July 26, became the last blockade runner to successfully clear the bay.[24]

By the beginning of August, it was clearly evident to the vigilant Confederates that the long expected enemy attack was imminent. *On the evening of the 4th of August, 1964,* wrote Commander Johnston, *it was plainly to be seen that the blockading fleet, which had recently been augmented by the arrival of the heavier wooden vessels and the monitors, was making preparations to attempt the passage of Forts Morgan and Gaines ... and to attack the Confederate squadron. Similar preparations were made by our vessels, which had been anchored just within the bay for nearly three months, in daily expectation of the impending encounter. During the night, a blockade runner entered the bay and was boarded by the executive officer of the Tennessee.*[25] The blockade-runner Johnston referred to was the *Red Gauntlet*. She had arrived, but would never see the blue waters of the Gulf again.

The first streaks of light had begun to appear in the eastern sky. Except for the watch on duty, most of the *Tennessee's* men were still sleeping, but the fragrant aroma coming from the galley stovepipe had awakened some of the hungry crew members. Because of the heat and humidity, Surgeon Daniel B. Conrad had found it impossible to sleep in his cabin. *I had been sleeping on the deck of the admiral's cabin for two or three nights,* he wrote, *when at daybreak, on the 5th of August, the old "quartermaster" came down the ladder, rousing us up with his gruff voice, saying: "Admiral, the officer of the deck bids me report that the enemy's fleet is under way." Jumping up, still half asleep, we came on deck, and sure enough, there was the enemy heading for the "passage" past the fort. The grand old admiral of sixty years, with his countenance rigid and stern, showing a determination for battle in every line, then gave his only order: "Get under way, Captain Johnston; head for the leading vessel of the enemy, and fight each one as they pass us."*[26]

The Federal fleet steaming slowly toward the channel in the dim early morning light, consisted of seven sloops-of-war in line astern, each with a smaller gunboat lashed to their port sides. First in line was the *Brooklyn* and the *Octorara*; followed by the *Hartford* (Farragut's flagship) and the *Metacomet*; the *Richmond* and the *Port Royal* were next; followed by the *Lackawanna* and the *Seminole*; then the *Ossipee* and the *Itasca*; and finally, the *Oneida* and the *Galena*. Off their starboard side between Fort Morgan and them, and also in line astern, steamed the four iron turreted monitors, the *Tecumseh*, the *Manhattan*, the *Winnebago*, and the *Chickasaw*.

Doctor Daniel B. Conrad, surgeon of the CSS *Tennessee*. Conrad found the wounded Buchanan doubled up against the shield on the smoking gun deck. Hoisting him on his soldiers, he carried the admiral to safety below.

Farragut also sent four small gunboats to the southeast of Fort Morgan to harass the garrison from the flank. Five light draft gunboats were ordered into Grant's Pass to fire on Fort Powell. Meanwhile, a Union ground force, which had landed on the western end of Dauphin Island two days before, was positioned to open fire with heavy artillery on Fort Gaines.[27]

As Buchanan continued to watch from the top of the *Tennessee*, the cables were slipped, and all stations reported ready for action. Descending to the gun deck, he addressed the assembled crew: *Now men, the enemy is coming, and I want you to do you duty; and you shall not have to say when you leave this vessel that you were not near enough to the enemy, for I shall meet them, and then you can fight them alongside of their own ships; and if I fall, lay me on the side and go on with the fight until you sink yourselves, but do not surrender.*[28]

The enemy ships were just about to enter the channel when a puff of dirty white smoke enshrouded the lead monitor, *Tecumseh*. The gunners in the fort watched as the big 15-inch shell appeared to scream directly toward each of them. With a tremendous crash, the monster exploded over the center compound of the fort, and at the same instant, scores of

Union and Confederate lanyards were pulled. The roar and thunder of heavy naval guns tore through the atmosphere, piercing and shattering the early morning silence. With the first thunderous discharges, flocks of frightened waterfowl rose from the water and along the shoreline. The action became more intensified as one by one, additional guns of Fort Morgan rumbled to life, sending their deadly missiles hurtling toward the approaching Federal fleet.

By now, Johnston had the *Tennessee* under way, and the *Gaines*, the *Morgan*, and the *Selma* moved into line abreast and slightly to the rear on her starboard quarter. Buchanan's plan was to steam his squadron across the channel, just inside the obstructions and torpedoes, and to rake the head of the Union column once it passed the hurricane of fire coming from the fort. He was determined to hold the *Tennessee's* fire until the enemy vessels had closed to within point-blank range, and had ordered Johnston to inform Wharton, who commanded the first gun division, "not to fire until the vessels are in actual contact." "Aye, aye, sir!" Wharton shouted as his fingers tightened on the lockstring of the bow pivot rifle.[29]

Fort Morgan's firing was becoming heavier and more accurate, as still more of her guns opened on the advancing Federals. The Union gunners, their vessels partially hidden by a dense cloud of white smoke that drifted toward the fort on a southwest breeze, courageously returned the fire with a vengeance. As the Federal monitors neared the obstructions, the *Tennessee* moved slowly across the channel to just west of the buoy, marking the beginning of the torpedoes. Her gunners were still nervously awaiting the order to open fire. Commander T. A. M. Craven of the *Tecumseh*, which was the lead Federal monitor, seeing the *Tennessee* cross his front, began edging to port, crossed in front of the *Brooklyn*, and headed straight for the Confederate ironclad. Unfortunately, he turned outside of the buoy and was now headed directly across the torpedo field.

Just as the *Tecumseh* was about to open fire on the *Tennessee*, there was a tremendous explosion, and the Federal monitor disappeared briefly behind a huge geyser of water. A Confederate torpedo had exploded against her bow, and within seconds, her forward section was beneath the waves. Her stern rose high into the air, and horrified onlookers watched aghast as she quickly went down with her exposed propeller still turning. In two minutes, there was nothing but steam and giant air bubbles where the *Tecumseh* had once been. Out of the 114 officers and men on board, only 21 scrambled out alive. Commander Craven was not among them.[30]

There was dead silence on board the Tennessee, Surgeon Conrad wrote; *the men peered through the port holes at the awful catastrophe, and spoke to each other only in low whispers; for they knew that the same fate was probably awaiting us, for we were then directly over the torpedo bed, and shut up tightly as we were in our iron capsule, in another moment it might prove to be our coffin.*[31] For a moment, all firing stopped, but soon it began anew. In Fort Morgan, General Page ordered his gunners to aim away from the spot where boats were picking up the pitifully few survivors.

By now the *Tennessee's* guns had roared to life sending their well-aimed Brooke shells crashing into the head of the Union column. The *Selma,* the *Gaines,* and the *Morgan* also opened fire causing heavy damage and many injuries on the enemy vessels. At this moment, the commander of the *Brooklyn*, the lead sloop-of-war, spotted what to him looked like torpedoes ahead, and he ordered his engines reversed. For a few minutes, the entire Union line was thrown into confusion, but Farragut courageously ordered the *Hartford* to take the lead, and the commander's flagship charged past the *Brooklyn*.

The *Hartford,* turning to avoid the *Brooklyn,* crossed the torpedo field, and Buchanan, seeing her slight change of course, ordered the *Tennessee* to ram her. With faulty torpedo primers snapping against the *Hartford's* bottom, the faster Union ship plowed through the water and easily maneuvered away from the charging ironclad. The Confederate's guns, however, poured in a devastating fire as she steamed past. Lieutenant Wharton was confident that his bow pivot could sink the *Hartford*. When the Union flagship pulled ahead of the *Brooklyn*, she passed across the *Tennessee's* bow no more than 200 yards away. *I took the lock-string from the captain of the gun myself, took a long deliberate aim, and gave the commands: 'Raise,' 'Steady,' 'Raise a little more,' 'Ready,' 'Fire!' I was as confident that our shell would tear a hole in the Hartford's side big enough to sink her in a few minutes as I was that I had fired it. It did tear the hole expected, but it was above the water-line. ...I have often speculated since upon the effect of not having raised the breech of our bow gun, and thus caused that shell to ricochet before striking the Hartford. I wish I had let the captain of the gun fire the piece himself.*[32]

In addition to the many guns of Fort Morgan aimed at her, the fire of the *Tennessee* and the three Confederate gunboats was now concentrated on the *Hartford*, and her decks were beginning to resemble a slaughterhouse. *The sight on deck was sickening beyond the power of words to portray,* wrote Signal Officer John C. Kinney. *Shot after shot came through the side, mowing down the men, deluging the decks with blood, and scattering mangled fragments of humanity so thickly that it was difficult to stand on deck. ...The bodies of the dead were placed in a long row on the port side, while the wounded were sent below until the surgeon's quarters would hold no more. A solid shot coming through the bow struck a gunner in the neck, completely severing head from body. One poor fellow lost both legs by a cannon ball; as he fell (he) threw up both arms, just in time to have them also carried away by another shot. At one gun, all the crew on one side were swept down by a shot which came crashing through the bulwarks. A shell burst between the two forward guns in charge of Lieutenant Tyson, killing and wounding 15 men. The mast upon which the writer was perched was twice struck, once slightly, and again just below the foretop by a heavy shell, by a rifle on the Confederate gunboat Selma. Fortunately, the shell came tumbling end over end, and buried itself in the mast, butt-end first, leaving the percussion cap protruding.*[33]

With the *Hartford* steaming on into the bay, Buchanan turned the *Tennessee* toward the *Brooklyn*, which had taken the second position in the Federal line. From the pilothouse, Johnston called down to the engine room and ordered full power in order to ram the Federal. Black smoke poured from the *Tennessee's* funnel, and tongues of orange-red flame streaked from her guns as she charged toward the *Brooklyn*. Again the superior speed of the Union ships displayed itself as the Federal vessel avoided a collision. The *Tennessee*, meanwhile, shuddered from a tremendous broadside fired by the *Brooklyn*, which slammed into the Confederate ironclad's armored casemate.

While the three Confederate gunboats steamed in front of the Federal column, firing on them with their stern guns, Buchanan turned the *Tennessee's* prow toward the next enemy in the line. This was the *Richmond*, and while the ironclad's guns sent their shells crashing into her, causing fearful carnage on board, the *Richmond* was also able to avoid the armored ram of the *Tennessee*. The *Lackawanna* and the *Monongahela* charged past, and they, too, felt the effect of the *Tennessee's* flaming guns.[34]

The last in line of Farragut's heavy wooden ships was the *Oneida*, with the gunboat *Galena* lashed to her port side. The Federal vessel had taken a beating from the guns of Fort Morgan, one shell having exploded in her boiler, killing or scalding all of her firemen and coal heavers. Totally disabled, she was dragged along by the *Galena* which remained undamaged. Buchanan drove the *Tennessee* along her side as she passed by and attempted to deliver a fatal broadside, but his gunners cursed and swore as faulty primers failed to fire the guns. Swinging around the *Oneida's* stern, the *Tennessee's* guns finally roared sending more death and destruction on board the stricken enemy vessel, but failing to sink her.

By the time the *Oneida* plowed past, the *Tennessee* had been in action for over an hour. While she had delivered devastating broadsides at the Union ships and had caused much damage, she had failed to stop them. The *Tennessee*, too, had been rocked by the heavy shells of the Federals. Fortunately, her armor plate had withstood the test; nothing had penetrated the shield, although some men had been wounded by small arms' fire that came through open gun ports. Outside, on the fore and after decks, everything had been swept away. Surgeon Conrad wrote that the Federal's *...fire was so destructive, continuous and severe that after we emerged*

*from it there was nothing left standing as large as your little finger. Every-
thing had been shot away, smokestacks, stanchions, boat devits, and in fact,
fore and aft, our deck had been swept absolutely clean. A few of our men
were slightly wounded, and when the last vessel had passed us and been
fought in turn, we had been in action more than an hour and a half; and then
the enemy's fleet, somewhat disabled, of course, kept on up the bay, and
anchored about four miles away—so ended the first part of the fight.*[35]

When Farragut observed that his line of ships were safely past the
torpedoes and the guns of Fort Morgan, he signaled for his gunboats
to be cast loose. Ordered to dispose of the three Confederate vessels
which were still causing so much havoc to the Federal fleet, the Union
vessels charged after the *Gaines*, the *Selma*, and the *Morgan* with grim
determination. Soon the *Gaines* was hulled below the waterline, and
another shell exploded in her hold flooding the magazine. With the
vessel sinking rapidly, Lieutenant Bennett ordered the helmsman to
steer for the protection of Fort Morgan. Hidden by a sudden passing
rain shower, the *Gaines* was beached approximately 500 yards from
the fort and set on fire. Later that night, using the ship's boats, the
crew silently rowed through the assembled Federal warships and
reached Mobile safely the next morning.[36]

With her engine pounding at full throttle, the *Selma*, under Lieutenant Murphy, had maintained her position off the starboard bow of
the *Hartford*, all the while delivering a blistering fire against her. Now,
however, the *Metacomet*, one of the fastest gunboats in the fleet, was
cast loose, and with her giant paddle wheels churning the waters,
charged after her. Within minutes she opened fire with her 9-inch guns
at close range, instantly killing six men and wounding seven others on
the *Selma*. Two of the *Selma's* four guns were disabled, and the gunboat's
deck was littered with debris and bloody body parts. With other Union
vessels closing in and being virtually surrounded, Murphy fired one
last defiant salvo from his two remaining guns and struck his flag.[37]

Lieutenant Harrison had maintained a position off the Federal
column's starboard front with the *Morgan* and had assisted the *Selma*
in her running fight with the *Hartford*. When the Federal gunboats were
cast loose, the *Morgan* turned her attention to the pursuing *Metacomet*,
but shortly Harrison disengaged and steamed for Fort Morgan. Later
that night, under heavy fire, the *Morgan* raced up the bay through the
Federal fleet to the protection of Mobile. Buchanan would bitterly censure
Harrison later for not being more aggressive during the passage of the
Federal fleet into the bay. A court of inquiry subsequently ordered by
Mallory, however, eventually exonerated Harrison from any blame.[38]

Meanwhile, by about 9:00 a.m., the bulk of the Federal fleet had
anchored about four miles up the bay, and while the wounded were

administered to, the rest of the exhausted Federal sailors were "sent to breakfast." Buchanan had ordered Johnston to make a slow, wide turn in the channel, and the *Tennessee* was now headed in the direction of Fort Morgan, while her officers assessed the condition of the ironclad. Surgeon Conrad graphically described this brief respite, and the reasons for Buchanan's decision to resume the fight:

Neither the officers or men of either fleet had as yet been to breakfast, and the order was given, "Go to breakfast!" For us on the Tennessee to eat below was simply impossible, on account of the heat and humidity. The heat below was terrific; intense thirst universally prevailed. The men rushed to the scuttlebutts, or water tanks and drank greedily. Soon "hard tack" and coffee were furnished, the men all eating standing, creeping out the ports on the after deck to get a little fresh air, the officers going to the upper deck.

Admiral Buchanan, grim, silent, and rigid with prospective fighting, was "stumping" up and down the deck, lame from a wound received in his first engagement in the Virginia, and in about fifteen minutes we observed that instead of heading for the safe lee of the fort, our iron prow was pointed for the enemy's fleet. Suppressed exclamations were beginning to be heard from the officers and crew: "The old admiral has not had his fight out yet; he is heading for that big fleet; he will get his fill of it up there!"

Conrad, as surprised as anyone, continued his narrative: *Slowly and gradually this fact became apparent to us, and I, being on his staff and in close association with him, ventured to ask him, "Are you going into that fleet, admiral?" "I am sir!" was his reply. Without intending to be heard by him, I said to an officer standing near me, "Well, we'll never come out of there whole!" But Buchanan had heard my remark, and turning around said sharply, "That's my lookout, sir!" And now began the second part of the fight.*

Ever since the smoke cleared over Mobile Bay, historians have debated the reasoning of Buchanan in choosing to attack the entire Federal fleet single-handedly after their passage into the bay. The crusty old admiral was, no doubt, determined that the *Tennessee* would not be abandoned and have to suffer the same fate as his first command, the *Virginia*. Surgeon Conrad, who accompanied Buchanan to the Federal hospital at Pensacola after the battle, explained: *He told me his reasons long afterwards as follows: He had only six hours' coal on board, and he intended to expend that in fighting. He did not mean to be trapped like a rat in a hole, and made to surrender without a struggle! Then he meant to go to the lee of the fort and assist General Payne in the defense of the place. This calculation was unluckily prevented by the shooting away of the rudder chains of the Tennessee in this second engagement.*[39]

With smoke pouring from her funnel, Johnston now had the *Tennessee* plowing through the swells of the bay toward the startled Federal fleet. The call to quarters sounded on the Confederate ironclad.

Galley fires were hurriedly extinguished and the magazines re-opened. Biscuits and coffee were quickly gobbled down as the men clambered back inside through the gunports and rushed to their guns. Down below, sweating coal heavers and firemen, black from coal dust, feverishly shoveled more coal into the already roaring furnace. With steam hissing through the valves and engine gauges quivering at the red line, the *Tennessee* pounded toward the enemy.

As we approached the enemy's fleet, Conrad wrote, *one after another of Farragut's ten wooden frigates swept out in a wide circle, and by the time we reached the point where the monitors were, a huge leading frigate* (the 1,278 ton *Monongahela*) *was coming at the rate of ten miles an hour, a column of white foam formed of the dead water piled in front of its bow many feet high.* With thirty feet of deck fore and aft of the casemate, and only 18 inches above the water, the Federals were convinced that they could sink the ironclad by simply running up on her and forcing her under.

Heavy cannonading from the monitors was going on at this time, Conrad continued, *when the leading wooden vessel came rapidly bearing down on us, bent on the destruction of the formidable ram, which we on board of the Tennessee fully realized as the supreme moment of the test of our strength. We had escaped from the torpedo bed safe and on top, and were now to take our chances of being run under by the heavy wooden frigates that were fast nearing us.*[40]

Just before impact, two of the *Tennessee's* guns roared sending their 6-inch shells crashing into the *Monongahela's* starboard bow and exploding in her berth deck. The Federal responded, but her 11-inch shells splintered into a thousand fragments against the Tennessee's armor. Conrad recalled, *Captain Johnston, in the pilot house, gave the word to officers and men: "Steady yourselves when she strikes! Stand by and be ready!" Not a word was heard on the deck, under its shelving roof, where the officers and men, standing by their guns, silent and rigid, awaited their fate.*[41]

Johnston had ordered the ironclad's wheel turned hard aport moments before the collision, and the onrushing Union warship struck at a slightly oblique angle. With a shattering crash the *Monongahela* rammed the *Tennessee,* and in spite of Johnston's warning, threw the ironclad's crew sprawling to the deck. *The Tennessee,* wrote Lieutenant Wharton, *yielded to the impact, and spun swiftly around as upon a pivot. I felt as if I were going through the air. "What is the matter, Captain Johnston?" I asked. "We've been rammed, sir," was the response from the pilot house where he stood.*[42]

The *Monongahela* sheered off and Conrad wrote that *Captain Johnston then shouted out: "We are all right! They can never run us under now!"* The Federal's iron prow had been wrenched off and carried away, while the *Tennessee,* though shaken, appeared unharmed. Scrambling to their feet, the ironclad's gunners were able to fire two of their broadside guns, sending their shells exploding deep into the *Monongahela's* interior as she scraped alongside.

The *Monongahela* had no more than cleared the *Tennessee's* side, when the 1,533 ton *Lackawanna* slammed into the ironclad at right angles near the aft end of her casemate. Again the *Tennessee's* gunners were sent sprawling. As the shaken Union ship backed away, two of the *Tennessee's* shells slammed into her twisted and leaking stem. The two vessels now swung bow to stern alongside each other and continued to trade horrendous broadsides at a distance of 12 feet. A nine-inch shot from the Union ship crashed into a port shutter on the *Tennessee*, jamming it, and driving spinning fragments the length of the casemate.

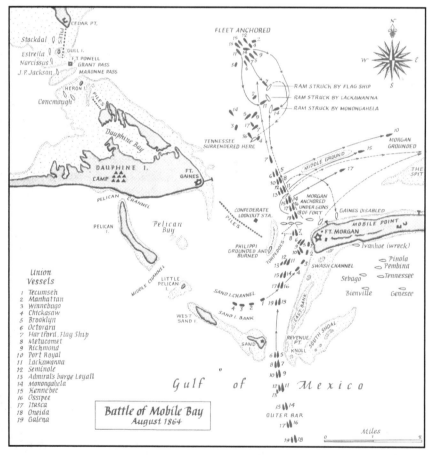

A map drawn from the chart which accompanied Admiral Farragut's official report, depicts the course and position of the individual vessels of his squadron as they entered Mobile Bay. The top portion of the chart illustrates the final engagement with the CSS *Tennessee*.

Federal marines fired muskets through the ironclad's open ports, and even hurled a spittoon and a holystone through the openings. The *Lackawanna* broke away and circled for another attack.[43]

Buchanan shouted for Johnston to set his course for the Federal flagship that was rapidly approaching. Amid the smoke of flaming guns and belching engines, the 1,273-ton *Tennessee* and the 2,900-ton *Hartford* charged bows at each other like two infuriated animals. With a bone-jarring crash, they collided just off their port bows. Sliding past, the two antagonists grated against one another, as the *Hartford* fired her entire port battery. The nine-inch shots struck the *Tennessee's* casemate, rebounded high in the air, and splashed into the turbulent waters of the bay. At the same instant, the *Tennessee's* gunners snapped their lanyards, but faulty primers again plagued the Confederates, and only one gun fired. That gun sent a shell ripping through the *Hartford's* berth deck, where it exploded, killing five men and wounding eight more. Red hot fragments continued spinning through the spar and lower decks, smashing a launch and injuring more men.[44]

Tending the wounded as they streamed below, Surgeon Conrad on the *Tennessee* wrote that, *Engineer Rogers, of the wounded, had a pistol ball through his shoulder. "How in the world did you manage to get this?" I asked him. He replied: "Why, I was off watch and had nothing to do, so while the Hartford was lying alongside of us a Yankee cursed me through the port-hole and I jabbed him with my bayonet in the body, and his comrade shot me with his revolver."*[45]

The *Hartford* now began a circle with the intent of making another run, and in so doing, she collided with the onrushing *Lackawanna*. The flagship stopped to inspect the damage, but the *Lakawanna* continued on, striking the *Tennessee* another shuddering blow. Conrad wrote of these constant rammings: *At the moment of impact they slid alongside of us, and our black wales came in contact. At a distance of ten feet they poured their broadsides of twenty eleven-inch guns into us. This continued for more than an hour, and as each vessel "rammed" the Tennessee and slid alongside, they followed, discharging their broadsides fast and furious, so that the noise was one continuous, deafening roar. You could only hear voices when spoken close to the ear, and the reverberation was so great that bleeding at the nose was not infrequent.*[46]

With their prows shattered and torn, the wooden ships now withdrew slightly, allowing the monitors to creep in close and hurl their huge 11 and 15-inch shells against the *Tennessee*. Johnston received word from Buchanan to steer for Fort Morgan, but it was too late. *At this time,* Johnston wrote, *it was reported to me that the wheel chains had been carried away; and, ordering the relieving tackles to be used, I made a personal examination of the broken chain to ascertain if it could be repaired.*

This was found to be impossible, without sending men outside of the shield to expose themselves several minutes to the fire of the enemy's vessels, by which the after-deck (over which the chains lead) was closely watched and constantly swept until the close of the action.[47]

By the time Johnston had made his way back to the pilothouse, the relieving tackles also had been shot away, and the tiller unshipped from the rudder head. With her smokestack down from the constant rammings, draft to the furnace was destroyed, and steam pressure had dropped to where the big ironclad's propeller was barely turning. The *Tennessee*, unable to steer, and with engine power failing was now nothing more than a floating target. Still, her sweating gunners continued to fire whenever they could bring one of their guns to bear.

The three Federal monitors took up positions near the hapless *Tennessee* and began to batter away at her iron shield. Lieutenant Wharton described the effects of their fire: *The Monongahela was hardly clear of us when a hideous-looking monster came creeping up on our port side, whose slowly revolving turret revealed the cavernous depth of a mammoth gun. "Stand clear of the port side!" I shouted. A moment after, a thundering report shook us all, while a blast of dense, suphurous smoke covered our portholes, and 440 pounds of iron, impelled by 60 pounds of powder, admitted daylight through our side where, before it struck us, there had been over two feet of solid wood, covered with five inches of solid iron. This was the only 15-inch shot which hit us fairly. It did not come through; the inside netting caught the splinters, and there were no causalities from it. I was glad to find myself alive after that shot.*[48]

With the *Manhattan* and the *Winnebago* taking up positions on either side, the commander of the *Chickasaw* moved in close on the *Tennessee's* stern and concentrated the fire of his 11-inch guns on the aft end of the casemate, delivering 52 accurate shots by the time the action ended. *In the midst of this continuous pounding,* Conrad wrote, *the port-shutter of one of our guns was jammed by a shot, so that it could neither open nor shut, making it impossible to work the piece. The admiral then sent for some of the firemen from below, to drive the bolt outward. Four men came up, and two of them holding the bolt back, the others struck it with sledgehammers. While they were thus standing there, suddenly there was a dull sounding impact, and at the same instant the men whose backs were against the shield were split in pieces. I saw their limbs and chests, severed and mangled, scattered about the deck, their hearts lying near their bodies. All of the gun's crew and the admiral were covered from head to foot with blood, flesh, and viscera. ...The fragments and members of the dead men were shoveled up, put in buckets and hammocks, and struck below.*[49]

During this period, the monitors continued to pound the *Tennessee* for nearly a half an hour, while the Confederate ironclad was unable to bring a single gun to bear. While attending the wounded, Conrad remembered, *an aide came down the ladder in great haste and said: "Doctor,* the admiral is wounded!" "Well, bring him below," I replied. "I can't do it," he answered; "I haven't time. I am carrying orders for captain Johnston." So up I went; asked some officer whom I saw: "Where is the admiral?" "Don't know," he replied. "We are all at work loading and firing. Got too much to do to think of anything else." Then I looked for the gallant commander myself, and lying curled up under the sharp angle of the roof, I discovered the old white-haired man. He was grim, silent, and uttered no sound in his great pain. I went up to him and asked: "Admiral, are you badly hurt?" "Don't know," he replied; but I saw one of his legs crushed up under his body, and, as I could get no help, raised him up with great caution and, clasping his arms around my neck, carried him on my back down the ladder to the cock-pit, his broken leg slapping against me as I moved slowly along. After I applied a temporary bandage he sat up on the deck and received reports from Captain Johnston regarding the progress of the fight.[50]

Johnston now received word that Buchanan was wounded, and he hurried through the smoking gun deck and down the ladder to see him. *The admiral sent for me,* he wrote, *and as I approached he quietly remarked, "Well, Johnston, They've got me. You'll have to look out for her now. This is your fight, you know." I replied, "all right, sir. I'll do the best I know how."* Johnston picked his way back to the pilothouse, but by now there was not much he could do. The Federal monitors were mercilessly pounding the aft end of the casemate which was threatening to cave in at any moment. With no steerage and little power, the *Tennessee* was not even able to stem the tide which was running at four miles per hour. Gun crews were becoming demoralized from not being able to fire at their tormentors because of jammed shutters. Johnston soon returned to the wounded admiral's side.

Realizing the impossibility of directing the firing of the guns without the use of the rudder, and that the ship had been rendered utterly helpless, I went to the lower deck and informed the admiral of her condition, and that I had not been able to bring a gun to bear upon any of our antagonists for nearly half an hour, to which he replied: "Well, Johnston, if you cannot do them any further damage, you had better surrender." Johnston hurried back to the pilothouse once more to make a another assessment of the situation. Squinting through the viewing slits he could see off the port quarter, the 1,240-ton *Ossipee* circling wide and gaining speed in preparation for a ramming attack. The *Chickasaw* and the two other monitors were continuing to batter the aft end of the shield, and if it were to fall, the casemate would become a death trap. Johnston acted quickly, and in his report to Buchanan, afterwards, he explained his decision:

Realizing our helpless condition at a glance, and conceiving that the ship was now nothing more than a target for the heavy guns of the enemy, I concluded that no good object could be accomplished by sacrificing the lives of

The CSS *Tennessee*, her smokestack gone and her flag down, is surrendered to overwhelming Federal forces, in this famous painting by J. O. Davidson. Note the twin-turreted *Chickasaw* to the right whose guns battered the rear of the *Tennessee's* casemate.

the officers and men in such a one-sided contest, and therefore proceeded to the top of the shield and took down the ensign which had been seized on the handle of a gun-scraper, and stuck up through the grating. While in the act, several shots passed close to me, and when I went below to order the engines to be stopped the firing of the enemy was continued. I then decided, although with an almost bursting heart, to hoist the white flag, and returning again on to the shield, placed it in the same spot where but a few moments before had floated the proud flag for whose honor I would so cheerfully have sacrificed my own life, if I could possibly have become the only victim; but at the same time it would have been impossible to destroy the ship without the certain loss of many valuable lives, your own among the number.[51]

With the appearance of the white flag, which was in reality a pocket handkerchief, all firing stopped. The commander of the onrushing *Ossipee*, on seeing the surrender signal, ordered his engines reversed, but the momentum still caused a final jarring blow to be delivered to the battered *Tennessee*. As the smoke of battle began to drift away, and sunshine streamed brightly through the grating of the gun deck roof, the dazed and exhausted men of the CSS *Tennessee* realized that after over four hours of constant fighting, the Battle of Mobile Bay was finally over.

Through the sheer determination of Admiral Farragut and his commanders, and the magnificent courage of the Federal sailors, the Union fleet was now in Mobile Bay,—however they had paid a terrible price. In addition to the monitor *Tecumseh*, in which 93 men went to a watery grave, the *Hartford* had 25 killed and 28 wounded; the *Brooklyn* accounted for 11 killed with 43 wounded; the *Lackawanna* listed only 4 men killed, yet had 35 wounded, and the *Oneida* had 8 killed and 30 wounded. The remainder of the vessels in the Federal fleet contributed 5 additional deaths and 34 others wounded. Total recorded Federal causalities were 146 killed and 170 wounded.

Confederate casualties, considering the forces arrayed against them, were surprisingly light. The little *Selma* suffered the most, with 8 killed and 7 wounded. The *Gaines* counted 2 dead and 3 wounded, while the *Morgan* had only one injured man on board. The builders of the *Tennessee* could be justifiably proud of the sturdy casemate that they had constructed. Out of a total complement of 190 men and officers on board, and after hours of constant pounding by the heaviest naval guns known to man, she counted but 2 killed and 9 wounded. Total Confederate casualties were 12 dead and 20 wounded.

While casualty figures are gruesome statistics, the numbers in this case illustrate that a tenacious Confederate naval force, consisting of only one ironclad and three small gunboats, had courageously delivered more than they had received. Some of the Federal casualties, to be sure, were inflicted by the guns of Fort Morgan. But the majority of the damage done to the Union fleet came from the roaring guns of the Confederate navy.[52]

The CSS *Tennessee* after her capture by Farragut's forces. She was photographed here in Mobile Bay with her awnings spread, and the United States flag flying from her stern.

Chapter Ten

The Overland Torpedo Expedition

Friday, February 23, 1865, dawned cold and overcast in Virginia. For the 120 Confederate sailors and marines stumbling into formation at Drewry's Bluff along the James River, below Richmond, it must have seemed especially dreary.[1] The navy's attempt to break through the obstructions in the river, and to attack the Federal fleet downstream had recently failed. Two of the Confederate ironclads, the *Virginia II* and the *Richmond*, had run aground before they could pass the obstructions, and with the element of surprise gone, the mission had to be aborted.[2]

After almost four long years of war, time was quickly running out for the Confederacy. With Sherman approaching from the south, and Grant's multitudes stretching Lee's lines to the breaking point, it was time for reckless action. When volunteers from the James River Squadron were requested, more than enough had stepped forward. A few men from local army units in the area were also present. Only when navy Lieutenant Charles W. Read, commander of the expedition, explained his plan, did they realize just how desperate things had become.[3]

If anyone could accomplish the impossible, it would be Lieutenant Read, who, along with other officers, was now personally inspecting every man's revolver and cutlass. After his service as a gunnery officer on the *Arkansas*, Read had joined Maffitt on the cruiser *Florida* and had been taken captive in the abortive *Caleb Cushing* affair in Portland,

159

Lieutenant Charles W. Read, shown here in his cadet uniform upon graduation from the United States Naval Academy at Annapolis, in 1860. Except for the traitor Lewis, Read did not lose a man nor beast on his mission behind Grant's army.

Maine. Exchanged in October of the previous year, he had spent an agonizing time as a prisoner of war at Fort Warren in Boston Harbor. His plan, now, was to transport four boats overland, traveling southwest of Petersburg beyond Grant's left flank, and gain the rear of the Union army. Once behind the Federals, he would turn his command east and continue on a course that would take them completely around the Union forces, cross the Blackwater River, and attempt to hit the James River somewhere in Surry or Prince George County.

After reaching the river, they planned to conceal themselves along its marshy banks until an opportunity presented itself to capture one or more of the Union tugs that were constantly passing up and down the river. Perhaps they might even be able to seize a Federal transport lying at anchor in Burwell's Bay. If this could be accomplished, they would then affix torpedo booms to the tugs and steam up the river to attack the Union vessels at Grant's huge supply base at City Point. At the same time, upon a signal from Read, the James River Squadron would break through the obstructions, and attack down the river. If the Federal fleet could be driven out of the James, Grant would lose his base at City Point and be forced to abandon his death grip on the Army of Northern Virginia. A desperate mission, perhaps, but it was time for such desperation.[4]

Master W. Frank Shippey, the commander of the small gunboat CSS *Raleigh* of the James River Squadron, kept a log during the expedition, and he wrote of the many dangers they expected to encounter: *The expedition was a hazardous one from its incipiency, the enemy having declared their determination to show no mercy to prisoners taken on torpedo service. We had to operate in the rear of Grant's army—a handful of men, with an army of one hundred and fifty thousand between us and our friends—and every man on the expedition fully understood and appreciated the danger we ran. If we were successful in reaching the James River our dangers would have but just commenced, as we would have to board and capture an unsuspicious craft, of whose fitness for our purpose we would have to judge from appearances at long range; the capture might attract attention of the men-of-war and make us the captured*

An engraving depicts the failed effort of the Confederate James River Squadron to force its way past the obstructions at Trent's Reach on January 23, 1865. It was this failure which led to Read's desperate overland mission.

Harper's Weekly

instead of the captors, or our plan discovered, we would have a long way to retreat in order to reach a place of safety. Added to these difficulties, the weather was very cold, the roads rough, and the path before us a 'terra incognito.'[5]

That Read was confident of success, however, was illustrated by one of his letters written to a member of the expedition not long after the war: *I am sure before they could possibly have known what was going on I could have run alongside and boarded a gunboat with my men, and, having thus captured the first gunboat, with this gunboat and my torpedoes, I could easily have sunk the rest of the gunboats ... My plans were made known to General Lee, and were also approved by President Davis himself.*[6]

The navy and Marine Corps veterans shivering in ranks on this bleak February morning were determined to carry out this plan. With the inspection finished, four wagons, each pulled by four mules, were driven up in front of the group. The wagon beds had been removed, leaving only the axles and wheels. A whaleboat was chocked in place onto each wagon frame, and spars, torpedoes, rations, and various other provisions were loaded aboard.

In mid-January, Lieutenant John Lewis had been dispatched to reconnoiter the route that Read intended to take. Lewis was to meet them at a ford on the Blackwater River, southeast of Petersburg, and guide them on to the James. With inspections concluded and everything loaded, Read and his men were ready to move out.[7]

Taking the rough frozen road south, the caravan left Drewry's Bluff, heading for Petersburg. Read, along with his second in command,

The CSS *Richmond* of the James River Squadron. At the time of Read's overland expedition, she was under the command of Raphael Semmes' former executive officer, Lieutenant John McIntosh Kell. Many of Read's volunteers were sailors from the *Richmond*.

Lieutenant William H. Ward, took the lead along with all of his sailors. Because most of these were crewmen from the ironclads that patrolled the James, marching over the winter roads would not be easy. Some may have reflected that serving on an ironclad warship in winter with steam up, while boring duty, meant that at least they could stay warm. Because of the nature of their expedition, five first-class engineers and five first-class firemen had been ordered to accompany the mission. They would be needed to operate the engines of the captured Federal vessels.[8] About one hundred yards behind the sailors, came the wagon train commanded by Master Shippey, whose logbook contains the only complete account of this naval expedition. Behind the wagons, and acting as a rear guard, was a detachment of Confederate Marines under the command of Lieutenant James T. Thurston, CSMC.[9] It is amusing to speculate what the grizzled veterans of Lee's army thought of the sight they were witnessing. Trudging along the frozen road through their midst were men in sailors' uniforms armed with cutlasses and revolvers. Mule teams dragged their boats behind them, followed by gray-coated marines carrying knapsacks and muskets. No doubt, some of Lee's ragged men shouted, "Hey boys! — The water's that way!" Despite the jibes, however, each man knew, that if he succeeded, these army comrades would soon be singing their praises.

The weather, after such a gloomy beginning, had turned out bright and sunny, and the men made good time over the frozen Virginia roads. Arriving in Petersburg, Read turned his little band southwest out the Boydton Plank Road. By evening, they had reached General Richard Anderson's headquarters on the right flank of the Confederate lines southwest of Petersburg. It had been a good start.[10]

The following morning, February 4, the expedition left Anderson's lines and continued trudging out the Boydton Plank Road. After a few miles they passed through the Confederate picket line, and they were now very much on their own. About ten miles southwest of Petersburg, just past Burgess Mills, Read turned their faces southeast. Keeping to unpopulated rural roads, the tired sailors and marines marched another fourteen miles before halting for the night. They were now well behind the Union lines. Fortunately, no Federal stragglers or foraging parties had been encountered. *Indeed,* Shippey wrote, *we were out of the line of travel, the Federals did all their business at City Point, and there was little more to attract anyone to this part of the country than to the Siberian deserts.* With high spirits and aching muscles, the men bivouacked for the night.[11]

Getting an early start the next day, Sunday, February 5, Read pressed his command forward over the rough country roads. The weather was clear and they made good time. Occasionally, however, someone would give an alarm that "Yankees" had been spotted, and the whole command would take to the woods. Fortunately, these all proved false, and they continued to move on. The wagon wheels clattered over the frozen ground as the sailors and marines, not being accustomed to long marches, began to feel the pain. At 9:00 p.m. that night they made camp, having covered an estimated thirty miles, a good day's march even for seasoned troops. When they built their campfires that night to cook their meager rations, it was with the realization that they were now deep within enemy-occupied territory.

The following day was uneventful, and other than an occasional alarm which caused them to take cover in the woods, the command moved along at a good pace. Fair weather continued, and they covered fifteen miles before camping near Wakefield Station on the Norfolk and Petersburg Railroad. They were now southeast of Petersburg, and the Blackwater and James Rivers were not much farther. That night, it turned bitterly cold. The men huddled closely around the fires in a futile attempt to keep warm, so close in fact that one of the junior officers, Master John A. G. Williamson, had a brush with "disaster." *He was lying close to a fire,* Shippey recalled with amusement, *and as I passed about midnight I saw that his coat-tail was on fire, and called him somewhat hurriedly from a sound sleep. He started up and rushed wildly through the woods, the fiery tail streaming out behind, and for awhile all efforts to stop him were futile, but we finally succeeded in capturing him, extinguishing the fire with the loss of one skirt of his coat. He afterwards cut off the other skirt and made it more 'uniform.'*[12]

Captain John K. Mitchell, commander of the James River Squadron at the time of Read's expedition. Mitchell's warships were to attack down the river upon a signal from Read.

As morning broke over the bleak Virginia landscape, the scene was truly a miserable one. It had begun to snow during the night and was alternating now between sleet and freezing rain. As the shivering marines and sailors crawled out from under their blankets, they discovered that everything which had been exposed to the elements was covered with a thick coating of ice. Breaking camp, the expedition assembled in the road, and braving the storm, they began to move out. Each man and wagon took up their assigned position in the line, but progress was slow because the mules had difficulty pulling the heavy wagons on the slippery road. As they struggled along, the wind gradually increased, until it became a howling gale. Men and animals, their heads bent against the shrieking wind, became blinded by the driving sleet and little headway was made. Time and again a mule team would fall or a wagon would slide into the ditch alongside of the road, blocking the way for those behind. With sleet stinging their faces, the half-frozen sailors struggled to push the heavy wagons back onto the icy road. Once they had succeeded, the column would again move slowly on. After two hours of this pain and frustration, Read ordered the command to halt and take shelter from the furious storm in a nearby abandoned farmhouse. They were now only a few miles from their rendezvous with Lieutenant Lewis on the Blackwater River.[13]

Securing the mules, as best they could behind the house, and away from the biting wind, the men crowded inside where fires were built in the large stone fireplaces. Huddled around the smoky fires, the sailors and marines began thawing out and drying their clothes. Read, impatient to continue, paced the floor and decided that as soon as the storm subsided they would press on. While they waited and listened to the howling elements whistling around the corners of their dilapidated shelter, crushing and inconceivable news arrived. Someone shouted that a rider was approaching and as Read stepped outside, an exhausted soldier in gray galloped up on a weary horse. The man was nearly frozen in the saddle and had to be helped from his mount and assisted inside. With anxious faces gathered around, he began to tell a tale that was almost inconceivable.[14]

The nameless Confederate related how he had been a prisoner of war at Fort Monroe, Virginia, and on one of the long dreary days of his imprisonment there, he had overheard from his cell window a conversation between a Confederate naval officer and his captors. The officer told of an overland torpedo expedition to the James River that was being planned, and offered to lead a Federal detachment to ambush and capture all those involved. The Confederate naval officer whom he had overheard, he claimed, was Lieutenant Lewis. Escaping from Fort Monroe shortly after this eavesdropping, the young soldier was determined to find the expedition and warn them of the awaiting danger. Read was stunned. He simply could not believe this story of betrayal. Lieutenant John Lewis, although northern born, had served the Confederate cause faithfully since the beginning of the war. Being in the United States Navy and stationed at Norfolk when Virginia seceded, Lewis had resigned and joined the Confederate army. Wounded at Manassas, he later resigned from the army in order to accept a commission on June 29, 1864, in the Confederate navy as a first lieutenant. During the latter part of 1864, he had served on the CSS *Drewry* and the CSS *Albemarle*. Read was sure Lieutenant Lewis' loyalty was above question.[15]

There was only one way to find out if the young soldier was telling the truth; Read would have to go and see for himself. After a council with his officers, and fearful that they might be discovered in the farmhouse by Federal foraging parties seeking shelter from the storm, Read decided to take the men and boats back down the road about a mile and conceal them in the woods. If he was not back by sundown the following day, he instructed, Lieutenant Ward was to turn the command around and retrace their route, and, hopefully, regain the Confederate lines. Reluctant to leave the warmth of the fireplaces, the men, nevertheless, filed out, hitched up the wagons, and started back down the road. After backtracking what Read considered to be a safe distance from the farmhouse, the command turned off the road and made camp in the dense woods. The wagons were hidden and their tracks erased using tree branches. Putting on a "disguise" (probably a civilian overcoat) as Shippey described it, Read mounted his horse and set out on his lonely ride. Hopefully, he must have thought, he would prove the young soldier wrong.[16]

Although the sleet and snow had stopped, it had turned bitterly cold. The frigid wind howled through the forest causing tree limbs to crack and break under the heavy load of ice. Because of the possible proximity of roving Federal patrols, Ward dictated that under no circumstances were campfires to be lighted. The cold windy night passed drearily by, while the men huddled together in a feeble effort to keep from freezing to death. When the long-awaited morning light finally broke over the eastern horizon on February 8, Ward ordered the men to remain hidden and out of sight in their secluded patch of woods. Worried over their leader's whereabouts, the cheerless day dragged by, and still the men saw no sign of Lieutenant Read. Anxiously they kept watch for their commander's return, when around 4:00 p.m., Read came riding down the road and turned off into their hiding place. His innermost fear had been confirmed; there was an ambush waiting and the Union cavalry was already scouring the countryside searching for them. If they had not been slowed by the storm, Read explained, they might have all been sitting in a Federal prison right then.[17]

There is an interesting record in existence at the U.S. National Archives. The records of the Headquarters Detachment, 3rd New York Cavalry, show that a Lieutenant Lewis of the C.S. Navy was forwarded from Benvard's Mills, Va. to Portsmouth, Va. on January 20, 1865. The remarks section of this record state, "A deserter from the C.S. Navy, Lt. Lewis has horse & equipment." Evidently the Federals did not trust him to lead the ambush, for he was forwarded from Fort Monroe to a prison in Washington, D.C. on February 4, 1865.[18]

Read knew they had only two choices: they could either surrender to the Federals, or turn around and then attempt to pass the rear of Grant's whole army again to gain the right flank of the Confederate lines. With surrender being unthinkable, there was no hesitation, and the order was given to hitch up and move out. They had come approximately eighty-five miles, and now they had to retrace those same miles to reach the safety of Confederate-held territory. Avoiding the main roads that were patrolled by Union cavalry, Read led his command along deserted and little-known farm traces. They marched all night, but concealed themselves during the daylight hours of February 9 to prevent being spotted by the Federals, who now seemed to be everywhere. The following night, the march was cautiously resumed. Every road seemed to be guarded by Federal pickets, and with hands nervously fingering their revolvers, they moved carefully on. Unexpectedly, an elderly gentleman, who was a resident of the area, approached the group and offered to be their guide. With little to lose, this offer was accepted and they continued the march. Traveling by night and hiding by day, and following the old man in the "stovepipe hat," as Shippey described him, the command kept moving westward. Taking a more roundabout route, they proceeded by way of Sussex Court House, Stony Creek, and then to Dinwiddle Court House.[19]

Approaching either Stony Creek or the Nottoway River (Shippey was not clear which), they found that the only way to cross, was by fording. The temperature was hovering around the freezing mark, and the stream was covered with a thin coating of ice. With Union cavalry sniffing at their heels, they plunged into the chest-high water and pushed across. *My teeth chatter yet to think of that cold wade through water waist deep, covered with a thin coat of ice,* Shippey wrote. There was no time to build fires to dry their clothes and warm themselves, so the whole command, including the mules, "double quicked" to keep their circulation going. In spite of this, their clothing froze stiffly on the men as they ran. Finally, on February 13, having been out for eleven days, and having marched

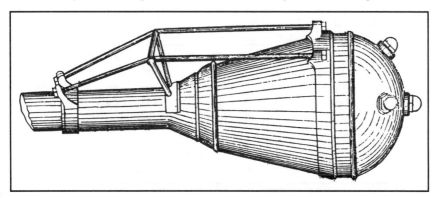

Spar torpedo most frequently used by the Confederates. This is most likely the same type carried by Read on his aborted mission to the James River.

Scharf's *History of the Confederate States Navy*

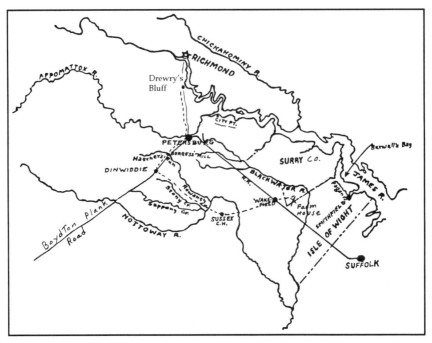

Map of the area below Petersburg, Virginia. The dotted line traces the approximate route taken by Read and his men in the Overland Expedition.

all the way around the Union army below Petersburg and back again, the weary column arrived back at their camps at Drewry's Bluff. Except for Lieutenant Lewis, every sailor and marine, every mule, and every wagon with its boat, had returned from the expedition.[20]

Thus ended the Confederate navy's last attempt to clear the James River of the enemy. Lieutenant Read would go on to another adventure, this time in Louisiana, before he would be forced to lay down his sword. Some of his officers would accompany him, while others, along with many of the sailors and marines, would end the war serving with the Semmes Naval Brigade. Shippey recalls, however, that upon the evacuation of Richmond in April, 1865, that at least seventy-five members of the expedition were still in the Richmond Naval Hospital suffering from severe exposure.[21]

While the expedition was unsuccessful, it was illustrative of the audacity and ability of the men of the Confederate States Navy and Marine Corps. It was proof once again, that one of the most outstanding features of the Confederate navy, regardless of overwhelming numbers and resources of the enemy, was its ingeniousness, and its courage. Above all, Read's aborted mission demonstrated the navy's willingness to try.

Conclusion

It is very understandable that the Confederate navy and Marine Corps have been largely overlooked in the accounts of the War Between the States. The role of the navy during the war was overshadowed in a conflict that saw one hundred thousand-man armies fighting bloody and protracted land campaigns. Most Confederate naval records were destroyed in the great fire that consumed a large part of Richmond during the evacuation of that city in April of 1865. This obviously makes any research into the navy's activities that much more difficult. Then too, with a total strength that probably never exceeded 6,000 men and officers, there was a scarcity of post-war writings and memoirs generated by Confederate navy participants. For an agriculturally oriented nation struggling to survive the loss of a war and the horrors of "reconstruction," the contribution of its navy at sea and on the nation's rivers and bays was uninteresting and unappreciated by most Southern readers. Naval leaders such as Semmes, Buchanan, Maury, Brown, and others never gained the fame and devotion of the Southern people as such army leaders as Lee, Jackson, Stuart, et al. This, too, is understandable, for the war on land, with its invading blue armies, tragically touched the lives of nearly every Southerner. The war on the rivers, bays and oceans was more distant, more remote. The capture and occupation of a particular bay

169

or river did not of itself mean that someone's home would be burned, their livestock slaughtered, and women raped and defiled.

If we turn our attention away from the land campaign, and diligently research what naval writings and records that are available, we find that the same superlative qualities that typified some of the most famous Confederate general officers, also existed in officers who wore the navy gray. Men such as Raphael Semmes, James D. Johnston, Isaac N. Brown, Franklin Buchanan, William L. Maury, Charles Read, Stephen Mallory, Charles Fuller, and Thomas M. Crossan, to name only those who are covered in this work, exhibited much the same character as the leaders of those gray armies on land. For the most part, they projected the same competency, intelligence, and resourcefulness as their army counterparts, and their crews proved by their actions that most naval officers earned similar respect and devotion from their men. The majority of Confederate naval officers were professional career officers prior to the outbreak of war. The typical naval commander had spent many years in the "old navy," and had been thoroughly trained to respect his God, love his country, and fight savagely for her cause. By the end of 1861, 373 of these officers, painful for them that it was, determined that their first allegiance as a citizen, was to their state. Discarding everything that they had earned in the old service, they resigned their commissions and swore allegiance to the Confederate States of America. Duty, honor, and country were not just mere words to these men. They were the principles by which their very lives were governed. If one should look for an example of this devotion to God, duty, and country, one need look no further than to Commander Isaac N. Brown of the CSS *Arkansas*.

The crewmen of such ships as the *Sumter*, the *Arkansas*, the *J. A. Cotton*, and the *Tennessee*, for example, also exhibited the same courage and devotion to their cause and country as the valorous soldiers in the ranks of the Confederate armies. Because of the lack of seafaring men in the South, many crews of Confederate vessels were composed of army units or former soldiers who had been transferred to naval service. It was their country, too, that was being invaded, and their peaceful homes and families that were being desecrated. Even on the sleek and speedy blockade runners, such as the *Advance*, whose crew was composed mostly of English sailors, men seemed to catch the spirit of this new nation struggling for its freedom. Army recruits, many of whom had never seen a boat or a warship, took their places inside the sweltering casemate of an ironclad monster and fought like demons for their country. When the time came, as it did for the crew of the *Arkansas* above Vicksburg, they would fight and die for that new nation in a way that is difficult for us, today, to grasp or understand. We who study the war are familiar with the depiction of long lines of blue and gray infantry, firing volleys of musketry at one another from close range. The image of those men on the Mississippi River firing 11 and 15-inch guns at one another from a distance of forty feet is incomprehensible.

When the limited resources of the Confederacy, both in manpower and raw materials, is considered, it is simply astounding that the Confederate navy accomplished as much as it did. The old adage that, "Necessity is the mother of invention," was never more applicable than it was for the Confederate navy during the war. Faced with an aggressive and brutal enemy within the very first weeks of its existence, this navy had to organize, begin operations, and fight an invader simultaneously. Because of this, many of the vessels initially thrown into the fray, which were nothing more than converted river steamers, had an "improvised" character about them. The characterization of the *J. A. Cotton* as a "warship" might have seemed comical to some—until they encountered her blazing guns. The improvised features of many Confederate warships should come as no surprise, for with the loss of Norfolk, New Orleans, and Pensacola early in the conflict, new construction facilities had to be found. It took months to construct new shipyards, and with a scarcity of skilled workers, even more time was needed to build new ships at these locations. Even if facilities were available, skilled workers and shipbuilding materials were not. One must remember that at the opening of hostilities, the timber for the vessels that the South was ultimately able to construct, was still growing in her forests, and the iron for their armor, engines, and machinery was still buried in the ground.

Yet, with all the shortages and difficulties that the South faced, approximately 150 warships were finally constructed within the borders of the Confederacy. The keels for approximately fifty ironclads were laid, and twenty-two of these were commissioned and put into operation. The Confederate navy lead the way in the deployment of the casemated ironclad, as illustrated by the *Arkansas* and *Tennessee*. The Confederacy was also a pioneer in the development and use of the underwater torpedo or mine, and she was the first to sortie forth with an operational submarine that actually destroyed an enemy warship. The predecessors of the fast torpedo boats of World War II, also made their debut with the Confederate navy.

Overseas, ship design leapfrogged into the twentieth century with the building and launching of the fast and sleek blockade runners. Often referred to as the "Lifeline of the Confederacy," these swift British-built steamers, particularly when commanded by regular naval officers, managed to consistently slip through the Federal blockade with near impunity.

The determination and brilliance of Confederate naval officers in Europe brought about the birth of what proved to be the ultimate combination of sail and steam. The English-built *Alabama* and *Florida* were acknowledged at the time, and still today, to be the finest cruisers the world has ever seen. Designed for a specific purpose, they accomplished that purpose devastatingly well.

In a letter written two years after the war, Secretary Mallory offered a brief and accurate appraisal of the Confederate navy: *I am satisfied that, with the means at our control and in view of the overwhelming force of the enemy at the outset of the struggle, our little navy accomplished more than could have been looked or hoped for; and if I have ever felt any surprise connected with its operations, it was that we accomplished so much.*

CHAPTERS 1 and 2

OFFICERS ASSIGNED TO THE CSS *SUMTER*

Name	Rank	From
Semmes, Raphael	Commander (Commanding)	Maryland
Kell, John M.	First Lieutenant (Exec. Officer)	Georgia
Chapman, Robert T.	Lieutenant	Alabama
Stribling, John M.	Lieutenant	South Carolina
Evans, William E.	First Lieutenant	South Carolina
Myers, Henry	Paymaster	Georgia
Galt, Francis L.	Surgeon	Virginia
Hicks, William A.	Midshipman	Mississippi
Armstrong, Richard F.	Midshipman	Georgia
Hudgins, Albert G.	Midshipman	Virginia
Holden, John F.	Midshipman	Tennessee
Wilson, Joseph D.	Acting Master	Florida
Howell, Becket K.	First Lieutenant, CSMC	Mississippi
Freeman, Miles J.	First Assistant Engineer	Louisiana
Brooks, William P.	Second Assistant Engineer	Louisiana
O'Brien, Matthew	Third Assistant Engineer	Ireland
Cummings, Simeon W.	Acting Third Assistant Engineer	New York
McCaskey, Benjamin P.	Boatswain	Louisiana
Cuddy, Thomas C.	Acting Gunner	South Carolina
Beaufort, Melville P.	Sailmaker	(Unknown)
Robinson, William	Carpenter	Louisiana

Appendix B

CHAPTERS 3 and 4
OFFICERS ASSIGNED TO THE CSS *ARKANSAS*

Name	Rank	From
Brown, Isaac N.	Commander	Kentucky
Stevens, Henry K.	Lieutenant	Connecticut
Grimball, John	First Lieutenant	South Carolina
Wharton, Arthur, D.	Second Lieutenant	Alabama
Read, Charles W.	Second Lieutenant	Mississippi
Barbot, Alphonse	Lieutenant	Louisiana
Gift, George W.	Lieutenant	Tennessee
Washington, H. W. M.	Surgeon	Virginia
Morfit, Charles M.	Assistant Surgeon	Maryland
Taylor, Richard	Assistant Paymaster	Virginia
City, George W.	First Assistant Engineer	District of Columbia
Covert, Ellison	Second Assistant Engineer	(Unknown)
Jackson, William H.	Third Assistant Engineer	Virginia
Brown, Eugene H.	Third Assistant Engineer	Virginia
Doland, James T.	Third Assistant Engineer	(Unknown)
Dupuy, John S.	Third Assistant Engineer	(Unknown)
Gettis, James S.	Third Assistant Engineer	(Unknown)
Milliken, Samuel	Acting Master	Kentucky
Phillips, John L.	Acting Master	Alabama
Bacot, Richard H.	Passed Midshipman	South Carolina

174

Name	Rank	From
Scales, Dabney M.	Acting Midshipman	Virginia
Tyler, Clarence W.	Acting Midshipman	North Carolina
Wilson, John A.	Midshipman	Maryland
Travers, Thomas B.	Acting Gunner	Virginia
Shacklett, James R.	Pilot	(Unknown)
Gilmore, William	Pilot	(Unknown)
Brady, James L.	Pilot	(Unknown)
Hodges, John	Pilot	(Unknown)

Appendix C

CHAPTER 6
BLOCKADE RUNNER - *ADVANCE*

Commander - Lieutenant Thomas M. Crossan, NCN

Arrivals and departures - Wilmington, North Carolina

Arrivals	Departures	From/Bound to
June 28, 1863		Nassau
	July 24, 1863	Bermuda
August 19, 1863		Bermuda
	September 23, 1863	Bermuda
October 10, 1863		Bermuda
	October 24, 1863	Bermuda
November 10, 1863		Bermuda
	November 19, 1863	Nassau
January 20, 1864		Bermuda
	February 6, 1864	Bermuda
February 21, 1864		Bermuda
	March 15, 1864	Nassau
March 30, 1864		Nassau
	April 12, 1864	Nassau
July 29, 1864		Bermuda
	August 6, 1864	Bermuda
August 27, 1864		Bermuda
	September 9, 1864	Bermuda (Captured)

CHAPTERS 7 and 8

OFFICERS ASSIGNED TO THE CSS *GEORGIA*

Name	Rank	From
Maury, William L.	Commander (Commanding)	Virginia
Chapman, Robert T.	First Lieutenant	Alabama
Evans, William E.	First Lieutenant	South Carolina
Ingraham, John H.	Second Lieutenant	South Carolina
Smith, ——	Third Lieutenant	(Unknown)
Bain, Robert M.	Carpenter	Virginia
Atchison, George	Master's Mate	(Unknown)
Walker, John T.	Passed Midshipman	South Carolina
Morgan, James M.	Midshipman	Louisiana
Curtis, R. W.	Paymaster	Arkansas
Wheeden, Thomas J.	Assistant Surgeon	Maryland
Pearson, ——	Chief Engineer	(Unknown)
Smith, Robert	Second Assistant Engineer	(Unknown)
Hannah, ——	Acting Third Assistant Engineer	(Unknown)
Dand, William	Gunner	England
Hunt, Cornelius E.	Acting Master's Mate	Virginia
Maltman, J. E.	Acting Boatswain	(Unknown)
Naylor, ——	Acting Gunner	(Unknown)

177

CHAPTER 9

OFFICERS ASSIGNED TO THE CSS *TENNESSEE*

Name	Rank	From
Buchanan, Franklin	Admiral (Commanding Mobile Squadron)	Maryland
Johnston, James D.	Commander (Commanding)	Kentucky
Bradford, William L.	First Lieutenant (Exec. Officer)	Alabama
Wharton, Arthur D.	First Lieutenant	Alabama
McDermett, Edward J.	Second Lieutenant	Arkansas
Molry, J. R.	Master	(Unknown)
Perrin, Henry W.	Master	Louisiana
Forrest, W. S.	Acting Master's Mate	(Unknown)
Beebee, Marcus J.	Acting Master's Mate	(Unknown)
Carter, Robert M.	Acting Master's Mate	(Unknown)
Lining, George D.	First Assistant Engineer	South Carolina
O'Connell, John C.	Second Assistant Engineer	Alabama
Hayes, John	Second Assistant Engineer	England
Benson, Oscar	Third Assistant Engineer	Alabama
Patterson, William B.	Third Assistant Engineer	Alabama
Cohen, Jacob H.	Paymaster's Clerk	(Unknown)
McCredie, John	Boatswain	Alabama
Smith, Heman S.	Gunner	Louisiana

178

Appendix F

CHAPTER 10
THE OVERLAND TORPEDO EXPEDITION

Officers Assigned to Overland Torpedo Expedition
February, 1865

Name	Rank	From
Read, Charles W.	First Lieutenant (Commanding)	Mississippi
Ward, William H.	First Lieutenant	Virginia
Wall, William H.	First Lieutenant	Virginia
Lewis, John	First Lieutenant (Deserted)	(Unknown)
Layton, James T.	Acting Master's Mate	(Unknown)
McBlair, William Jr.	Acting Master's Mate	(Unknown)
Peters, James A.	Passed Midshipman	Tennessee
Scott, Henry H.	Passed Midshipman	North Carolina
Shippey, W. Frank	Master	Florida
Skinner, Edwin C.	Acting Master's Mate	(Unknown)
Thurston, James J.	First Lieutenant, CSMC	South Carolina
Turner, James E.	Pilot	(Unknown)
Williams, John A. G.	Master	Virginia

Endnotes

CHAPTER 1
"GIVE ME THAT SHIP, ..."

1. Raphael Semmes, *Memoirs of Service Afloat* (Baltimore: Kelly, Piet, 1869), pp. 80–81.
2. Ibid., pp. 93–94.
3. Ibid., p. 96.
4. Ibid., p. 98.
5. Chester G. Hearn, *Gray Raiders of the Sea* (Camden: International Marine Publishing, 1992), p. 10.
6. J. Thomas Scharf, *History of the Confederate States Navy* (New York: Rogers & Sherwood, 1887), p. 785.
7. Charles G. Summersell, *The Cruise of the CSS Sumter* (Tuscaloosa: The Confederate Publishing Company, Inc., 1965), p. 30.
8. Ralph W. Donnelly, *The Confederate States Marine Corps* (Shippensburg: White Mane Publishing Company, Inc., 1989), p. 18.
9. Summersell, p. 43.
10. Semmes, p. 105.
11. Summersell, p. 42.
12. Ibid., p. 45.
13. Semmes, p. 114.
14. John McIntosh Kell, *Recollections of Naval Life, Including the Cruises of the Confederate Steamers Sumter and Alabama* (Washington: Neale, 1900), p. 147.
15. Semmes, p. 115.
16. Ibid., p. 116.
17. Ibid.
18. Ibid., pp. 117–118.

19. Ibid., p. 121.
20. Summersell, p. 52.
21. Semmes, p. 122.
22. Ibid., pp. 127–128.
23. Ibid., pp. 128–129.
24. Kell, pp. 147–148.
25. Hearn, pp. 16–17.
26. Semmes, p. 135.
27. Ibid., pp. 136–137.
28. Hearn, p. 18.
29. Summersell, pp. 68–71; Hearn, pp. 18–19; Semmes, pp. 139–144.
30. Hearn, p. 20.
31. John M. Taylor, *Confederate Raider, Raphael Semmes of the Alabama* (Washington: Brassey's Inc., 1994), p. 66.
32. Semmes, p. 154.
33. Ibid., p. 160.
34. Ibid., pp. 162–164

CHAPTER 2
FAREWELL AT GIBRALTAR

1. Raphael Semmes, *Memoirs of Service Afloat* (Baltimore: Kelly, Piet, 1869), pp. 162–164.
2. Chester G. Hearn, *Gray Raiders of the Sea* (Camden: International Marine Publishing, 1992), p. 22.
3. Charles G. Summersell, *The Cruise of the CSS Sumter* (Tuscaloosa: Confederate Publishing Company, Inc., 1965), pp. 85–86.
4. Semmes, p. 176.
5. Ibid., pp. 184–185.
6. Ibid., p. 193.
7. Hearn, pp. 24–25.
8. Semmes, p. 197.
9. Semmes, pp. 197–199.
10. Ibid., p. 203.
11. Hearn, p. 26.
12. Semmes, p. 208.
13. Hearn, pp. 27–28.
14. Summersell, pp. 116–117.
15. Ibid., pp. 118–119.
16. Semmes, pp. 226–228.
17. Ibid., pp. 237–238.
18. Ibid., p. 253.
19. Ibid., p. 254.
20. Ibid., pp. 252–262
21. Hearn, p. 33.
22. Summersell, p. 140.
23. Hearn, pp. 33–34.
24. Semmes, p. 276.
25. Hearn, p. 34.
26. Semmes, pp. 280–281.
27. Ibid., p. 281.
28. Hearn, p. 35.
29. Semmes, p. 296.
30. Hearn, p. 36.
31. Ibid., p. 37.

32. Ibid., p. 41.
33. Ibid.
34. John McIntosh Kell, *Recollections of a Naval Life, Including the Cruises of the Confederate Steamers "Sumter" and "Alabama"* (Washington: Neale, 1900), p. 176.

CHAPTER 3
THUNDER ON THE YAZOO

1. J. Thomas Scharf, *History of the Confederate States Navy* (New York: Rogers & Sherwood, 1887), p. 310.
2. William N. Still, Jr., *Iron Afloat* (Nashville: Vanderbilt University Press, 1971), p. 62.
3. Ibid.
4. Scharf, p. 306.
5. Ibid.
6. Isaac N. Brown, "The Confederate Gunboat *Arkansas*," *Battles and Leaders of the Civil War*, vol. 3 (New York: The Century Company, 1884–1888), p. 572.
7. Ibid.
8. Scharf, p. 307.
9. Brown, p. 572.
10. Scharf, pp. 307–308.
11. Brown, p. 572.
12. Ibid.
13. George W. Gift, "The Story of the *Arkansas*," *Southern Historical Society Papers*, vol. 12, p. 212.
14. Scharf, p. 388.
15. M. Jeff Thompson, *The Civil War Reminiscences of General M. Jeff Thompson* (Dayton: Morningside House, Inc., 1988), pp. 168–169.
16. Charles W. Read, "Reminiscences of the Confederate States Navy," *Southern Historical Society Papers*, vol. 1, no. 5, pp. 350–351.
17. Ibid., p. 351.
18. Maurice Melton, *The Confederate Ironclads* (New York: A. S. Barnes and Co., Inc., 1968), p. 119.
19. Read, p. 352.
20. Tom Z. Parrish, *The Saga of the Confederate Ram Arkansas* (Hillsboro: Hill College Press, 1987), p. 159.
21. Brown, p. 573.
22. Read, p. 353.
23. Brown, p. 573.
24. Ibid.
25. Ibid.
26. Ibid.
27. Melton, pp. 121–122.
28. Gift, p. 50.
29. Read, p. 353.
30. Scharf, pp. 310–311.
31. ——, *Official Records of the Union and Confederate Navies in the War of the Rebellion*, ser. 1, vol. 19, pp. 5–7.
32. Gift, p. 51.
33. Ibid., pp. 51–52.
34. Ibid., p. 52.
35. Brown, p. 574.
36. Read, p. 354.
37. Brown, pp. 574–575.
38. Gift, p. 53.
39. Ibid.
40. Brown, p. 575.

41. Gift, p. 53.
42. Brown, p. 575.

CHAPTER 4
THUNDER ON THE MISSISSIPPI

1. Isaac N. Brown, "The Confederate Gunboat *Arkansas*," *Battles and Leaders of the Civil War*, vol. 3 (New York: The Century Company, 1884–1888), p. 575.
2. Ibid.
3. George W. Gift, "The Story of the *Arkansas*," *Southern Historical Society Papers*, vol. 12, p. 115.
4. Brown, p. 576.
5. ——, *Official Records of the Union and Confederate Navies in the War of the Rebellion* (Washington: Government Printing Office, 1894–1922), ser. 1, vol. 19, pp. 3–75
6. Brown, p. 576.
7. Gift, p. 116.
8. Brown, p. 576.
9. Ibid.
10. Gift, p. 117.
11. Ibid.
12. Ibid.
13. Ibid.
14. Ibid., p. 118.
15. J. Thomas Scharf, *History of the Confederate States Navy* (New York: Rogers & Sherwood, 1887), p. 318.
16. Brown, p. 576.
17. Gift, p. 119.
18. Ibid.
19. Martha Goodwin, "The Ram *Arkansas*," *Confederate Veteran*, July 1920, p. 263.
20. Brown, p. 577.
21. *Official Records.*
22. Ibid.
23. Gift, p. 164.
24. Brown, p. 577.
25. Gift, pp. 164–165.
26. *Official Records.*
27. Ibid.
28. Brown, p. 577.
29. Charles W. Read, "Reminiscences of the Confederate States Navy," *Southern Historical Society Papers*, vol. 1, no. 5, p. 357.
30. Brown, p. 577.
31. Gift, pp. 168–169.
32. Ibid., p. 169.
33. Scharf, p. 332.
34. *Official Records.*
35. Brown, pp. 578–579.
36. Maurice Melton, *The Confederate Ironclads* (New York: A. S. Barnes and Co., Inc., 1968), p. 138.
37. Gift, p. 207.
38. Brown, p. 579.
39. Read, p. 359.
40. Gift, p. 207.
41. Ibid.
42. Read, p. 360.
43. Gift, p. 209.
44. Ibid., pp. 209–210.

45. *Official Records*, ser. 1, vol. 19, p. 136.
46. Ibid.

CHAPTER 5
CAPTAIN FULLER AND THE *J. A. COTTON*

1. Richard Taylor, *Destruction and Reconstruction* (New York: Longmans, Greem and Co., 1955), p. 142.
2. Thomas T. Moebs, *Confederate States Navy Research Guide* (Williamsburg: Moebs Publishing Co., 1991), p. 335.
3. Maurice Melton, *The Confederate Ironclads* (New York: A. S. Barnes and Co., Inc., 1968), pp. 143–144.
4. Taylor, pp. 141–143.
5. Melton, p. 145.
6. ———, *Official Records of the Union and Confederate Navies in the War of the Rebellion* (Washington, D.C.: Government Printing Office, 1884–1927), ser. 1, vol. 19, p. 342.
7. Ibid.
8. Ibid.
9. Ibid.
10. Ibid.
11. Ibid.
12. Ibid.
13. Ibid.
14. Ibid.
15. Ibid.
16. Ibid.
17. Ibid.
18. Taylor, p. 143.
19. *Official Records*, ser. 1, vol. 19, p. 342.
20. Ibid.
21. Ibid.
22. Ibid., & Taylor, p. 144.
23. Moebs, p. 352.

CHAPTER 6
FAST SHIPS AND DARK NIGHTS

1. Stephen R. Wise, "Blockade Runners," *Encyclopedia of the Confederacy* (New York: Simon & Schuster, 1993), vol. 1, pp. 183–184.
2. John G. Barrett, *The Civil War in North Carolina* (Chapel Hill: The University of North Carolina Press, 1963), p. 254.
3. Stephen R. Wise, *Lifeline of the Confederacy* (Columbia: University of South Carolina Press, 1988), p. 105.
4. William R. Trotter, *Ironclads and Columbiads* (Winston-Salem: John F. Blair, Publisher, 1989), p. 284.
5. Adam Tredwell, "North Carolina Navy," *Histories of the Several Regiments and Battalions From North Carolina in the Great War 1861–'65* (Goldsboro: Nash Brothers, Book and Job Printers, 1901), vol. 5, pp. 299–313.
6. William Morrison Robinson, Jr., *The Confederate Privateers* (Columbia: University of South Carolina Press, 1990), pp. 102–103.
7. Hamilton Cochran, *Blockade Runners of the Confederacy* (New York: The Bobbs-Merrill Company, Inc., 1958), p. 172.
8. James Sprunt, "Blockade Running," *Histories of the Several Regiments and Battalions From North Carolina in the Great War 1861–'65* (Goldsboro: Nash Brothers, Book and Job Printers, 1901), vol. 5, p. 361.

9. Sprunt, pp. 359–360.
10. Trotter, p. 286.
11. Sprunt, pp. 360–361.
12. John Wilkinson, *The Narrative of a Blockade Runner* (New York: Sheldon & Company, 1877), p. 199.
13. Moses D. Hoge, "Running the Blockade on the Advance," *Histories of the Several Regiments and Battalions From North Carolina in the Great War 1861–'65* (Goldsboro: Nash Brothers, Book and Job Printers, 1901), vol. 5, p. 341.
14. Hoge, p. 342.
15. Hoge, pp. 342–343.
16. Hoge, pp. 343–344.
17. Hoge, p. 344.
18. James MaGlenn, "The Steamer Advance," *Histories of the Several Regiments and Battalions From North Carolina in the Great War 1861–'65* (Goldsboro: Nash Brothers, Book and Job Printers, 1901), vol. 5, pp. 335–336.
19. Cochran, pp. 174–175.
20. MaGlenn, p. 337.
21. Trotter, p. 293.
22. MaGlenn, pp. 337–338.
23. Wise, pp. 200–201.
24. Sprunt, pp. 353–354.
25. Cochran, p. 175.

CHAPTER 7
THE *GEORGIA* IS LOOSE

1. Chester G. Hearn, *Gray Raiders of the Sea* (Camden: International Marine Publishing, 1992), p. 237.
2. Hearn, pp. 237–238.
3. Hearn, p. 238.
4. Ethel S. Nepveux, *George Alfred Trenholm and the Company that Went to War* (Charleston: Ethel S. Nepveux, 1994), p. 50.
5. Milton F. Perry, *Infernal Machines* (Baton Rouge: Louisiana State University Press, 1965), pp. 13–15.
6. Hearn, p. 239-240.
7. Warren F. Spencer, *The Confederate Navy in Europe* (Tuscaloosa: The University of Alabama Press, 1983), p. 138.
8. Hearn, p. 240.
9. Spencer, pp. 138–139.
10. Spencer, p. 139.
11. Thomas Truxtun Moebs, *Confederate States Navy Research Guide* (Williamsburg: Moebs Publishing Company, 1991), p. 240.
12. Spencer, p. 140.
13. Hearn, p. 242.
14. James Morris Morgan, *Recollections of a Rebel Reefer* (New York: Houghton Mifflin Company, 1917), p. 115.
15. Ibid.
16. Morgan, pp. 116–117.
17. Morgan, p. 117.
18. ———, *Official Records of the Union and Confederate Navies in the War of the Rebellion* (Washington: Government Printing Office, 1894–1922), ser. 1, vol. 2, p. 811.
19. Morgan, pp. 117–118.
20. Morgan, p. 120.
21. Morgan, p. 121.

22. *Official Records*, ser. 1, vol. 2, p. 812.
23. Morgan, p. 125.
24. Morgan, pp. 125–126.
25. Morgan, pp. 127–128.
26. Morgan, pp. 128–129.
27. *Official Records*, ser. 1, vol. 2, p. 813.

CHAPTER 8
REQUIEM FOR A CRUISER

1. ——, *Official Records of the Union and Confederate Navies in the War of the Rebellion* (Washington: Government Printing Office, 1894–1922), ser. 1, vol. 2, p. 213.
2. James Morris Morgan, *Recollections of a Rebel Reefer* (New York: Houghton Mifflin Company, 1917), p. 134.
3. Morgan, pp. 135–136.
4. Morgan, p. 137.
5. Morgan, pp. 137–138.
6. Morgan, pp. 138–139.
7. *Official Records*, ser. 1, vol. 2, p. 814.
8. Morgan, pp. 142–143.
9. Morgan, p. 145.
10. *Official Records*, ser. 1, vol. 2, pp. 815–816.
11. Morgan, p. 147.
12. Morgan, pp. 149–150.
13. Morgan, p. 148.
14. Morgan, p. 153.
15. *Official Records*, ser. 1, vol. 2, p. 816.
16. *Official Records*, ser. 1, vol. 2, p. 817.
17. Morgan, p. 156.
18. Morgan, pp. 156–158.
19. *Official Records*, ser. 1, vol. 2, p. 816.
20. Morgan, pp. 158–159.
21. *Official Records*, ser. 1, vol. 2, pp. 817–818.
22. Morgan, pp. 163–164.
23. Morgan, p. 165
24. Morgan, p. 173.
25. William F. Spencer, *The Confederate Navy in Europe* (Tuscaloosa: The University of Alabama Press, 1983), pp. 183–184.
26. Morgan, p. 183.

CHAPTER 9
"...YOU HAD BETTER SURRENDER"

1. Arthur W. Bergeron, Jr., *Confederate Mobile* (Jackson: University Press of Mississippi, 1991), pp. 4–5.
2. Chester G. Hearn, *Mobile Bay and the Mobile Campaign* (Jefferson: McFarland & Company, Inc., Publishers, 1993), p. 45.
3. ——, "Opposing Forces at Mobile," *Battle and Leaders of the Civil War* (New York: The Century Company, 1884–1888), vol. 4, p. 400.
4. Hearn, p. 22.
5. James D. Johnston, "The Ram 'Tennessee' at Mobile Bay," *Battles and Leaders of the Civil War* (New York: The Century Company, 1884–1888), vol. 4, p. 401.
6. Hearn, pp. 22–24.
7. Johnston, p. 401.

8. Hearn, p. 25.
9. Ibid.
10. Maurice Melton, *The Confederate Ironclads* (New York: A. S. Barnes and Co., Inc., 1968), p. 209.
11. Hearn, p. 27.
12. Ibid., p. 28.
13. ——, *Official Records of the Union and Confederate Navies in the War of the Rebellion* (Washington: Government Printing Office), ser. 1, vol. 21, p. 934.
14. Melton, pp. 209–210.
15. Hearn, p. 29.
16. William N. Still, Jr., *Iron Afloat* (Nashville: Vanderbilt University Press, 1971), p. 197.
17. J. Thomas Scharf, *History of the Confederate States Navy* (New York: Rogers & Sherwood, 1887), p. 555.
18. Ibid., p. 559.
19. Johnston, p. 401.
20. Still, p. 201.
21. *Official Records*, ser. 1, vol. 21, p. 935.
22. Still, p. 203.
23. Ibid., ser. 1, vol. 21, p. 204.
24. *Official Records*, ser. 1, vol. 21, p. 936.
25. Johnston, p. 402.
26. Dr. Daniel B. Conrad, "Capture of the CSS Ram Tennessee in Mobile Bay, August, 1864," *Southern Historical Society Papers*, vol. 19, p. 73.
27. Hearn, p. 81.
28. Melton, p. 216.
29. Scharf, pp. 560–561.
30. Hearn, pp. 87–89.
31. Conrad, pp. 73–74.
32. Scharf, p. 562. (Footnote)
33. John C. Kinney, "Farragut at Mobile Bay," *Battles and Leaders of the Civil War* (New York: The Century Company, 1884–1888), vol. 4, pp. 389–390.
34. Scharf, p. 564.
35. Conrad, p. 74.
36. *Official Records*, ser. 1, vol. 21, pp. 588–590.
37. Ibid., pp. 587–588.
38. Scharf, p. 583.
39. Conrad, pp. 74–75.
40. Ibid., p. 75.
41. Ibid., pp. 75–76.
42. Hearn, p. 103.
43. Ibid., pp. 103–105.
44. Ibid., pp. 105–106.
45. Conrad, p. 77.
46. Ibid., p. 76.
47. Scharf, p. 577.
48. Hearn, p. 107.
49. Conrad, pp. 76–77.
50. Ibid., p. 77.
51. Scharf, pp. 577–578.
52. Ibid., p. 573.

CHAPTER 10
THE OVERLAND TORPEDO EXPEDITION

1. Ralph W. Donnelly, "A Confederate Navy Forlorn Hope," *Military Affairs*, Summer, 1964, p. 73.

2. J. Thomas Scharf, *History of the Confederate States Navy* (New York: Rogers & Sherwood, 1887), p. 742.
3. Donnelly, p. 74.
4. W. F. Shippey, "A Leaf From My Logbook," *Southern Historical Society Papers*, vol. 12, 1884, p. 416.
5. Shippey, p. 417.
6. Charles L. Dufour, *Nine Men in Gray* (Garden City: Doubleday & Company, Inc., 1963), p. 152.
7. Shippey, p. 416.
8. Donnelly, p. 75.
9. Ralph W. Donnelly, *The Confederate States Marine Corps* (Shippensburg: White Mane Publishing Company, Inc., 1989), p. 57.
10. Shippey, pp. 416–419.
11. Ibid.
12. Ibid.
13. Donnelly, p. 75.
14. Shippey, p. 416.
15. Donnelly, p. 77.
16. Shippey, p. 417.
17. Ibid.
18. Donnelly, p. 77.
19. Shippey, p. 418.
20. Donnelly, p. 78.
21. Shippey, p. 419.

Bibliography

——"Opposing Forces at Mobile." *Battles and Leaders of the Civil War.* Vol. 4. New York: The Century Company, 1884–1888.

——. *Official Records of the Union and Confederate Navies in the War of the Rebellion.* 31 vols. Washington, D.C.: Government Printing Office, 1894–1927.

——. *The War of the Rebellion: A Compilation of the Official Records of the Union and Confederate Armies.* 130 vols. Washington, D.C.: Government Printing Office, 1880–1901.

Barrett, John G. *The Civil War in North Carolina.* Chapel Hill: The University of North Carolina Press, 1963.

Bergeron, Arthur W., Jr. *Confederate Mobile.* Jackson: University Press of Mississippi, 1991.

Brown, Isaac N. "The Confederate Gunboat *Arkansas.*" *Battles and Leaders of the Civil War.* 3 vols. New York: The Century Company, 1884–1888.

Bulloch, James D. *The Secret Service of the Confederate States in Europe, or How the Confederate Cruisers Were Equipped.* 2 vols. New York: Putnam Publishers, 1883.

Cochran, Hamilton. *Blockade Runners of the Confederacy.* New York: The Bobbs-Merrill Company, Inc., 1958.

Davis, William C. *Jefferson Davis, The Man and His Hour.* New York: Harper Collins Publishers, 1991.

Delaney, Norman C. *Ghost Ship, The Confederate Raider Alabama.* Middletown: Southfarm Press, 1989.

Donnelly, Ralph W. *The Confederate States Marine Corps.* Shippensburg: White Mane Publishing Company, Inc., 1989.

Donnelly, Ralph W. "A Confederate Navy Forlorn Hope." *Military Affairs,* (Summer 1964).

Dowdey, Clifford (Editor). *The Wartime Papers of R. E. Lee.* New York: Bramhall House, 1961.

Dufour, Charles L. *Nine Men In Gray.* Garden City: Doubleday & Company, Inc., 1963.

Durkin, Joseph T. *Confederate Navy Chief: Stephen R. Mallory.* Chapel Hill: The University of North Carolina Press, 1954.

Gift, George W. "The Story of the *Arkansas.*" *Southern Historical Society Papers,* vol. 12 (1887), Richmond.

Goodwin, Martha. "The Ram *Arkansas.*" *Confederate Veteran* (July 1920).

Gosnell, H. Allen.. *Guns on the Western Waters.* Baton Rouge: Louisiana State University Press, 1949.

Hearn, Chester G. *Gray Raiders of the Sea.* Camden: International Marine Publishing, 1992.

Hearn, Chester G. *Mobile Bay and the Mobile Campaign.* Jefferson: McFarland & Company, Inc., Publishers, 1993.

Hoge, Moses D. "Running the Blockade on the Advance." *Histories of the Several Regiments and Battalions From North Carolina in the Great War 1861–'65,* vol. 5 (1901), Goldsboro: Nash Brothers, Book and Job Printers.

Horner, Dave. *The Blockade Runners.* Port Salerno: Florida Classics Library, 1992.

Johnston, James D. "The Ram 'Tennessee' at Mobile Bay." *Battles and Leaders of the Civil War.* Vol. 4. New York.

Jones, Virgil C. *The Civil War at Sea.* 3 vol. New York: Holt, Rinehart, and Winston, 1960–1962.

Kell, John McIntosh. "Cruise and Combats of the *Alabama.*" *Battles and Leaders of the Civil War.* 4 vol. New York: The Century Company, 1884–1888.

Kell, John McIntosh. *Recollections of a Naval Life, Including the Cruises of the Confederate Steamers "Sumter" and "Alabama."* Washington: Neale, 1900.

Kinney, John C. "Farragut at Mobile Bay." *Battles and Leaders of the Civil War.* Vol. 4. New York: The Century Company, 1884–1888.

MaGlenn, James. "The Steamer Advance." *Histories of the Several Regiments and Battalions From North Carolina in the Great War 1861–'65,* vol. 5 (1901), Goldsboro: Nash Brothers, Book and Job Printers.

Melton, Maurice. *The Confederate Ironclads.* New York: A. S. Barnes and Co., Inc., 1968.

Merli, Frank J. *Great Britain and the Confederate Navy.* Bloomington: Indiana University Press, 1970.

Moebs, Thomas Truxtun (Compiler). *Confederate States Navy Research Guide.* Williamsburg: Moebs Publishing Co., 1991.

Morgan, James Morris. *Recollections of a Rebel Reefer.* New York: Houghton Mifflin Company, 1917.

Morgan, James Morris. "The Pioneer Ironclad." *United States Naval Institute Proceedings,* p. 2277.

Nepveux, Ethel S. *George Alfred Trenholm and the Company that Went to War.* Charleston: Ethel S. Nepveux, 1994.

Outlaw, P. J. & R. W. Betterton. "Home Is the Sailor." *Confederate Veteran,* (July–August 1994).

Parker, William H. *Recollections of a Naval Officer.* New York: Charles Scribners' Sons, 1883.

Parrish, Tom Z. *The Saga of the Confederate Ram Arkansas.* Hillsboro: Hill College Press, 1987.

Perry, Milton F. *Infernal Machines.* Baton Rouge: Louisiana State University Press, 1965.

Read, Charles W. "Reminiscences of the Confederate States Navy." *Southern Historical Society Papers,* vol. 1 (May 1876).

Robinson, William Morrison, Jr. *The Confederate Privateers.* New Haven: Yale University Press, 1928.

Scharf, J. Thomas. *History of the Confederate States Navy.* New York: Rogers & Sherwood, 1887.

Semmes, Raphael. *Memoirs of Service Afloat During the War Between the States.* Baltimore: Kelly, Piet, 1869.

Shingleton, Royce Gorden. *High Seas Confederate, The Life and Times of John Newland Maffitt.* Columbia: University of South Carolina Press, 1994.

Shingleton, Royce Gorden. *John Taylor Wood, Sea Ghost of the Confederacy,* Athens: University of Georgia Press, 1979.

Shippey, W. F. "A Leaf From My Logbook." *Southern Historical Society Papers,* vol. 12 (1884).

Sinclair, Arthur. *Two Years on the Alabama.* Boston: Lee and Shepard Publishers, 1895.

Spencer, Warren F. "Raphael Semmes." *Encyclopedia of the Confederacy.* New York: Simon & Schuster, Inc., 1992.

Spencer, William F. *The Confederate Navy in Europe.* Tuscaloosa: The University of Alabama Press, 1983.

Sprunt, James. "Blockade Running." *Histories of the Several Regiments and Battalions From North Carolina in the Great War 1861–'65,* vol. 5 (1901), Goldsboro: Nash Brothers, Book and Job Printers.

Stern, Philip Van Doren. *The Confederate Navy, A Pictorial History.* New York: Bonanza Books, 1962.

Still, William N., Jr. *Iron Afloat.* Nashville: Vanderbilt University Press, 1971.

Still, William N., Jr. *Confederate Shipbuilding.* Columbia: University of South Carolina Press, 1987.

Strode, Hudson. *Jefferson Davis, Confederate President*. New York: Harcourt, Brace & World, Inc., 1959.

Summersell, Charles G. *The Cruise of the CSS Sumter*. Tuscaloosa: The Confederate Publishing Company, Inc., 1965.

Taylor, John M. *The Confederate Raider, Raphael Semmes of the Alabama*. Washington: Brassey's Inc., 1994.

Taylor, Richard. *Destruction and Reconstruction*. New York: Longmans, Green and Co., 1955.

Taylor, Thomas E. *Running the Blockade*. Annapolis: Naval Institute Press, 1995.

Thompson, M. Jeff. *The Civil War Reminiscences of General M. Jeff Thompson*. Dayton: Morningside House, Inc., 1988.

Tredwell, Adam. "The North Carolina Navy." *Histories of the Several Regiments and Battalions From North Carolina in the Great War 1861–'65*, vol. 5 (1901), Goldsboro: Nash Brothers, Book and Job Printers.

Trotter, William R. *Ironclads and Columbiads*. Winston-Salem: John F. Blair, Publisher, 1989.

Wells, Tom Henderson. *The Confederate Navy, A Study in Organization*. Tuscaloosa: The University of Alabama Press, 1971.

Wilkinson, John. *Narrative of a Blockade Runner*. New York: Sheldon & Company, 1877.

Wise, Stephen R. *Lifeline of the Confederacy*. Columbia: University of South Carolina Press, 1988.

Wise, Stephen R. "Blockade Runners." *Encyclopedia of the Confederacy*. Vol. 1. New York: Simon & Schuster, 1993.

Index

193

Profile

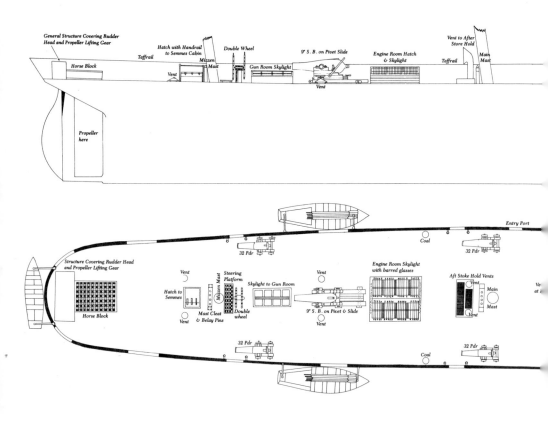

General Structure Covering Rudder
Head and Propeller Lifting Gear

Horse Block

Taffrail

Hatch with Handrail
to Semmes Cabin

Mizzen
Mast

Vent

Double Wheel

Gun Room Skylight

9' S. B. on Pivot Slide

Vent

Engine Room Hatch
& Skylight

Taffrail

Vent to After
Store Hold

Main
Mast

Propeller
here

Structure Covering Rudder Head
and Propeller Lifting Gear

Horse Block

Vent

Hatch to
Semmes

Vent

Mizzen Mast

Mast Cleat
& Belay Pins

Steering
Platform

Double
wheel

Skylight to Gun Room

Vent

Vent

9' S. B. on Pivot & Slide

Engine Room Skylight
with barred glasses

Aft Stoke Hold Vents

Vent

Vent

Main
Mast

Entry Port

Coal

32 Pdr

32 Pdr

32 Pdr

Coal

32 Pdr